NEW ATLANTIS

A NARRATIVE HISTORY OF SCIENTIFIC ROMANCE

VOLUME I:
THE ORIGINS OF SCIENTIFIC ROMANCE

NEW ATLANTIS

A NARRATIVE HISTORY OF SCIENTIFIC ROMANCE

VOLUME I:
THE ORIGINS OF SCIENTIFIC ROMANCE

BRIAN STABLEFORD

WILDSIDE PRESS

Copyright © 2016 by Brian Stableford
All rights reserved.

Published by Wildside Press LLC.
www.wildsidebooks.com

CONTENTS

ACKNOWLEDGEMENTS 7
INTRODUCTION 8
SCHEMA 9
PROLEGOMENON 13
CHAPTER ONE: THE ROOTS OF THE GENRE 53
CHAPTER TWO: THE DISCOVERY OF NEW
    ATLANTIS 124

ACKNOWLEDGEMENTS

I am greatly indebted to Heather Datta for scanning *Scientific Romance in Britain 1890-1950* for me, and thus making the text available for manipulation in electronic form. I should also like to thank John J. Pierce for reading the first draft of the present work and offering useful comments thereon. In the forty years that have somehow slipped by while I was engaged in the research for this book numerous people have lent me valuable assistance in one way or another, and I should like to record my gratitude to John Gloag; Nigel, Margaret, Patricia and Augustine Fowler Wright; John Squires; Bill Russell, Everett Bleiler; Robert Reginald; John Clute; Peter Nicholls; David Langford; Michael Rosenblum; Chris Morgan; Andy Sawyer; and Farah Mendlesohn.

INTRODUCTION

This volume is the first of four, and is not intended to be read independently. The schema of the entire project can be found in volume one, and the index to all four volumes in volume four.

SCHEMA

VOLUME I: THE ORIGINS OF SCIENTIFIC ROMANCE

PROLEGOMENON
1. The Definition of Scientific Romance
2. The Idea of Scientific Romance
3. The Problems of Heterocosmic Creativity

CHAPTER ONE: THE ROOTS OF THE GENRE
1. Philosophical Speculation
2. Travelers' Tales
3. Tainted Reputations
4. The Elements of Science

CHAPTER TWO: THE DISCOVERY OF NEW ATLANTIS
1. The Prospects of Science
2. The Pleasures and Perils of Imagination
3. The New Prometheia
4. The Prospect of the Future
5. The Future of Destiny
6. The Poetry of Science
7. Triumph of Evolution
8. The Shadows of Science

VOLUME II: THE EMERGENCE OF SCIENTIFIC ROMANCE

CHAPTER THREE: SCIENTIFIC ROMANCE BEFORE THE GREAT WAR
1. The Historical Background of Scientific Romance, 1887-1914
2. The Evolution of the Literary Marketplace

3. H. G. Wells
4. George Griffith
5. Robert Cromie
6. Fred T. Jane
7. C. H. Hinton
8. C. J. Cutcliffe Hyne
9. M. P. Shiel
10. Arthur Conan Doyle
11. William Hope Hodgson
12. J. D. Beresford
13. Adventures in Space
14. Adventures in Time
15. Adventures in Possibility
16. The Carnival of Destruction
17. The Discovery of the Future

VOLUME III: THE RESURGENCE OF SCIENTIFIC ROMANCE

CHAPTER FOUR: SCIENTIFIC ROMANCE BETTWEEN THE WARS

1. The Historical Background of Scientific Romance, 1914-1939
2. Economic Factors in the Further Development of Scientific Romance
3. Speculative Essays on the Future of Science
4. H. G. Wells
5. Arthur Conan Doyle
6. M. P. Shiel
7. J. D. Beresford
8. S. Fowler Wright
9. Olaf Stapledon
10. Neil Bell
11. John Gloag
12. J. Leslie Mitchell
13. Katherine Burdekin
14. Muriel Jaeger
15. J. Storer Clouston
16. Aldous Huxley
17. Eden Phillpotts
18. C. S. Lewis
19. The People of the Ruins

20. The Age of Frustration
21. The Transcendent Tomorrow
22. Metaphysical and Metaphorical Digressions
23. Shadows of Science Fiction

VOLUME IV: THE DECADENCE OF SCIENTIFIC ROMANCE

CHAPTER FIVE: SCIENTIFTIC ROMANCE AFTER WORLD WAR II

1. The Socioeconomic Fallout of World War II
2. Scientists in the Nuclear Age
3. H. G. Wells
4. J. D. Beresford
5. Olaf Stapledon
6. John Gloag
7. Neil Bell
8. S. Fowler Wright
9. Aldous Huxley
10. Eden Phillpotts
11. C. S. Lewis
12. Gerald Heard
13. Edward Hyams
14. George Orwell
15. The Desolation of the Future
16. British Science Fiction
17. Science Fiction and Fantasy
18. The Ambitions and Achievements of Scientific Romance
19. The Future of Scientific Romance

APPENDICES

1. A Chronology of Significant Texts
2. A Chronology of Major Genre Writers

BIBLIOGRAPHY

1. Bibliographical Reference Works
2. Historical and Critical Works
3. Studies of Individual Authors

INDEX

PROLEGOMENON

1. THE DEFINITION OF SCIENTIFIC ROMANCE

What this history means by "scientific romance" is a genre of imaginative fiction that enjoyed a brief vogue in the British isles in the late 1890s, when the term was popularized in connection with a sequence of novels and short stories by H. G. Wells, and which continued to enjoy a certain popularity until the outbreak of the Great War. After that interruption, similar works of fiction enjoyed a gradual resurgence in the 1920s and a second flourishing in the 1930s, until the outbreak of World War II. After that war, the term "scientific romance" fell into almost complete disuse, although fiction of a recognizably similar stripe continued to be produced for a while in Britain, before being eclipsed and displaced by a rising tide of fiction produced under the borrowed American label of "science fiction."

In an earlier book, *Scientific Romance in Britain 1890-1950*, published in 1985 by Fourth Estate, I attempted to map the broad outline of that history, attempting to identify the most important texts that could reasonably be deemed, on the grounds of their kinship with the Wellsian exemplars, to belong to the genre in question, and to explain why they formed a loose set possessed of a certain coherency. I argued that the genre, thus conceived, was significantly different in its typical interests and attitudes from the American imaginative fiction that evolved in the same sixty-year period, acquiring its own generic label half way through it. The two genres were never entirely distinct, because the Wellsian texts held in Britain to be exemplary of scientific romance were also reckoned in America to be significant precursors of science fiction, and numerous texts originating in one or other genre were published on both sides of the Atlantic. It was nevertheless the case that, during the period in question, the British and American writers picking up the themes that Wells had used took them in different directions, with a different set of imaginative and esthetic priorities in mind.

The present project is an attempt to complete the earlier one, extending the time span of its concern, filling in data that was not available to me when I wrote the earlier text, and revising assessments of the significance of some of the information recorded with the aid of fuller knowledge and hindsight. I hope to be able to supplement this volume in a few years' time with a parallel sketch of the early development of the French tradition of *roman scientifique*, which became manifest and robust before the advent of British scientific romance, but was also confused with science fiction once the American label was imported to Europe after the end of World War II. In the same way that the dissimilarities and contrasts between the British and American traditions, while they were largely separate, are interesting and illuminating, the addition of the French tradition into the picture will hopefully establish an interesting and illuminating triangular set of dissimilarities and contrasts. Because of the inherent flexibility of the term *roman*, *roman scientifique* could be translated in various ways, but the most reliable is "scientific fiction" rather than "scientific romance" or "scientific novel," because the idiosyncratic connotations of the British word "romance" make the former translation misleading and the latter term is inappropriate because the description, while it was in use, was routinely applied to short works as well as long ones.

The fact that the "science fiction" label achieved a universal dominance in the latter half of the twentieth century, making other labels seem redundant—although many of the people to whose works it was applied were dissatisfied with it, and some tried hard to invent more satisfactory substitutes—ensured that attempts to map the history of British scientific romance, either as a whole or in part, were usually subsumed into "histories of science fiction" prior to 1985. Such histories tend to take the view that all previous fiction having a significant similarity to the kinds of fiction to which the science fiction label was applied from 1930 onwards ought to be reckoned to be ancestral to science fiction, and that the history of the entire pattern of endeavor can be regarded as an essentially integral and international one.

There are a few exceptions to that rule, however. The first such history to be published, J. O. Bailey's *Pilgrims Through Space and Time: Trends and Patterns in Scientific and Utopian Fiction* (1947), was written in an era when the term "science fiction" was used almost entirely in downmarket popular magazines and had a slightly bad odor; Bailey therefore elected to describe his subject matter as "scientific fiction" and declared in its preface that the text "describes a large number of scientific romances,"[1] subsequently classifying all those texts in the Bibliography under the heading "scientific romances." Once the science fiction label had spread into books, genre historians largely abandoned the use of euphemisms, and employed "science fiction" as a generic description, but Everett F. Bleiler's massive and scrupulously-annotated bibliography of *Science Fiction: The Early Years* (1990) does use the term "scientific romance" to indicate a separate subsection of British works, for the same reasons as the present history.[2]

Many critics and historians continue to take the view that all of what Bailey calls "scientific fiction" should be considered under one heading, irrespective of its national origins. That is entirely understandable, given that the American label, and many of the assumptions and connotations associated with it, became standardized throughout the world within a decade of the appearance of *Pilgrims Through Space and Time,* and before it had any significant supplement.

The notion of the international integrity of science fiction is also supported by the fact that when the American category label was formally launched, with the founding of the first specialist magazine of "scientifiction," *Amazing Stories*, in 1926, the proprietor of the magazine in question, Hugo Gernsback, represented "scientifiction" as a genre whose solid foundations had already

---

1   J. O. Bailey. *Pilgrims Through Space and Time: Trends and Patterns in Scientific and Utopian Fiction*. New York: Argus, 1947. p.2.
2   Everett F. Bleiler, with the assistance of Richard J. Bleiler. *Science Fiction: The Early Years*. Kent, Ohio: Kent State University Press, 1990. p.xxi.

been laid in France and Britain by Jules Verne and H. G. Wells, many of whose works he reprinted in the early issues.

When Gernsback subsequently founded *Wonder Stories*, and substituted the term "science fiction" for "scientifiction," the latter magazine initially used numerous translations from both French and German. That policy deliberately maintained the notion that "science fiction" ought to be seen as an international project and as an ensemble, in conscious reflection of the fact that science is a question of universal truth, to which national, ethnic and linguistic boundaries are essentially irrelevant, and deliberately ignoring the fact that such boundaries had frequently been reflected in various ways in the fiction produced by different ethnic groups in different languages and different nations.

In spite of its initial internationalism and focus on the universality of science, however, the material published in America under the label of science fiction soon forsook translated works to become an English language project, which rapidly came to seem typically, and perhaps quintessentially, American. The labeled genre developed and evolved in its own highly distinctive fashion within the marketing category initiated by Gernsback's magazines, all the more tightly focused simply because the label had been attached to a marketing category, soon confined to a very narrow stratum of the literary marketplace, the popular "pulp magazines."

The word "pulp" was descriptive of the kind of paper on which such magazines were printed, but it also became steeped in pejorative connotations denigrating the kinds of fiction typically contained in such magazines, by comparison with that contained in more expensive "slick" magazines printed on paper of better quality. Even within the pulp milieu, science fiction soon became an eccentric isolated enclave; many of the people most heavily involved with it as readers, writers and editors came together to form a curious community of fanatic loyalists, assisted by Hugo Gernsback's encouragement of readers to become members of a "Science Fiction League" endorsed and publicized by *Wonder Stories*.

The relative enclosure and isolation of American science fiction was one of the factors that encouraged its rapid and idiosyncratic evolution; some of its fanatics compared it to a ghetto, but also to a hothouse where, in their view, a crucial transformation was taking place, by comparison with which, anything that was being done with similar themes in other locales was simply a matter of the irrelevant stirring of obsolete materials. At any rate, American science fiction soon became markedly different in its typical concerns and narrative strategies from the more loosely-aggregated genres of British scientific romance and French *roman scientifique*—a difference that remained discernible, even though the latter labels were only used in a desultory fashion, having never been generally adopted as descriptive terms, let alone as marketing labels.

It was mainly because it did become a marketing label as well as a perceived set of resemblances that the American term was able to achieve such dominance as a descriptor all over the world, in spite of the fact that some of its most diehard fanatics would have preferred to get rid of it and substitute something free from the pollution of the pejorative connotations of pulp fiction. "Speculative fiction" was the most common term of choice, and it remains the best option to identify the entire category of imaginative fiction of which American science fiction, British scientific romance and French *roman scientifique* are subsets; that is the manner in which the term will be used in the present work.

* * * *

In view of this pattern of development, it is hardly surprising that the most detailed academic study covering a part of the ground mapped out in the present project—Darko Suvin's painstaking study of *Victorian Science Fiction in the UK: The Discourses of Knowledge and Power* (1983)—is perfectly content to refer to its subject-matter as "Victorian science fiction" even though no such label was current at the time; nor is it surprising that the study embraces all the relevant works published in England in the relevant period, irrespective of their ultimate origin. Genres are, inevitably, artificial constructs defined for historical and critical consideration as well as categories represented in marketing strategies, and Suvin's operational definition is entirely justifiable. However, given that my own intention in this book, and the study of the *roman scientifique* with which I hope to supplement it, is to identify, analyze and emphasize the differences between the British, French and American traditions of speculative fiction rather than their similarities, my own strategy is also perfectly justifiable.

The two different approaches exemplified by Suvin's project and mine are not in competition. Suvin's purpose was to attempt to link the typical concerns of the writers he identifies with their socioeconomic situation—a kind of exercise that could equally well have been carried out on the writers of books published in France or America during the same period, and whose implications are intended to be universal. By contrast, the core of my concern is that literary reflections of the scientific imagination in different places are strongly influenced by idiosyncratic historical circumstances, and I shall attempt to demonstrate that the different historical experiences of the three relevant nations resulted in distinct and significant differences in the manner in which their respective traditions of speculative fiction developed prior to 1950—differences that did not entirely disappear thereafter, in spite to the universal triumph of the American label.

In his book, Suvin is so scrupulous in defining exactly what it is that qualifies a text to be described retrospectively as "Victorian science fiction" in his reckoning that he includes "An Annotated Checklist of Books Not to Be Regarded as SF, with an Introductory Essay on the Reasonable Reasons Thereof" in his survey, which is a useful exercise in deft boundary-marking. Having every sympathy with Suvin's definitive criteria, I have no quarrel with his procedure, and, in fact, my list of books identifiable as "British scientific romances" from the period covered by his book is not much different from the set of locally-originated items in his list of "science fiction novels," although I have cast my net somewhat wider and have included mention of a considerable number of works that did not qualify for inclusion in his study, on the grounds that they help to establish the intellectual and literary contexts in which the centrally relevant texts appeared.

I do not intend to offer a definition of "scientific romance" as strict as Suvin's definition of "science fiction" in terms of the contents of the works to be included, partly because I think such strict definition to be impracticable, but mainly because "scientific romance," unlike "science fiction," was a term in usage throughout the nineteenth century, and that contemporary usage needs to be taken into account in assessing its relevance to contemporary texts. It cannot be said that it was a common term—indeed, it was relatively rare—nor can it be said that it was used consistently, but it was used, and the pattern of its earlier usage has considerable relevance to its eventual adoption in the 1890s as a category description that seemed to fit many of H. G. Wells' early works. The story of the term's fugitive evolution is odd and complex, but certainly not irrelevant to an understanding of the "prehistory" of the genre that was identified in the 1890s.

* * * *

As with the use of the term "science fiction," the use of "scientific romance" as a generic term has been complicated by the fact that some of the people to whom others tried to apply it did not like it, and a few made active attempts to deny or avoid it. H. G. Wells was not initially been averse to it himself; in an interview with Arthur H. Lawrence published in *The Young Man* in 1897 he stated straightforwardly that he was thinking of starting "another scientific romance,"[3] and Lawrence used the term freely as a generic description without apparently giving rise to any objection or quibble on Wells' part. Other journalists were using the term copiously by then; St. Loe Strachey, reviewing *The War of the Worlds* in the *Spectator* in January 1898, referred nonchalantly to Wells as "a writer of scientific romances,"[4] clearly assuming that his readers would know what he meant and would not think the description at all controversial, while R. A. Gregory, reviewing the same work in *Nature* the following month, referred to Wells' "contributions to scientific romance"[5] in a similarly casual manner.

It did not take long, however, for Wells to begin to feel some discomfort with the term, and he soon abandoned its use in personal

---

3   Arthur H. Lawrence. "The Romance of the Scientist." Reprinted in J. R. Hammond, ed. *H. G. Wells: Interviews and Recollections*. London: Macmillan, 1980. p.6.
4   Quoted in Patrick Parrinder, ed. *H. G. Wells: The Critical Heritage*. London: Routledge & Kegan Paul, 1972. p.63.
5   Quoted in ibid. p.75.

references to his own works; in the classified lists of previous publications included in his books in the early years of the twentieth century, Wells generally filed the supposedly-archetypal scientific romances with other works under the rubric "Fantastic and Imaginative Romances." It was not until 1933, when Victor Gollancz issued an omnibus edition of eight novels as *The Scientific Romances of H.G. Wells,* that Wells consented to allow the phrase to reassume its authoritative status, and even then he only did so tacitly; in the preface he supplied to the volume, presumably by request, he only referred to his "fantasies" and his "scientific fantasies," and included a long argument to the effect that they were, indeed, fantasies, and did not belong to the same literary category as the works of Jules Verne. Instead, he argued that "they belong to a class of writing which includes the *Golden Ass of Apuleius*, the *True History of Lucian, Peter Schlemihl* and *Frankenstein*."[6]

That argument obviously had not convinced Victor Gollancz, who plainly felt that his title was appropriate, at least in marketing terms, but the contest between the author and the publisher makes it abundantly clear that the term "scientific romance" was always somewhat problematic, and that it suffered in Britain from image problems not dissimilar to those that led J. O. Bailey to refrain from the use of the term "science fiction" in his pioneering academic study. Although there will be occasion to refer back more than once in the course of this history to H. G. Wells' equivocation on the matter of whether his works ought or ought not to be classified as "scientific romances," there are reasonable grounds to side with Gollancz, who had sound reasons for insisting on his title, even though it provoked a surly response in his author's prefatory essay. The dispute might well have caused Wells to insist on including at least one item in the omnibus that Gollancz would rather have left out, and excluding at least one that the publisher would probably have put in, but that is a matter of conjecture.

The eight novels actually contained in the 1933 Gollancz omnibus are *The Time Machine* (1895), *The Island of Doctor Moreau* (1896), *The Invisible Man* (1897), *The War of the Worlds* (1898), *The First Men in the Moon* (1901), *The Food of the Gods* (1904), *In the Days of the Comet* (1906), and *Men Like Gods* (1923),

6 H. G. Wells. "Preface." *The Scientific Romances of H. G. Wells.* London: Gollancz, 1933. p.vii.

although some commentators would argue that the last two do not belong in the set. The initial sequence of Wells' works in the genre also included *When the Sleeper Wakes* (1899), of which Wells had issued a revised edition in 1910 as *The Sleeper Awakes*, which the same hypothetical commentators would doubtless have preferred to see included.

Wells presumably considered that the ideas for social reform contained in *When the Sleeper Wakes* had been superseded by those developed in *Men Like Gods*. *The War in the Air* (1908) is also omitted from the omnibus, perhaps because it was considered that its anticipation of the politics and armaments of a future war had been rendered obsolete by the actual war of 1914-18. *The World Set Free* (1914) had suffered the same fate.

Quibbles aside, however, it was the first four novels featured in the omnibus, along with a number of shorter stories, that had initially prompted the widespread adoption of "scientific romance" as a descriptive term by commentators, and it was that material which effectively framed and anchored understanding of what people meant in the late 1890s when they said "scientific romance."

By the time the Gollancz omnibus appeared, many of Wells' shorter scientific romances had already been reprinted in an omnibus of *The Short Stories of H. G. Wells* issued by Ernest Benn in 1927, but they had not been sorted by genre in the collections combined in that volume, although *Tales and Space and Time* (1899), which included the long novella "A Story of the Days to Come" (1897), was almost a specialized collection. There is, therefore, no single book that contains the whole set of the works that Wells produced in 1895-98, which created and formulated the notion of "scientific romance," and any attempt to draw up a definitive list is bound to run into problems at the margins. However, a reasonable core of a dozen items could be established by supplementing the first four novels in the Gollancz omnibus and "A Story of the Days to Come" with "The Flowering of the Strange Orchid (1894), "The Remarkable Case of Davidson's Eyes" (1895), "The Plattner Story" (1896), "In the Abyss" (1896), "The Sea Raiders" (1896), "The Crystal Egg" (1897) and "The Star" (1897).

Some of Wells' subsequent works, including *When the Sleeper Wakes*, were quite rightly viewed as being sufficiently similar to those dozen items to be reckoned as belonging in the same bag, and many more were seen as having some affinity with it, in spite of Wells' increasing aversion to the judgment that there really was a bag, or, if there was, that it was his. Indeed, many of Wells' subsequent works can be construed as deliberate attempts to change, break, expand or confuse the limits of the framework in which those twelve early works had been placed, and which he had evidently come to consider too restrictive in terms of his reputation and the manner in which his work was viewed.

Although the original characterization remained secure in the minds of many readers and commentators, therefore, it was inherently unsteady and controversial almost as soon as it was first applied. Most of Wells' relevant works published in the twentieth century can not only be considered as hybrids, in which elements of scientific romance are deliberately combined with other kinds of enterprise, but as works actively engaged in a combative dialogue with the notion of the genre and its limitations. The same is also true of many of the writers who followed in Wells' footsteps, although there were a few who were proud to adopt the label and proclaim their allegiance to it.

The reasons for Wells' increasing reluctance to be considered as a writer of "scientific romance" are easy enough to comprehend. Any label carries a threat of restriction, and it is a rare author who is happy to be "pigeon-holed" or "typecast" by the expectations of readers and the editorial gatekeepers positioned between writers and readers. Authorial resentment of perceived pressure to do "more of the same" is a common and well-known problem, and writers have not been shy about dramatizing its frustrations in their work. Some labels, however, seem more threatening than others, because they seem to embody insulting implications.

Wells was an exceedingly ambitious man, to say the least, and he was justifiably fearful of the potential contempt of critics who felt that "scientific romance" was intrinsically unworthy of consideration as "serious literature." It is significant that the only contemporary work he cites in his preface to the Gollancz *Scientific Romances* as an example of the "class of writing" to which his "fantasies" belong is *Lady into Fox* by David Garnett; there were dozens of other contenders, but that was the only one written by a member of the "Bloomsbury Group," whose members were widely considered at the time to be the ultimate arbiters of literary taste in England.

More specifically, Wells also seems to have reacted against the term because the use of the label tacitly placed his work in the same category as Jules Verne, to some of whose works it had previously been applied. Wells, understandably, did not want to be accounted as a mere follower—especially of a writer whose reputation in Britain was that of a producer of "boys' books": a term whose dismissive implication is perfectly obvious. It is not surprising that he went out of his way in the 1933 "Preface" to deny that particular similarity:

"These tales have been compared to the work of Jules Verne and there was a disposition on the part of literary journalists at one time to call me the English Jules Verne. As a matter of fact there is no literary resemblance whatever between the anticipatory inventions of the great Frenchman and these fantasies. His work dealt almost always with actual possibilities of invention and discovery, and he made some remarkable forecasts. The interest he invoked was a practical one.... But these stories of mine collected here do not pretend to deal with possible things."[7]

Jules Verne was entirely in agreement with this judgment, and had protested against the comparison on his own behalf in an interview with Robert H. Sherard published in *T. P.'s Weekly* on 9 October 1903, to the delight of journalists eager to discover dissent, and the amusement of future critics in search of controversy. The authors' denials of close literary kinship did not, however, prevent the association between Verne's work and Wells' becoming firmly fixed in the minds of many readers and commentators, and their names remain welded together in retrospective consciousness as the key pioneers of scientific romance and science fiction alike.

In fact, both writers were justified in their denials; there is a fundamental difference between their approaches to their subject matter and the import of their works. That does not, however, mean that there is no essential kinship between their endeavors. To some extent, the differences reflect differences between the entire tradition of the *roman scientifique* and that of scientific romance, but those initial differences were deeply confused when Wells' works were translated into French, and became as influential in France as

7   Ibid. p.vii.

they were in Britain and America. Numerous French writers and commentators, as well as numerous English writers and commentators, considered that what the relevant works of the two writers had in common was more important than what distinguished them.

In one small but significant respect, too, Wells' denial is clearly excessive. The last sentence quoted above is blatantly disingenuous. It is true that Wells' scientific romances do not deal with possible things, but it is not true that they do not *pretend* to do so. They *do* pretend, and they pretend with considerable rhetorical force; and when Wells gave up that effort of pretence, as he very obviously did, perhaps unable to maintain it any longer in his own mind and heart, he became a very different writer, who did not entirely abandon the raw materials of scientific romance, but began to deploy them in a manner so deliberately casual as to be contemptuous. That was the spirit in which he wrote the 1933 preface, but it was not the spirit in which he wrote the first dozen works that established and characterized the notion of "scientific romance" in the minds of the reading public during the final years of the nineteenth century.

2. THE IDEA OF SCIENTIFIC ROMANCE

Jules Verne was not the only writer to whom the term "scientific romance" had been applied by English reviewers and critics prior to the late 1890s, but a significant group of Verne's works, especially the trio known in English as *Journey to the Centre of the Earth* (English publication 1872), *Twenty Thousand Leagues Under the Sea* (English publication 1873) and *From the Earth to the Moon...and a Trip Around It* (English publication 1873), seemed to have special affinities with a group of Wells' early works, which justified linking the two sets of works and applying the same collective term. In its application to Verne's work by English reviewers, the term had probably been consciously adapted from the French *roman scientifique*, which had been used by commentators on the French originals, and it is entirely possible that some of its users did not realize that it had been previously bandied about in various English language publications. The fact that it had is, however, by no means irrelevant to the manner in which the term was used in and after the 1870s.

It is impossible to determine with any certainty who coined the English term "scientific romance" or when it was first used in print, but the earliest use of the phrase that it was possible to find in December 2012 by means of searching for the phrase among the digital documents indexed by the Hathi Trust and Google Books is in a footnote to a dissertation on Saxon law by the barrister James Ibbetson, first published in 1780. In that essay, Ibbetson refers scathingly to a suggestion that a Medieval Saxon legal custom might have originated in Troy, and the corollary account of its importation to England, as "the dreams of prejudice and scientific romance."[8]

The idea that refugees from Troy, led by one Brutus, credited by legend as England's first lawgiver, had once settled in Britain, was already ancient in 1780. It had been credited by scholars to Celtic legends allegedly preserved in Welsh Chronicles, and had become sufficiently familiar for many English writers, including Edmund Spenser and John Milton, to make allusion to it, but it is certainly fanciful. Indeed, the entire legendary "history" of Britain prior to William I's acquisition of the English throne in 1066 is a vast tissue of fantasies, much of it invented by the Normans in the wake of the "conquest," in the spirit of "romance," and it was subsequently subjected to a continual process of remolding as subsequent litterateurs and scholars attempted to reconcile Norman fancy with previous Saxon and Celtic fancy.

In all probability, James Ibbetson, as a man of law, meant to imply little more by his scathing dismissal of the Trojan origins of British law than the mere fact that it was nonsense—but given that, the fact that he chose not merely the term "romance," but the phrase "scientific romance," is revealing. If we are to understand why that particular portmanteau term came into existence in the latter half of the eighteenth century, it will be helpful briefly to examine the contemporary implications of both of its components a little more closely.

The English word "romance" comes from a group of French words, including both *roman* and *romance*, derived from the Old

8   James Ibbetson. *A Dissertation on the Judicial Customs of the Saxon and Norman Age*. London: B. White, 1780. p 36.

French *romanz*, whose approximate meaning was "vernacular" and was usually used to refer to documents translated from Latin. "Romance" was imported to the English language by the Normans after the conquest, but its French equivalents were in the midst of a striking evolution by then. They were used in a general sense with reference to "romance languages" descended from Latin, but in the eleventh century they were more frequently and more particularly used with reference to a genre of poetry and prose fiction that had begun with translations of Latin epic poetry but had soon given birth to prolific original composition. Just as the translations had referred to what was by then a distant mythologized past, the imitations and pastiches also looked back nostalgically to a whole series of mythologized distant pasts.

By the middle of the twelfth century—the heyday of the conquering Normans, who had originated as invaders from Scandinavia—such works had become enormously popular, and had become a kind of ideological enshrinement of the feudal political system, glorifying the contemporary hierarchy of kings, barons and knights by extending it backwards into imaginary pasts and crediting it with imaginary virtues. In the late Middle Ages the rulers of both France and England had long been descended from northern invaders—the Franks and the Saxons—who had partly displaced and partly absorbed previous cultures, loosely describable as Gauls and Celts, which had been previously conquered by the Romans, so the mythological pasts cooked up in France and England in the twelfth century were blessed with a rich complexity and confusion of inherited and improvised materials.

Literary "Romance" was, in consequence, an inherently syncretic genre, tacitly celebrating the kind of unification obtained by conquest and reorganization that was inherent in the actual history of feudalism as well as the flattering ideological image that romancers tried to construct. Although the "chivalric romance" glorifying knightly prowess in combat was at its heart, it also embraced "courtly romance," which offered an idealized depiction of intimate relationships, and it was enthusiastic to embrace all kinds of local superstitions and gather them into a generalized melting-pot—always, of course, with the proviso that threats originating from such dubious apparatus could not withstand the ideological forces of Christian faith and knightly heroism.

In France, where political domination was shared by two sets of northern invaders whose mastery was by no means total or wholly secure, the key imagery of chivalric and courtly romance was nostalgically attached to, and partly derived from, cultures with a longer local history: the courtly apparatus was associated with the southern region of Provence, whose Roman roots had been confused with Arabic influences imported via Moorish Spain, and the chivalric apparatus had a particular link with the western region of Brittany, the population of which had strong ethnic links with those of Cornwall and Wales. When the Normans imported Romance into England, therefore, it was only natural that the romances relating to the island should concoct an imaginary history that was distinctly affiliated to the Breton chivalric strand of French romance, with a relatively light seasoning of courtly romance. The imaginary history in question focused primarily on legends of King Arthur, the Knights of the Round Table and the wizard Merlin, to which was added—by courtesy of an unfinished allegory penned by Chrétien de Troyes—the striking original element of the quest for the Holy Grail. The tale of Brutus and his earlier refugees from Troy became a minor element in that vast tissue of invention.

The entire substance of Medieval Romance is deliberately fanciful. It is an extravagant, fantastic, magnificent and beautiful tissue of blatant lies. Like all fiction, however, it relied to some extent for its rhetorical effect on the assertion of its truth, and the more blatant its lies were, the harder it had to emphasize its pretence: a necessary paradox. It would probably be unsafe to say that composers of romances were never fooled by their own inventions, because charlatans are notoriously liable to fall prey to their own patter, but in the main, the inventors of romances cannot have been unaware of the fact that they were weaving pure fantasies, even though they were obliged to assert the opposite in order to pay due court to their readers' "willing suspension of disbelief."

The vast majority of hearers and readers of Medieval Romances cannot have been fooled by that imposture, any more than modern children can really believe in Santa Claus, but in the same spirit of preserving rhetorical effect, they might well have pretended to believe, at least temporarily. Subsequent scholars, however, were sometimes much less certain of the total falsehood of romance, having an innate tendency of their own to suspect and to judge that, even if the stories could not be literally or entirely true, something preserved *in writing* must surely have a seed of some kind of reliability within it. Indeed, one of the primary activities of scholarship throughout the ages, if not *the* primary activity, has been the sustained and determined endeavor to prove the false true, especially if it has been written down.

Paradoxical as it may seem, that tendency coexists with a strong desire on the part of scholars to pose as hard-headed skeptics, partly out of sincerity but partly because of the necessity to establish and conserve their own rhetorical effect. Scholars are inherently far more likely to fall prey to their own patter than inventors of romance; indeed, it is a rare scholar who does not. There is no fantasy that tries harder to pretend to be fact than scholarly fantasy, although it is the case, perhaps sadly, that all scholarship, including scientific scholarship, contains a weighty component of fantasy—which, by virtue of its scholarly nature, tends to be very insistent in its denial of its own fantastic quality. Scholarship dealing with fanciful subject-matter—and there is none more fanciful than Romance—is, inevitably, particularly vulnerable to its own inherent tendency to fantasy.

There is too much that is obviously fantastic in the substance of Medieval Romance for its assertions ever to have been taken at face value by scholars, but that never prevented scholars from looking for "the truth behind the fiction." In the British context, that has included searching for the "real" King Arthur and the "real" Merlin behind the myths—or, at least, for "authentic" Celtic myths, legends and folklore underlying the supposedly-bastardized Norman "fakelore."

Such are the fashions of scholarship that quests for those particular unholy grails were largely conducted in terms of arguments from authority for centuries after the initial documentation had taken place, but as the perceived weight of arguments from authority began to decline by comparison with the perceived force of arguments based on objective evidence—scientific arguments—thus bringing about "the Age of Reason," and "the Enlightenment," the manner in which scholars interested in Romance conducted their research, interpreted their findings and reported their conclusions inevitably shifted.

Some scholars of the Enlightenment took up the position that, because there was not an atom of worthwhile objective evidence, the rational conclusion was that the substance of Romance was unworthy of scholarly attention, but some did not, preferring to recruit scientific—or, at least, seemingly scientific—methods and theories to the analysis of their data, in the hope of teasing out whatever precious grains of insight were lurking within it, whether ethnographic, psychological or linguistic in character.

The latter tendency became intricately involved with a spectacular resurgence in the latter part of the eighteenth century of a new kind of self-declared and unrepentant Romanticism, which deliberately took up an ideological position opposed to allegedly-obsolete but firmly-entrenched notions in art and scholarship. The boundaries of the movement in question were vague, and its manifestations in different European countries exhibited spectra of concern that were markedly different in different places, and temporally staggered in terms of the emergence of actual groups of individuals who considered themselves as members or leaders of new schools of thought and endeavor, but there were certain crucial common elements, of which the most important were an emphasis on innovation rather than convention, and a focus on emotion rather than reason as a factor in explaining what had happened in history and a source of inspiration in artistic creativity.

In Germany, where such a movement first became clearly and assertively manifest it was represented by the extrapolation of idealism in philosophy, an emphasis on *sturm und drang* [storm and stress] in art, and an interest in searching for the essential German *volksgeist* [the spirit of the race] in the folklore that was supposedly common to the people of the disunited German nation.

In France, inevitably, the equivalent movement became intricately entangled with the sources and the problematic unfolding of the 1789 Revolution, taking its artistic and philosophical cues from Voltaire, Rousseau and Diderot, and attempting to bring about Revolutions in the arts that were simultaneously, and perhaps paradoxically, progressive and disrespectful of the supposedly perverting effects of "civilization."

In Britain, where the political establishment had long forestalled one of the principal causes of the French Revolution by substituting a constitutional monarchy for an absolute one, but which nevertheless shivered in the chill of the Republican wind, Romanticism was working against a much more secure opposition, which marginalized it to a far greater extent than was possible in Germany or France, reducing its impact in philosophy as well as politics, and perhaps forcing its artistic elements to be—or, at least, to seem—more adventurous by contrast.

Although the Romantic emphasis on emotion as a factor in human motivation, at the expense of reason, and the corollary interest in intrinsically-magical folklore and mythology, might seem to run contrary to trends in the development of science, that was not necessarily the case. Emotion and folklore could be—and did, indeed, become—significant foci of scholarly investigation, using methods that at least pretended, and usually honestly inspired, to be scientific. Then again, there was no doubt that the science of the period was genuinely innovative, and at least threatened to bring about a complete revolution in human thought, thus posing a serious threat to some of the most cherished traditions of all, enshrined by the most rigid and jealous of all conventions: faith. In some respects, therefore, the evolution of scientific ideas seemed to be profoundly and quintessentially Romantic.

It was doubtless his awareness of the existence and ambition of the burgeoning movements in question, and his attitude to them, that prompted James Ibbetson to refer in his footnote to scholarship willing to entertain the thesis that British law had Trojan foundations not simple as "romance" but as "scientific romance." Ibbetson was not simply dismissing the idea of Brutus the Trojan lawgiver as a fantasy but as a scholarly fantasy—which he doubtless considered, being a hard-headed lawyer, to be a uniquely silly, and perhaps dangerous, kind of fantasy. "Scientific romance" was, in his view, something particularly pernicious, and something menacing. He was not alone in that view. It was, inevitably, shared by many practitioners of science, who were all the more enthusiastic to attack the scholarly fantasies of others while remaining in fierce denial regarding their own, no matter how evident the mote/beam relationship might seem to distanced observers.

* * * *

The phrase "scientific romance" crops up infrequently but repeatedly in documents indexed by the Hathi Trust and Google

Books published throughout the first six decades of nineteenth century, used in the same way that Ibbetson had used it—which is to say, deploring any tendency of scientists to make supposedly fanciful claims and any tendency on the part of anyone making supposedly fanciful claims to sanctify them as "scientific." The phrase seems to have been particularly common, as might be expected, in works dealing with the perceived ideological conflict between science and religion, religion's defenders routinely wanting to write off scientific ideas that challenged dogmatic belief as illegitimate "romances."

There are, however, two significant British literary works published early in the century that employ the term in their supplementary material in a revealing manner, given their fictional contents, and which will therefore warrant more detailed consideration in Chapter Two: the satirical novel *Flim-Flams! Or the Life and Errors of My Uncle and the Amours of my Aunt*, first published in 1805 under the by-line "Messieurs Tag, Rag and Bobtail," written by Isaac D'Israeli, and a story series by the Irish Catholic writer Gerald Griffin, reprinted in volumes with various different titles, including *The Christian Physiologist* (1830) and *The Offering of Friendship* (1854). For the moment, it is sufficient to observe that both authors use it in a derisory and dismissive fashion, in the same spirit of denigration as Ibbetson and various defenders of religious dogma.

The Ibbetson/D'Israeli/Griffin usage of "scientific romance" was also repeated, naturally enough, in 1845, by at least one reviewer of Robert Chambers' evolutionist account of *Vestiges of the Natural History of Creation*, prompting the introducer of the second American edition, George B. Cheever, to observe, with deliberate unrepentance, that "This book has well been called a scientific romance."[9] Other writers then began to use the term in a more neutral fashion, ignoring its insulting intent, and even attempting to construe it as a compliment. When Archibald Tucker Ritchie's *The Dynamical Theory of the Earth* was reviewed in *Annals and Magazine of Natural History* in 1851 the reviewer compared it to Chambers' *Vestiges*, calling the latter a "delightful

---

9   Rev. George B. Cheever. Introduction to *Vestiges of the Natural History of Creation* [by Robert Chambers]. Second U.S. Edition. New York: Wiley & Putnam, 1845. p.vii.

scientific romance." In the same year, a reviewer in *Macphail's Edinburgh Ecclesiastical Journal and Literary Review* described Robert Hunt's *Panthea*—another text requiring discussion in Chapter Two—as a scientific romance, in a similarly approving manner. The geological account of the Earth's past popularized by Chambers and rhapsodized by Hunt continued to attract the use of the phrase; in 1884, a reviewer in *Popular Science Monthly* applied it, as if it were the natural term to use, to Alexander Winchell's pioneering endeavor in "astrogeology," *World-Life; or, Comparative Geology*.

The abandonment of insulting implication by some of the mid-century users of the phrase presumably helped clear the way for the development of the somewhat different meaning that was later appropriated for reference to Wells. The French-derived usage that crops up in comments on translations of Jules Verne's early works was also used in the frame narrative of Henry Holt's 1867 translation of Edmond About's *L'Homme à l'oreille cassée* (1862), published in the U.S.A. as *The Man with the Broken Ear*, in which it is a straightforward translation from the French *roman scientifique*. A reference in William Stanley Jevon's *Principles of Science* (1874) to Bernard de Fontenelle's *Entretiens sur la pluralité des mondes* as a scientific romance was probably inspired in the same way.

The use of the term in Moritz Kauffmann's *Utopias; or, Schemes of Social Improvement from Sir Thomas More to Karl Marx* (1879) might be reckoned particularly significant, in that it combines the idea of scientific romance with other notions that were to remain closely linked with it, with specific reference to Francis Bacon's *New Atlantis*. Kauffmann states that *New Atlantis*: "embodies Bacon's visions of the future, and is remarkable not only as a philosophical speculation or scientific romance, but as being the outcome of sane reflection, containing but few, if any, of those chimerical extravagancies to be found in other Utopias. In the description of the conditions of mankind here we have nothing but the practical results he anticipated from a practical and diligent study of nature according to his own principles."[10] Although not intended as a definition of or manifesto for scientific romance,

---

10   Rev. M. Kauffmann. *Utopias; or, Schemes of Social Improvement from Sir Thomas More to Karl Marx*. London: Kegan Paul, 1879. p.18.

the remark highlights the more serious ambitions of that form of "philosophical speculation."

The use of "scientific romance" as a descriptive term with no pejorative implications was continued in the 1880s. In 1884 the publisher William Swann Sonnenschein issued a pamphlet entitled *Scientific Romances No. I: What is the Fourth Dimension?* by C. H. Hinton, and followed it up with four further pamphlets in the series, numbered II-V, which were then bound up into a book as *Scientific Romances: First Series* (1886). As promised, other pamphlets followed, but the series was interrupted after two more, for reasons explained in the detailed discussion of Hinton's work in Chapter Three.

The Swann Sonnenschein series presumably helped to make the phrase sufficiently familiar to invite pedantic modification on the part of hesitant users. A reviewer in *Blackwood's Magazine* in 1885 referred to the Earl of Lytton's *Glenaveril; or, The Metamorphoses* as "a scientific romance in verse." In 1889 a review in the *English Illustrated Magazine* referred to "the quasi-scientific romance of Jules Verne and his imitators," and the following year a reviewer in the *Athaeneum* referred to Robert Cromie's *A Plunge into Space* as "a pseudo-scientific romance of the Jules Verne type." The meaning of "scientific romance" that referred to works of fiction rather than conjectural essays in non-fiction seems to have become more frequent than its insulting rival after 1870, but the other did not disappear entirely, and it continued to crop up in popular science magazines in the early twentieth century.

The quasi-oxymoronic ambiguity of the phrase, mischievously exploited by D'Israeli and still retained in the odd admixture of speculative essays in Hinton's series, is a thoroughly Romantic phenomenon. The notion that scientific writing should not only stick to reportage but to dour reportage, from which all metaphor, illustration and decorative style has been ruthlessly eliminated, along with more vulgar forms of inexactitude, seemed innately conservative by the end of the eighteenth century, even though it had good arguments to support it. The proposition that literary romance ought not to allow itself to be fettered by any allegiance to a discipline intrinsically opposed to enchantment and fancy also had eloquent advocates, but that too seemed obsolete to some eighteenth-century writers eager to employ fanciful apparatus for serious rhetorical purposes. There was, therefore, every reason why the dismissive use of the term "scientific romance" should at least be counterbalanced, and perhaps displaced, by a more generous implication.

Several notable British scientists of the nineteenth century had a definite poetic streak in their writing, which often led them to rhapsodize about the wonderful implications of their discoveries. To some extent, this arose from a desire to dramatize their findings for the layman, communicating something of the excitement of enlightenment, but it was also intimately connected with the ongoing battle of ideas whereby men of science were trying to displace or modify the dogmas and prejudices of religion. In that contest, it was often considered strategic folly simply to argue flatly that certain beliefs encouraged by religion had been found to be false, and that the actual truth of some of some such matters had now been ascertained. The war was not so much about individual items of belief, but a struggle of world-views, to which aesthetic and moral considerations were far from irrelevant, and many would-be champions of science who went in search of converts to their cause were very sensitive to the esthetic considerations of their work.

Running parallel to the Romantic traditions of poetry and prose fiction paying heed to scientific ideas, therefore, is a tradition of scientific non-fiction that is intrinsically Romantic in its speculative and futuristic dimensions, frequently blessed with an elegance of style and a delicate irony. It is hardly surprising that some works of nineteenth century science, including works on geology by James Hutton and Charles Lyell, Lord Kelvin's essay on the potential lifetime of the sun and Charles Darwin's *Origin of Species* and *Descent of Man*, had such a considerable impact on literary endeavor, given their literary quality as well as the quality of their ideas. H. G. Wells began his journalistic career with the writing of speculative essays, which then became springboards for stories, and many other exponents of scientific romance were essayists as well as novelists.

* * * *

The impact of geology, cosmology and evolutionary theory on traditional views of "man's place in nature," and on moral and metaphysical philosophies relating to that question, inevitably became one of the central themes of British scientific romance. In dealing with such notions, the best writers of scientific romance exhibited a philosophical ambition that was quite remarkable, and noticeably different in its tone and implication from those of French and American writers of speculative fiction. The greater reluctance of French and American writers to involve themselves in that particular war of ideas, and their typical manner of handling it when they did, inevitably reflected differences in the religious cultures of the three nations, and the different influences of religious culture on publishing policy. French Romanticism and American Romanticism each had their own distinct flavor—as, for that matter, did French anti-Romanticism and American anti-Romanticism—and those differences affected the way that science was viewed, by scientists as well as laymen.

The most obvious difference of that kind is perhaps the heavy American emphasis on technology and the practical application of science, at the expense of theory and philosophy, as reflected in the glorification of Thomas Alva Edison as an archetype of pragmatic American genius. That emphasis not only affects the typical patterns of American science fiction but American attitudes to speculative fiction from Europe, and hence attempts to locate writers like Verne and Wells within the generalized "history of science fiction." Although Wells became a very popular writer and a key exemplar in France and America as well as in Britain, it does not follow that readers in those various countries were paying attention to the same aspects of the fiction, and it is undeniable that the patterns of his influence in France and America were different, and different from the pattern of his influence in Britain.

This is one reason why attempted "definitions of science fiction" produced by historians of the genre have created so many difficulties of application and so much controversy. Darko Suvin, in *Victorian Science Fiction in the UK,* refers back to an earlier definition of his own, which is certainly as good as any, whereby the distinguishing feature that separates science fiction from narratives of other kinds is "a fictional novelty," which, while not referring to anything in the experiential world of writer and reader, is nevertheless "valid" because of its continuity with the aspects of that experience and with beliefs about what *could* exist. The account of the novelty given in the story then becomes a kind of "thought experiment." The problems that arise in passing judgment on what Suvin calls the "validity" of the innovations in science fiction stories help to illustrate certain key differences between the typical slants of science fiction and scientific romance.

If, for instance, the most famous "fictional novelty" invented by Wells—the time machine—is considered in terms of its influence on subsequent writers of science fiction and scientific romance, it is obvious that the extrapolation of the "thought experiment" is handled differently on opposite sides of the Atlantic.

In America, where the time machine was treated as an imaginable gadget whose technical "validity" could be posited, the extrapolation of the notion eventually gave rise to hundreds of stories in which such machines were employed, individually or generally, to produce exotic and often frankly paradoxical outcomes, spawning or shoring up whole subgenres such as the "time paradox story" and the "alternative history story."

British scientific romance, however, is largely unconcerned with time machines as potential gadgets, tending to treat them as purely literary devices for launching examinations of the remote past or the eventually destiny of humankind. The "thought experiments" carried out within the two genres are markedly different in design. It is significant that Wells, having invented the machine, never used it again once he had rewritten the particular story in which it featured several times, in order to bring out the future history mapped out therein more dramatically.

American accounts of the "history of science fiction" tend to have acute problems with the notion of the "validity" of the innovations featured in speculative fiction, arguing extensively about whether certain hypothetical notions are rationally plausible or not, always wanting to demand that they ought to be devices that an Edison might actually be able to invent, while somehow veering around the obvious inconvenience that the vast majority of such devices are blatantly incapable of standing up to rational analysis.

This too can be seen as a reflection of the oxymoronic character of the two terms, but an attempted characterization of "scientific romance," rather than "science fiction" would probably be wise to put the emphasis elsewhere, admitting frankly that the "fictional novelties" typically employed in scientific romances are purely literary devices, whose merit lies not in their "validity" as rationally plausible hypotheses but in their narrative utility in opening windows of apparent possibility through which interesting vistas can be glimpsed, from which scientific discovery has drawn back the curtain. It might be a dubious contention, in this instance as in others, that the ends really justify the means, but it nevertheless remains true that one cannot always look to the means to justify the ends, as "definitions of science fiction" often attempt, overtly or covertly, to do.

It would be misleading to claim that the things that tend to happen in scientific romances really are rationally valid possibilities, or that they could be seen as possibilities in terms of the limited and defective scientific knowledge of their day. The fact is that they routinely include "plausible impossibilities" that are only tokenistically supported by an apologetic jargon borrowed from scientific discourse. H. G. Wells knew perfectly well enough that his invisible man would not be able to see with invisible eyes, and knew that the Cavorite that provided his characters with a means of flying to the moon was an arbitrary invention cooked up for the sake of convenience. That is why he felt perfectly justified in describing the romances in question as fantasies—but that does not mean that any pretence of rational plausibility offered by such endeavors is irrelevant to their nature and their effect.

The point of identifying some romances as scientific is not to make them into a species of scientific speculation, to be judged by scientific standards, but rather to separate them from those other kinds of imaginative fiction, variously describable as "supernatural fiction" or "fantasy." The distinguishing characteristic is not that scientific romances employ conceivable technologies as hypothetical narrative levers, but that they set out to exert a kind of narrative leverage that claims plausibility from a scientific worldview, rather than a supernatural world-view, in order to serve some rhetorical purpose bearing upon the supposed revelations or implications of scientific theory or discovery.

If assessment of the "validity" of the novelties employed in scientific romances is liberated from the narrow straitjacket of rational plausibility, it becomes easier to refrain from the kind of strict boundary-marking undertaken by Suvin, by virtue of which a particular text either is or is not "science fiction," and therefore either warrants full consideration or none at all. It is surely more reasonable to accept that there are matters of degree involved in characterizing stories, and that the "proportion" of scientific romance compounded with other elements in an individual text might vary considerably, not merely in its "quantity" but also in its "configuration."

It makes sense, for example, to speak of some of H. G. Wells' stories as "pure" scientific romance—*The Time Machine* and *The War of the Worlds* being typical examples—while recognizing that the elaborate spectrum of his works includes many stories that are clearly of some interest as scientific romance, while not belonging purely to that category, including fantasies that adopt a supernatural world-view in a manifestly skeptical fashion, such as *The Wonderful Visit*, "The Man Who Could Work Miracles," *The Undying Fire* and *All Aboard for Ararat*, such evident genre-hybridizing exercises as *A Modern Utopia, In the Days of the Comet, Star Begotten* and *The Croquet Player*, and also contemporary novels that have minor elements of scientific romance in their plots, such as *Tono-Bungay*. In view of this variability, a history of scientific romance cannot entirely isolate its subject matter from the other literary spectra with which it intersects and overlaps, and, while endeavoring to avoid excessive digression, I have not attempted to do.

* * * *

Historians of science fiction are usually wary, in attempting to define the nature of such fiction, to avoid any claim that science fiction is or can be predictive of the future. Indeed, science fiction writers seeking a defense against that perennially tedious supposition eventually came up with a formula, frequently used in verbal discourse by Ray Bradbury and John Brunner, among others, to the effect that: "I'm not trying to predict the future; I'm trying to prevent it." Even so, the temptation of the error sometimes proved too much to resist. Hugo Gernsback's prospectus for "scientifiction" repeatedly trumpeted the anticipatory successes of past science fiction and the predictive potential of new science fiction.

In the same way, H. G. Wells' scientific romances are often described as "prophetic," encouraged by the fact that Wells subsequently did, indeed, develop prophetic ambitions and spent the latter part of his life trying simultaneously to predict the future and to steer it in the direction of his predictions. It is certainly mistaken, however, to regard Wells' early scientific romances, or scientific romances in general, as endeavors in prediction. In many instances, they too are more interested in attempting to prevent the possibilities outlined in their futuristic visions than to predict them, but even when they are not, they remain well aware that they are dealing with futures of contingency rather than destiny—with the significant exception of the eventual extinction of the sun. Indeed, one of the cardinal implications inherent in the notion of scientific romance is that it assumes a world-view in which the future requires to be constructed by human endeavor rather than already being determined by divine diktat, and in which the whole point of investigating possibilities is to enhance the scope and expertise of choice.

Scientific romance is essentially the romance of the disenchanted universe: a universe in which new things can and must appear, quite unpredictably, by virtue of the discoveries of scientists and the ingenuity of inventors; and a universe that is already rich in strange phenomena that humans have not yet discovered, the range of which can only be tentatively estimated with the aid of scientific notions of conceivability. It remains a kind of romance, although it is skeptical of received ideas and frequently mischievous in the manner of the challenges that it opposes to them. There is an irreducible element of "flim-flam" in it, but one that aspires to enhance its seriousness rather than detracting from it, however paradoxical that might seem.

The genre varies widely in the earnest and comic inspiration of its individual inclusions, extending from the heavily didactic and passionately earnest, exemplified by Wells' careful Utopian novels and Olaf Stapledon's "essays in myth-creation," to the blithely frivolous and overtly farcical, as exemplified by the flamboyant extravaganzas of Fred T. Jane and the amiable comedies of J. Storer Clouston. The existence of this extensive spectrum should not be allowed to obscure the fact that scientific romance is always inherently playful and is never without at least a hint of seriousness. Both of these aspects are inherent in the nature of the exercise and we should not fall into the trap of considering playfulness and seriousness to be contradictory; Johann Huizinga points out emphatically in his study of *Homo ludens* (1938), that this is not the case. Scientific romances play with scientific notions in different ways, sometimes painstakingly and sometimes exuberantly, but the outcome of their play always reflects back into everyday experience. The lessons of scientific romance always have the power to change our minds by modifying our world-views, and they always have that intention, no matter how thickly coated they are with the sugar of mere amusement.

This combination of playfulness and seriousness makes scientific romance inherently iconoclastic. The better writers of scientific romance have shared with Francis Bacon a heightened awareness of the extent to which our ideas about the world are confused by "idols"—false but persuasive beliefs intricately entangled with our true ones. There is a crusading fervor about much scientific romance, because many writers consciously employed it as a way of taking up arms against false beliefs handed down by tradition, and popular follies of the day. The weapons adapted to this purpose were varied, including melodrama and satire as well as reasoned argument, but in every scientific romance, the clash of the battle can be heard.

3. THE PROBLEMS OF HETEROCOSMIC CREATIVITY

Alexander Baumgarten, who attempted to redefine esthetic philosophy in the middle of the eighteenth century, represented artistic creativity as "secondary creation"—primary creation being the divine endeavor assumed to have formulated reality. Baumgarten belonged to a philosophical school associated with Christian Wolff, a follower of Gottfried Leibniz, and therefore subscribed to the opinion Leibniz had put forward in his *Theodicy* that since God is good, he would naturally want to create the best possible world. The good artist, in Baumgarten's view, ought to have the same ambition in formulating a secondary creation.

The problem with Leibniz's proposition, of course—as Voltaire was to illustrate memorably in *Candide*—is that the world in which humans find themselves does not seem to be the best possible one at all, being rife with manifest evils and apparent flaws. Leibniz accounted for this by suggesting that God's goodness had been thwarted by the limitations of his process: in effect that, even though he was not a poor workman, his tools and his materials had left a lot to be desired. This argument might seem to be saving God's benevolence at the expense of his omnipotence, but, given the evident state of creation, something obviously has to go, and on the whole, a weak dictator seems preferable to a malevolent one.

Secondary creators need not be assumed to be omnibenevolent, and do not always want to create the best of all possible secondary worlds, but that is what Baumgarten expected of the ambition of good artists. They too, he assumed, would have to struggle against the limitations of their materials and tools—language, in the case of storytellers and writers, along with all the subsidiary problems of generic forms, narrative devices and so on—and would inevitably fall short of perfection, but some would fall further than others.

Because the creation of storytellers is secondary rather than primary, however, they have the additional consideration to take into account that the primary creation is already in place. To what extent, therefore, should their creation attempt to imitate that one, and to what extent, or in what ways, should it aim to differ from it? Baumgarten's response to this question was forthright. Since the primary creation was the best possible world, the best possible secondary creation had to be one that imitated it most faithfully, and represented it most accurately. Any variation must, *ipso facto*, be bad. Baumgarten described such variation as "heterocosmic" creativity: the attempt to create a world within a work of art significantly different in some respect from the world found and experienced by the artist.

The fact that almost all the secondary creation that had occurred within the fields of storytelling and literary endeavor prior to Baumgarten's analysis of esthetics had, in fact, been heterocosmic, did not seem particularly problematic to him. After all, the Age of Enlightenment had only just arrived, and things had apparently been improving. It was at least arguable that representations in drama, poetry and prose had become more accurate over time as techniques had improved, and the kinds of creation that seemed most distant from accurate representation—fantastic folktales, for instance—could easily be regarded as primitive forms of creativity, ripe for supersession.

Voltaire, of course, disagreed. So did many others. Nevertheless, Baumgarten's argumentative strategy permitted him to set aside a whole class of esthetic problems, and to pay them no heed. If heterocosmic creativity were to be dismissed as an error or a moral failure in itself, there was no need for him to investigate its techniques. If it ought not to be done at all, there was no need to analyze the problems that arose in trying to do it, let alone offer any suggestions as to how those problems might best be solved.

One might expect that subsequent esthetic philosophers would have rushed in where the angelic Baumgarten had feared to tread, even at the cost of seeming foolish, but there was no stampede, and, in fact, the issue continued to suffer a certain theoretical neglect. The esthetics and methodology of heterocosmic creation have not often been assiduously addressed, as theoretical issues, even by enthusiastic heterocosmic creators. Nevertheless if one is to attempt to analyze the history of a genre that is, by definition, defiantly and proudly heterocosmic, it is at least convenient, and perhaps necessary, to confront the question of what materials and tools are available to the secondary creator, and what skills are involved in their use.

In the course of compiling the history that follows, some previous attempts to do that will be encountered, notably in the subsection entitled "The Pleasures and Perils of Imagination," which gives brief consideration to contemporaries of Baumgarten who took a very different approach to esthetic philosophy. It might, however, be useful, by way of introduction, to skip ahead of those pioneering endeavors and introduce some recent perspectives and terminology that help to provide an analytical framework for the consideration of the origins and evolution of scientific romance.

* * * *

The definition of the genre, as outlined in the previous subsection, already addresses the most fundamental problem facing the heterocosmic creator—which, as every heterocosmic creator who has ever been questioned about the creative process knows from tedious experience, is: "Where do you get your ideas from?"

The secondary creator who follows Baumgarten's advice to stick to representation of the primary creation has the materials for the task already defined, and must adopt and adapt tools appropriate to those materials. The heterocosmic creator, by contrast must find additional materials: elements of potential worlds-within-texts that are not to be found in primary creation. There are ready-made stocks of such elements, conserved by tradition and folklore: notions that are immediately recognizable to potential hearers and readers even though they are not aspects of the experienced or believed-in world. They are the basic materials of most fantastic fiction, and a significant fraction of the stock-in-trade of "Romance." Scientific romance, however, defines itself in terms of a different source: it takes its elements of difference not from the traditional imagination—from the imaginary past of myth, legend and folklore—but, ostensibly at least, from rational conjecture.

As the last subsection pointed out, the idea of "scientific romance" first arose in order to refer to apparent follies of scholarship: to fancies or "flim-flams" that were new rather than traditional, having been spontaneously generated by philosophical effervescence. Unlike traditional romance, which is only heterocosmic in that it refers back to notions largely discarded from common belief, or at least rendered problematic in the context of common belief, scientific romance is more determinedly heterocosmic, tending not so much toward the no-longer-believed but toward the potentially-believable. Not all scientific romance is futuristic, but there is a sense in which it is all futuristically orientated; it does not deal with notions once believed but now condemned as obsolete, but—ideally, at least—with hypothetical possibilities yet to be put to the proof.

The necessity of dealing with materials of that sort inevitably creates problems for the design and manipulation of the tools required to shape them. To some extent, the narrative instruments adapted to shape the materials of imitative creation and those of traditional heterocosmic creativity can be borrowed—and inevitably are, since there is no other readily-available starting-point—but their adaptation cannot be straightforward.

The relevant problems of adaptation apply to all scientific romance, but are most obvious in the fraction that is most straightforwardly futuristic, because the standard "narrative voice" of literary representation is couched in the past tense. Narrative authority—the storyteller's entitlement to be telling the story—is largely based on the assumption, or pretence, of experience: either "this happened to me" or "this happened to a friend of mine," or, at the very least, "I heard this story…." The problem is not diminished for depersonalized narrative voices that adopt a stance of impersonal objectivity; their authority too is bound up in the assurance that "this is what happened," or, at the very least, "this is what is said to have happened."

There is a sense in which that problem has now disappeared, or at least faded to negligibility. Twenty-first century listeners, readers and viewers know that it is possible for a narrative voice to speak as if it were speaking, not in the assumed local present, but from some hypothetical distant or future viewpoint. Being aware of that possibility, twenty-first century consumers of scientific romance are well enough attuned to signals identifying and locating such viewpoints that the narrative labor necessary to set them up within a text can now be minimized. The labor in question still has to be done, but secondary creators know that most of the addressees of their creation will be sufficiently skilled in construing such clues that it need not be hard or brutal.

That was not always the case; in fact, it is a recent achievement. For most of the twentieth century, the only consumers possessed of the skills necessary to identify, locate and comfortably relate to futuristic hypothetical viewpoints were specialists who had cultivated and gained a particular expertise in that kind of exercise: "science fiction fans." In the early part of the century, and throughout previous history, such expert consumers were exceedingly rare. In order for a narrative voice to adopt a futuristic viewpoint—or, indeed, any viewpoint from which the raw materials of *scientific* romance could be deployed for shaping—the secondary creator had to do a good deal of introductory narrative labor, which usually had to be hard, and frequently brutal.

Just as there are two principal ways to imagine primary creation, there are two principal approaches to the construction of a literary heterocosm. Primary creation can be envisaged as creation *ex nihilo*: from nothing to something; alternatively, it can be envisaged as a rearrangement, bringing order out of chaos—or, somewhat conversely, bringing variety out of uniformity. A literary heterocosm can be constructed as a whole, as it were, in advance of the beginning of the narrative; alternatively, it can be constructed by degrees within the narrative. In either case, of course, it will have to be displayed by degrees, but in the former case, the narrative viewpoint will encounter the heterocosm already integrally present in the world within the text, whereas in the latter, the heterocosm will develop by a process of evolution.

Nowadays, as has just been pointed out, it is possible for a secondary creator simply to set up a heterocosm within a text, and plunge potential readers into that heterocosm without any kind of introduction or preamble, expecting them to have the skills to orientate themselves rapidly and accommodate themselves to the specific heterocosm even though it is new to them. Once upon a time, however, the vast majority of listeners and readers were only able to orientate themselves swiftly and easily within heterocosms with which they were already vaguely familiar, engaging a set of ready-made expectations that could be evoked by the use of a formula such as "once upon a time." It was not easy to get here from there, even to the extent that today's readers really have arrived, and the history of scientific romance is, in part, a narrative of how they were guided as they made their way.

Heterocosms into which readers are plunged directly are categorized by Farah Mendlesohn, in a taxonomy sufficiently accurate for its terminology to be useful, as "immersive fantasies": stories set entirely within "secondary worlds" in which the characters are already at home, because it is the world of their everyday experience, their normality. The consumption of immersive fantasy depends on the consumer's readiness, willingness and ability to take a plunge, to dive straight in and adopt the secondary creation as a temporary mental residence.

Consumers have always been ready and willing to do that with respect to certain kinds of heterocosms. Indeed, there are certain kinds of heterocosms in which at least some consumers feel more at home than they do in the world of real experience, which can be very difficult to orientate oneself within, especially for children. As Michel Butor has pointed out in his essay "La Balance des fées" (1954 tr. as "On Fairy Tales"; reprinted in *Répertoire*, 1968; tr. as *Inventory*), the great utility of fairy tales as a medium of fictional communication between adults and children is that the child listener knows fairyland as well as the adult does, and far better than the real world that the adult inhabits. The function of the ritual opening "Once upon a time" is to engage a set of assumptions on the listener's part regarding the kind of fictional world in which the story is set. Writing immersive fantasies set in the future, however, poses very different problems, because there is no such set of shared assumptions on which to draw.

One of the principal reasons for the existence of the kind of secondary creation of which Alexander Baumgarten approved is that such creations provide advice and guidance that can be useful in helping its consumers adapt themselves better to the real world. The same is true of all the other kinds of secondary creation, although their methods are subtler. That is one of the reasons why many consumers thought and found that it might be useful, in the course of the twentieth century, to develop the skills necessary to orientate themselves within a wider range of heterocosms, including the problematic heterocosms of scientific romance.

Because the skills involved in consuming immersive fantasies other than those in which it is easy for consumers to make themselves at home pose a challenge, other ways were long ago developed of dealing with literary heterocosms, which seemed, until recently, to be far more convenient as vehicles for any heterocosm possessed of novelty. The most seemingly-convenient of all is what Mendlesohn calls "portal fantasies": stories that begin in a simulacrum of the experienced world, in which characters of a kind that a listener or reader can easily recognize are then led by the narrative thread *into* a ready-made heterocosm located within or alongside the simulacrum of the experienced world. That process of guidance is often represented as a literal journey, but it sometimes involves a more abrupt process of passing through some kind of "portal," and the fact that the destination to be reached is hypothetical means that the unorthodox journeys employed to reach them can also be considered as portals

Portal fantasy is very convenient as a narrative strategy, because it provides potential listeners and readers with a protagonist to whom the heterocosm is just as unfamiliar as it is to them, who can and will explore it on their behalf, seeking explanations on their behalf, and building an understanding on their behalf. It is particularly convenient with respect to scientific romance, not only because of the intrinsic novelty of the heterocosms involved but also because of the manner in which those novelties are supposedly derived: by the logical extrapolation of ideas. The protagonist who passes through the portal can not only learn the configuration of the heterocosm but its innate logic, the process by which it has been extrapolated—which is, in essence, the whole point of the exercise.

Portal fantasies do, however, have certain innate inconveniences as well as their fundamental convenience. One is the matter of location. In an immersive fantasy, a heterocosm can simply be presumed to exist; although the question of its location relative to the consumer's world of experience might well be raised and addressed, it is a subsidiary issue; from the viewpoint of the characters in the story, the world within the text is simply the reality in which they live, and although visiting readers are perfectly entitled to wonder how it relates to their own world, they are only present, as it were, in spirit, and must simply take it as given. In a portal fantasy, however, the world within the text is initially defined as a simulacrum, within which the heterocosm requires a geographical or geometric location, or an alternative existential status. To put it more simply, the heterocosm within a portal fantasy needs to be either a hypothetical place or a dream. Both alternatives come with awkward corollaries, and the history of scientific romance provides graphic illustrations of the difficulties involved in handling those kinds of baggage.

The other seemingly-convenient way of accommodating heterocosms within narratives without requiring an immersive plunge is the approach that Mendlesohn terms "intrusive fantasy": beginning a story in a simulacrum of the experienced world and then introducing a single novelty into it, whose existence and effects occasion a partial transformation of the world within the text into a heterocosm.

This strategy can also be useful, especially with respect to scientific romance, because it can actually display the logic of the extrapolation, step by step, but, by the same token, it has the monstrous inconvenience of having to go through a long-winded process one step at a time. An intrusive fantasy can eventually produce a heterocosm very different from its initial simulacrum, but it has to do so gradually. The literary forms that permit something of that sort to happen rapidly are necessarily synoptic. Any literary form that attempts or pretends to describe events as they happen is direly handicapped in the extrapolation of any intrusive novelty beyond a few relatively simple steps, and the production of any but a very modest heterocosm.

As Mendlesohn points out, the tacit existence of this problem has had a profound effect on the history of intrusive fantasies, whose principal corollary has been that in the vast majority of such fantasies, the intrusive novelty—the "bringer of chaos," as she aptly calls it—is only allowed a temporary effect. In most such stories, a seemingly-natural narrative arc moves toward a conclusion in which the novelty is removed, restoring the simulative nature of the world within the text. The narrative tidiness of that kind of conclusion carries an innate charge of satisfaction, which offers a powerful resistance to the extrapolation of the novelty, so that the urge to remove the intrusion almost invariably triumphs over any temptation or desire to follow its logical consequences very far.

The existence and attraction of that seemingly-natural story arc within the history of intrusive fantasy has created severe problems for secondary creators employing that strategy for the purposes of scientific romance—except for those creators intent on or content to represent the relevant hypotheses as mere follies thoroughly deserving of being put away in that fashion. Indeed, insofar as scientific romance is construed as a kind of flim-flam, intrusive fantasy is very attractive format, to the extent that it makes any attempt to use the format in a different spirit look a trifle silly, in spite of any creative attempt to be serious.

There is nothing actually preventing the use of intrusive fantasy to display novelties pregnant with some kind of future possibility, thus offering a glimpse of the possibilities inherent therein, but it is impractical for any conventional narrative actually to develop the possibilities in question, so as to bring about a complete and comprehensive transmutation of the world within the text, one step at a time. Either the process has to be presented synoptically, or it has to involve a temporal leap that will effectively transform the narrative into a portal fantasy. If, on the other hand, the intrusive fantasy is allowed to follow its customary story arc, removing the novelty, then any future possibilities glimpsed are, tacitly if not explicitly, subverted.

Portal fantasies are better pre-adapted to accommodate futuristic possibilities than intrusive fantasies, but the fit has acute problems there too. If a heterocosm is provided with a geographical location within a portal fantasy, then it is fundamentally bound to the present of the simulacrum, and any "futuristic" novelties it displays will require special explanation. The idea that the inhabitants of a hidden enclave might have made a more rapid social evolution than familiar cultures, thus becoming "more advanced," carries a certain innate implausibility, even in an era that is completely accustomed to such notions of evolution and advancement—the era in question is, of course, historically recent—and that kind of notion has severe limitations of elasticity.

Before the conceptual foundations of such narrative moves were laid, and for some time afterwards, it seemed to the great majority of dealers in future possibility that the best, if not the only, option for locating any kind of ambitious heterocosm within a portal fantasy was to locate it beyond the "gates of dream" eloquently described in Homer's *Odyssey* as the gate of horn and the gate of ivory. Unfortunately, and inevitably, not only is one of those Homeric gates assumed to lead to cruel deception rather than accurate revelation, but it is supposedly difficult to tell them apart. Once again, therefore, any future possibilities glimpsed or developed in portal fantasies of that sort are tacitly, if not explicitly, subverted from the start.

* * * *

Whichever narrative strategy is employed in a scientific romance, it is required to cope with the problem of the unfamiliarity of the hypothetical materials involved in the particular heterocosmic variations employed in the story. There is, of course, abundant scope for innovation within any kind of heterocosm, and scientific ideas may become familiar even if they are always new to begin with, but in general, writers of scientific romance are likely to have more narrative labor to do in explaining the variations in their heterocosms than writers employing traditional materials. That additional burden of explanation causes problems with regard to rhetorical strategy, narrative pace and narrative flow.

Scientific romances are obliged by their nature to carry more exposition than stories set in simulacra of the experienced world or in heterocosms whose variations mostly follow a familiar pattern. That additional exposition takes up narrative space, which inevitably puts pressure on the other elements of composition that make up stories: dialogue, the description of locations, the reportage of action and the analysis of character. In some instances, exposition might crowd out some or all of those aspects to the extent that the romance bears a closer resemblance to an essay than a story, and it does, in fact, make good sense to identify a genre of "speculative non-fiction," suspended somewhere between orthodox philosophical discourse and speculative fiction, just as it makes good sense to identify a genre of "scholarly fantasy," in which much of what James Ibbetson and Isaac D'Israeli identified as "scientific romance" exists.

For this reason, readers accustomed and attuned to naturalistic fiction or to conventional forms of heterocosmic fiction sometimes find scientific romance awkward and slightly alien, requiring more effort than ordinary reading, or effort of a different sort. Some readers find a particular pleasure in that: an opportunity to exercise "mental muscles" that might otherwise be unused; others find a particular displeasure, as the metaphorical muscles in question feel the strain and begin to ache. The effort in question is not evenly distributed across the various narrative strategies identified above; intrusive fantasy and portal fantasy are designed in such a way as to minimize, or at least to spread out, the effort concerned; immersive fantasies tend provide more abrupt and more immediate challenges.

A further problem that has a particular relevance to the development of scientific romance, and to which this history will be required on occasion to refer, is that of "melodramatic inflation." In any discernible sequence of texts, ranging from a single story series by an individual author to an entire genre, each work produced is obliged, to some extent, to take account of those that have gone before. Part of that accountancy is, inevitably, a desire to avoid mere repetition: to do something different and, if possible, better. In scientific romance more than any other genre, "better" can easily be construed as "bolder"—more exotic, or more "spectacular."

Once a particular narrative move has been made, and is, so to speak, "on record," there is always an incentive to take any vaguely similar move at least a little further. Within a single author's oeuvre, therefore, and within an imaginative genre as a whole, there tends to be an unsteady but continual increase in melodramatic pitch. The challenges faced by heroes become gradually more difficult; villains become gradually more evil and more ingenious in their villainy; battles become more violent, and are fought on a larger scale. Those factors are applicable to all genres of fiction, but there are extra ones limited to and typical of scientific romance, which enable more dramatic narrative shifts. Near futures, alien worlds and new inventions become increasingly complex and surprising; further futures envisaged become increasingly distant; catastrophes increase in magnitude; the average narrative expenditure on a conclusive *deus ex machina* creeps ever upwards.

Naturally, writers who go swiftly to new extremes cannot be expected to exceed their own limits every time; nor can other writers be expected to outdo them consistently. There is always more narrative labor to be done in filling in the gaps left by daring new leaps of the imagination. On the whole, though, the general tendency is always inflationary: upwards and outwards. That is one of the major features of the evolution of any genre, and it applies more forcefully to scientific romance than any other. It is one of the principal aspects of the overall narrative of the genre, reflected as untidily and fragmentarily as any other aspect of that narrative, but obtrusive nevertheless.

One might expect that melodramatic inflation would actually kill off some sequences of narrative development by taking them as far as they can go, eventually leaving no more scope for further expansion. In fact, that rarely happens, not only because of the scope left by mighty leaps for ingenious filling in but also because limits tend to be more elastic than they sometimes seem, rarely running out of scope for the envelope to be pushed any further. Even so, lines of narrative development do occasionally fall into desuetude, and excessive melodramatic inflation is one of the potential causes of that kind of decline.

Scientific romance is so multivarious, in terms of its themes, and is so copiously supplied with new stimuli by the advancement of science and technology, that it would never have run out of scope for new ventures had the genre continued all the way to the end of the twentieth century and beyond. Indeed, looking back at its sum, one is obliged to conclude that a very large fraction of the scope potentially available to it went unexploited. Even so, the deleterious effects of melodramatic inflation were frequently manifest, at the level of individual authorship and that of the entire genre, and there will be occasion to comment on a number of instances in the chapters to come.

* * * *

These matters of narrative technique are, admittedly, rather abstract, but their consideration will hopefully help readers of the present text, perhaps enormously, to understand the peculiar history of scientific romance—in particular, to understand why that history is so awkward, so diverse and so extensively strewn with apparent absurdities. It might also help to understand why it makes sense to record the history in question as a *narrative* history, embodying a definite evolutionary process, rather than merely as a catalogue of texts that have certain thematic resemblances to one another.

Scientific romance is a difficult genre in which to work, because there is no narrative strategy comfortably adapted to it, and whichever strategy is selected brings with it innate difficulties that a secondary creator must work hard to overcome, sometimes against the active opposition of the format. It is, in fact, arguable that those difficulties are insuperable and that no one has ever fully succeeded in overcoming them—and that it is partly in consequence of that fact that scientific romance is now a dead genre, whose brief intrusion on to the literary scene brought nothing but chaos, and which was ultimately required by the legislation of narrative logic and the devaluation of its imaginative currency to be put away.

Perhaps that is so—but even if it is, the fact that some secondary creators thought the Herculean labor worth attempting is not insignificant or uninteresting. It is, at the very least, Romantic. The knights errant of scientific romance might, in the end, have failed to slay any giants, and mostly seemed quixotically absurd while they were merely tilting at windmills, but they were heroes nevertheless, worthy of study and admiration. Most of them were not even wholly confident themselves that what they had actually achieved, when their labor was complete, had lived up to their initial hopes, and many gave up after falling at the first hurdle, but some pressed on anyway, trying at least to fail better, sometimes with a great deal of determination, intelligence and ambition. That surely entitles them to the respect of serious consideration.

CHAPTER ONE

THE ROOTS OF THE GENRE

1. PHILOSOPHICAL SPECULATION

There is a sense in which every emergent literary genre is built on the foundations of all those that have gone before, with deep roots that go back even beyond the limits of history, into the genres of oral discourse that provided the raw materials for the first written texts. Scientific romance has an extra set of roots, equally deep, related to the development of the ideas that provided its stimulation. It would obviously be impractical, therefore to study the roots of the genre is full detail, but it would be taking too much for grated not to study them at all. There are several particular threads within the vast pattern of prior circumstance that are of particular relevance to the eventual development of scientific romance, and which made vital contributions to the pattern of its weave. There is an inevitable awkwardness and artificiality about the isolation of individual threads from a tangle that contains seamless fusions as well as overlaps and knots, but for the purposes of this history it will be helpful to separate out four such threads for special consideration.

The first of these crucial ancient threads of consists what I shall call "philosophical speculation," borrowing the phrase that Moritz Kauffmann used as tentative synonym for "scientific romance" in speaking of Francis Bacon's *New Atlantis*. That saves the slight awkwardness of adapting the French phrase *conte philosophique* into English as "philosophical tales," although the latter designation, favored by Voltaire for an eighteenth century genre of fanciful skeptical fiction that helped to lay the foundations for the French *roman scientifique*, would by no means be inappropriate, in emphasizing the playful element of the exercise as well as its serious side. That playful element was not something that Voltaire arbitrarily added to a kind of philosophical speculation that he, like Kauffmann, defined by its sanity, but goes back all the way to Classical sources, most particularly to the uses of exemplary fictions—including, and perhaps especially, the invention of the tale of Atlantis by Plato.

Plato, who lived from approximately 428 to 347 B.C., was by no means alone in using fanciful tales to illustrate philosophical points, but the survival rate of documents produced by his forebears and approximate contemporaries is so low that it is not easy to identify the sequence of their use by other pioneers. If Plato's account of his mentor can be trusted, Socrates was not much given to the strategy in his own teaching methods, and Plato's pupil Aristotle—who, having set up the Lyceum as a rival to Plato's Academy, then made it a point of principle to disagree with Plato in every regard where disagreement seemed possible—refused to make any significant use of it. For those reasons, Plato's devices stand out as a pioneering enterprise

Plato founded the Academy, organized its syllabus and produced many of his dialogues in a spirit of outrage against the manner in which Socrates had been treated by the citizens of Athens, who had condemned the great educator to death for "corrupting" the city's youth. Socrates' trial is described in some detail, fictionalized for effect, in the *Phaedo*, and many of Plato's other dialogues feature Socrates in the leading role, preserving and promulgating his ideas and displaying the "Socratic method" of education, in which a teacher constructs a persuasive argument to guide a pupil from truths already admitted to a further conclusion.

Plato's dialogues provided a key model for philosophical discourse and established the key principle that knowledge ought to be obtained by intellectual effort rather than the mere acceptance on faith of authoritarian statements. Those of his surviving works that seem to be early are primarily devoted to the quest for clear definitions of qualities such as courage, excellence and soundness of mind, and often occupy themselves with the puzzling question of why men in pursuit of good so often commit evil acts. In those works, the character of Socrates usually takes up a critical position, ruthlessly exposing flaws in the reasoning of others. In a second, probably later, group of dialogues, the Platonic Socrates sets out his own convictions and speculations more elaborately, although it seems likely that Plato was no longer quoting his old teacher but using a fictitious version of him as a mouthpiece.

That seeming shift in emphasis takes place in the course of the *Republic*, which commences as a critique of the idea of justice in the standard dialogue form, but becomes much more elaborate in its rhetorical method, setting several significant and highly influential precedents in the philosophical use of literary method. It includes a pioneering attempt to design an ideal society, and three striking exercises in didactic fabulation: the allegory of the cave; the story of the ring of Gyges; and the story of Er.

The allegory of the cave likens the imperfections of human perception to the plight of prisoners in a cave, chained with their backs to the mouth, so that they are aware of the underlying reality of the world—its constituent Forms—only by means of a series of reflections cast upon the wall by firelight. The story of Gyges describes the discovery of a ring that confers the ability to make oneself invisible, so that any action can be performed with impunity, and poses the question of whether a man equipped with such a device would be likely to act in accordance with moral prescriptions. The story of Er, which concludes the dialogue, is an afterlife fantasy and cosmic vision, in which a dead soldier is borne away to an Elysian Meadow in order to be judged, before seeing the Spindle of Necessity, on which the cosmic whorl—a primitive version of the cosmology subsequently refined by Aristotle and Ptolemy, owing much to ideas credited in legend to Pythagoras—is spun, to the accompaniment of the music of the spheres.

Another dialogue of considerable importance to the development of fabular manufacture is the *Symposium*, which, set at a banquet, is the only Platonic dialogue in which all the participants can be assumed to be drunk—an appropriate state for a discussion of the intoxications of love. The contributors to the dialogue include the famous writer of comedies Aristophanes, whom Plato had criticized for harming Socrates' reputation with the satirical caricature featured in *The Clouds*, but whose narrative method he nevertheless appreciated. It is in the mouth of the unsober Aristophanes that he places a tale suggesting that human beings must once have been compound spherical entities, rolling along quite happily, until the gods split them up into misshapen fragments as a practical joke, condemning them all to spend their lives longing for reunion with their relevant "other halves" in the hope of recovering a more rounded character. The tale is generally represented as an account of "the Hermaphrodite" or "the Androgyne," although the pairs in the original spheres include homosexual unions as well as heterosexual ones, so they are by no means all androgynous.

The most relevant of Plato's dialogues to the subsequent development of science, and to Plato's subsequent literary influence, is the *Timaeus*, which includes a more elaborate version of his cosmology, as well as his comments on physics and biology. The *Timaeus* attempts to combine the mathematical ideas of the Pythagoreans with the Empedoclean theory of the elements, crediting the atoms of the four elements with different geometrical forms and employing a spatial void as the basic metaphysical substrate containing such atoms. Significantly, the *Timaeus* also makes further use of literary method, further elaborating the hypothetical construction of an ideal state in the *Republic* by hypothetically incarnating that state on the fictional vanished island of Atlantis. Plato continued the description of Atlantis more elaborately in the *Critias*, but if that dialogue was ever completed, the full version did not survive.

Plato's usage of fanciful literary methods of rhetorical exposition was often seen as an embarrassment by later philosophers, who frequently marginalized that aspect of his work. The subtleties of his method sometimes went unappreciated; it is still commonplace to find references to "Plato's theory of the Hermaphrodite," as if that tale—deliberately presented as a fictitious invention by a drunken comedian famous for fantastic satire—represented something Plato might actually have believed rather than a playful fantasy contrived to dramatize and highlight the absurdity of a puzzling feature of human behavior.

The mistake of believing that ancient writers in general always meant what they said in a crudely literal fashion remains surprisingly common, even among Christians, who somehow contrive to forget that Jesus' fundamental teaching instrument, according to the gospels, was the parable: a form of story that depends on the ability and willingness of its audience to perceive a much more important meaning behind and beyond the trivial literal one. Jesus never wrote a single line, alas, but if the accounts of his teaching contained in the gospels are accurate, he was far too sophisticated a thinker and storyteller ever to have thought that the tales contained in the Torah should be taken literally rather than viewed as exemplary fables constructed in a spirit of philosophical speculation.

Few people made that mistake with respect to Plato's story of Er or the allegory of the cave, but the tale of Atlantis became an archetypal focal point of scholarly fantasy, the effects of which extended so far that they eventually found a considerable space in the intimate entrails of modern literature, including a significant appendix of scientific romance. Nobody makes the same mistake about Aristophanes' fancies—Nephelococcygia, as featured in *The Birds* and Anglicized as "Cloudcuckooland" has become a significant emblem of non-existence—but the earnest tone of Greek tragedy has often encouraged people to construe such works as reflections of the actual beliefs of the authors rather than the deliberate transfiguration of mythical materials from an essentially skeptical viewpoint.

The mythical and folkloristic materials contained in the Old and New Testaments, in Greek theogony and tragedy, and in the literary inclusions of Plato's dialogues, all remain crucially important to modern imaginative literature because they provided an important component of its vocabulary of ideas. They are still present within it, and the overwhelming probability is that they have not changed their nature as much as some commentators are willing to assume. If they are not to be reckoned scientific romances themselves, because such "science" as they contain is too primitive to be worthy of the name, they are nevertheless romances, and they are, for the most part and probably invariably, *conscious* romances, deliberately formulated as philosophical speculations rather than blunt expressions of belief. It is therefore not surprising that they echo so plangently in modern literature in general, and scientific romance in particular.

* * * *

In addition to its included tales, Plato's *Republic* also contains the beginnings of literary theory: a fundamental analysis of the methods of storytelling, which calls attention, among other things, to the different narrative strategies of *mimesis* (representation, as by the actors in a drama) and *diegesis* (reportage, as by the chorus in a kind of drama that was already obsolete by Plato's day). Plato argues that although drama performed by actors is wholly mimetic, the mimetic and the diegetic are artfully combined in epic poetry. He does not bother to point out, perhaps because he thought it obvious, that fables, being wholly diegetic, form a spectral terminus opposite to that of sophisticated drama. The *Republic* is itself an artful combination of the two strategies, as any dialogue may be in which the participants use diegetic strategies akin to those employed in the stories of Gyges and Er.

Platonic dialogue and epic poetry became gradually marginalized by the subsequent evolution of philosophy and literature, although both survived into the eighteenth century, but the new forms of endeavor that took up some of their methods retained that artful combination of the mimetic and diegetic. Medieval romances carried forward the methods of epic poetry in verse before and after their gradual transition into prose, while the adaptation of dialogue as a significant mode of mimetic literary discourse helped to bring about a crucial transformation of prose fiction in the course of the evolution of the novel. Diegetic narrative voices tended to fade further and further into the background as the characters in novels loomed ever larger and their dialogue became more naturalistic, but they retained their function, while prose romances also benefited increasingly from more skilled use of mimetic dialogue.

In work continuing the tradition of Medieval romances into later centuries, however, all the way through to the renaissance brought about by the Romantic Movement, diegetic discourse held its own much more forcefully, not only in the narrative background, but also in the ways that characters tended to talk to one another; the artistry of that combination, and its gradual modification by mimetic methods, was a crucial factor in the eventual evolution of scientific romance. Platonic allegory and fabulation, and the method of exemplification that established the archetypal republic of Atlantis, became key strategies of modern diegetic enterprise, elaborately displayed in scientific romance—perhaps more ingeniously than anywhere else, by virtue of the imperatives of its ambition.

Philosophical speculation not only drew upon the supernatural world-view in the course of its evolution from its Classical origins, but made a considerable contribution to the continual reformulation and repopulation of that world-view. By the time Medieval romance became a popular genre, the calculated manufacture of mythical, legendary and folkloristic materials had become an industry, as the makers of romances fused the chivalric pretences of the feudal system of social organization with the saintly legendry of the church, expanding both in the process. Of particular relevance to the subsequent evolution of British literature, including scientific romance, is the remarkable invention by Britain's Norman conquerors and their relatives in France of "the matter of Britain": an imaginary history of the islands, complete with a lexicon of fictional characters and exploits, whose absolute unreality still remains difficult for many commentators to accept.

The mythological resources of European literature broadened out by means of a cultural syncresis that supplemented Graeco-Roman and Hebrew sources with Scandinavian and Teutonic mythology, and a significant component of the Romantic Movement of the late eighteenth and early nineteenth centuries was a dramatic renewal of interest not only in the "rediscovery" of local mythology and folklore as a kind of national heritage, but also the wholesale recycling and transfiguration of such materials, and the continued manufacture of new supplementary elements.

One striking example of the process is provided by the reinvention of philosophical speculation in France by Voltaire, who made the most of materials borrowed from the exotic tales of wonder recently popularized in France by Antoine Galland's *Les milles et une nuits* (1704-17)—which had recycled a quantity of Arabic folklore and covertly supplemented it with pastiches—in the satirical extrapolation of various philosophical issues of his day. Although Voltaire devised the term *conte philosophique* by analogy with *conte populaire* (folk-tale) the works to which he attached the label were very various in length; what he meant to emphasize was that the works needed to be read as fabulations, their artificiality being plainly manifest. The first of them "Le Monde comme il va, vision de Babouc" (1746; tr. as "The World as It Is") summarized in its title the nature of the exercise, which was to show the world as it really is, and not as contemporary ideologies deceptively represented it to be, by means of fantastic devices whose distancing from mundane expectation created a kind of sarcastic objectivity, and a special sanity.

Although only one of Voltaire's *contes philosophiques* fully qualifies as *roman scientifique*—*Micromégas* (1752; tr. as *Micromegas*), a fierce assault on religious vanity, the distanced viewpoint of which is that of a giant visitor from Sirius, who picks up a local giant from Saturn on his way to Earth—several others are close in spirit to modern skeptical fiction. *Zadig, ou la Destinée* (1748; tr. as "Zadig; or, Destiny") tracks the misfortunes of a master of logical deduction whose brilliance is unappreciated by various interrogators, thus becoming a significant precursor of detective fiction as well as a comment on the popular reception of scientific discoveries. *Candide, ou l'Optimisme* (1759; tr. as *Candide; or, Optimism*) is a scathing juxtaposition of the Leibnizian insistence that ours is the best of all possible worlds—here credited to Dr. Pangloss—with a cynical analysis of the world as a cauldron of evils and horrors. "Les Oreilles du Comte de Chesterfield, et le Chapelain Goudman" (1775; tr. as "The Earl of Chesterfield's Ears") subjects an anatomist's views on the immortal soul to a painstaking thought-experiment.

English translations on Voltaire's works exerted an obvious influence of subsequent British devotees of philosophical speculation, and they had themselves been influenced by the English satirist Jonathan Swift, whose masterpiece, *Travels into Several Remote Nations of the World in Four Parts...by Lemuel Gulliver* (1726; revised 1735), better known as *Gulliver's Travels,* includes one of the key precursors of scientific romance in its account of Gulliver's adventures on and around the flying island of Laputa. The latter work also serves to illustrate the crucial importance in the ancient history of scientific romance of the second of the four major threads connecting scientific romance to the most ancient stories of all: the traveler's tale.

2. TRAVELERS' TALES

We only have historical examples to go on, but we can undoubtedly presume, not only that travelers' tales go back to the remotest origins of travel, but that they shared from the very beginning the one invariable characteristic of all such tales: exaggeration. It would be going too far to suggest that all travelers narrating accounts of the things they have seen while they were away are flagrant and unrepentant liars, but the temptation to make a journey and its spectacles more dramatic in the retelling is undoubtedly forceful, and perhaps irresistible, by would-be saints as well as admitted sinners. The natural temptation is further boosted by the occasional requirement to explain and excuse an absence; one does not have to be away from home for as long as twenty years, as Odysseus allegedly was, to feel compelled to think of an out-of-the-ordinary *Odyssey* by way of an apologetic explanation.

The first corollary of the observable temptation to exaggerate is that inventors making up stories of imaginary travels are always inclined to go to extremes. Imaginary voyages to non-existent places rarely bother to feature milieux that are only moderately different from the next village, city or country. There is a tendency to go the whole hog, often in the interests of parody and satire—a process that inevitably attracts parody and satire itself. There are, in consequence, imaginary travelers' tales whose extremism is doubled by the intention of poking fun at other travelers' tales. The cardinal example of that redoubling of effect is a tale by the second-century Greek satirist Lucian, which is generally known, by virtue of an altogether-understandable sarcasm, as the *True History*.

The *True History* attempts to highlight the innate tendency of travelers' tales to exaggeration by describing the most impossible of journeys to the most unreachable of places: a flight to the Moon. The journey also takes in a close passage of the Sun and numerous remote islands on Earth—following a splashdown in the sea—but it is the trip to the Moon that established a key archetype, and a fundamental reference-point for future inventors of traveler's tales. Lucian could not have known it, but it was also fated, eventually, to be a highly ironic reference-point, transformed in its significance by the subsequent evolution of scientific knowledge and mechanical technology to the extent that the most conscientiously improbable of all barely-imaginable voyages not only became gradually more imaginable, but was actually accomplished after a mere 1,800 years. The story thus became accidentally illustrative of an important feature of the human imagination: that the limits of actuality sometimes lie beyond its reach.

Travelers' tales are not, however, mere lies, even when they have no manifest didactic purpose. As Philip Babcock Gove dutifully points out in *The Imaginary Voyage in Prose Fiction*, literary examples of the imaginary voyage are not only unified by the trivial circumstance that they all involve journeys, but by the fact that they necessarily provide "evidence of the activity of the human mind."[11] The imaginary voyage—especially, but not exclusively, in its literary forms—is an authentic form of exploration. There is a sense in which the study of fictitious Moons is as illuminating, in providing us with insight into the human condition—and a good deal less depressing in its indications—as the exploration of the actual Moon eventually turned out to be.

Historians in search of a noble ancestry for the genre of science fiction have co-opted ancient tales of imaginary journeys to strange lands in a wholesale manner, but they have always had a special affection for voyages to the Moon, however absurd and calculatedly unlikely the specific examples might be. The tradition of fanciful lunar voyages leads in a direct, if rather unsteady, line to what eventually became one of the "classical" themes of science fiction, and one of the most spectacular achievements of human technology. The history of such voyages, as detailed in such academic texts as Marjorie Hope Nicolson's *Voyages to the Moon* (1948) and such popularizing accounts as Russell Freedman's *2000 Years of Space Travel* (1963), makes a reasonably coherent narrative in its own right, and the way that imagined lunar landscapes and populations have changed along with scientific theories and speculations reveals a fascinating pattern.

The evolution of such voyages, from deliberate nonsense and farcical satire to a recognition and understanding of the actual situation of the Moon within the solar system and its nature as a world, gave them a significant role to play in propagandizing and popularizing the heliocentric theory of the solar system in the seventeenth and eighteenth centuries. The awareness of that role generated a certain sense of responsibility, although one that was admittedly more honored in the breach than the observance. A significant nonsensical flourish was added to the satirical tradition when Ludovico Ariosto dispatched Astolpho to the moon astride a "hippogriff" in *Orlando Furioso* (1516), to discovery a repository of everything wasted on Earth: misspent time, broken

---

11   Philip Babcock Gove. *The Imaginary Voyage in Prose Fiction*. New York: Columbia University Press, 1941. p.3.

vows, unanswered prayers, and so on; but Copernicus published his account of the heliocentric model of the solar system not long afterwards, in 1543, and paved the way for a significant imaginative reconfiguration.

Galileo's telescopic observations heated up the Copernican debate considerably in the early years of the seventeenth century, with an immediate influence on such philosophical and literary works as Ben Jonson's masque *News from the New World Discovered in the Moon* (1621), John Kepler's didactic *Somnium* (1634) and John Wilkins' earnestly-argued *The Discovery of a New World* (1638; expanded 1640). Farcical and satirical developments continued to dominate 17th century imagery, but such images were conspicuously enriched by new notions spun off by the acceptance of the heliocentric theory. The notions in question are obvious in Francis Godwin's *The Man in the Moone* (1638), and are given even greater prominence in Savinien Cyrano de Bergerac's *L'Autre monde* (1657), as well as affecting Aphra Behn's farcical comedy *The Emperor of the Moon* (1687).

The satirical tradition continued forcefully in such eighteenth-century British works as Daniel Defoe's *The Consolidator* (1705), Samuel Brunt's *A Voyage to Cacklogallinia* (1727), Murtagh McDermot's *A Trip to the Moon* (1728) and William Thomson's *The Man in the Moon* (1783), but Thomas Gray's poem "Luna Habitabilis" (1737, in Latin) earnestly imagined English colonialism extended to the lunar continents. The supplementation of satirical fantasy with a spirit of pure adventure became increasingly noticeable, in such works as Ralph Morris' *The Life and Wonderful Adventures of John Daniel* (1751).

The gradual increase in the apparent plausibility of lunar voyages became clearly manifest in the nineteenth century, even though the notion was still treated in a tongue-in-cheek fashion, any assertion that such a voyage might be possible carrying an embarrassing likelihood of attracting ridicule. John Banim's futuristic satire *The Revelations of the Dead-Alive* (1824), set in 2023, adds the news, almost as an afterthought, that the moon has been colonized and is now the object of fierce territorial battles fought with the aid of "balloon-ships."

In America, Edgar Allan Poe's "The Unparalleled Adventure of One Hans Pfaal" (1835 as "Hans Phaal"; exp. 1840), was set solidly in the satirical tradition, but included a few observations drawn from contemporary popular astronomy. Poe was then annoyed when an account of lunar life that he thought suspiciously similar to his own was passed off as reportage in one of the most celebrated newspaper hoaxes of its era, written by Richard Adams Locke for the New York *Sun* in August 1835. Locke's series of articles, which began with modest revelations of lunar geographical features but grew gradually more extravagant and absurd as they appeared over five days, was swiftly reprinted in other newspapers and as a pamphlet, causing a sensation not only in America but also in Europe, where it was widely translated for the sake of repetition.

Locke's articles purported to be reprints from the *Edinburgh Journal of Science* publishing observations made by the English astronomer Sir John Herschel in South Africa. John Herschel's father, William Herschel, had convinced himself that the moon was habitable, and other astronomers exercising the eye of faith had also discovered "evidence" of that habitation. Johann Schröter had reported surface formations of an artificial nature, while Francisco de Paula Gruithuisen had announced the discovery of an entire lunar city. Other observers, including William Beer and J. H. Mädler, correctly deduced from contemporary observations that the moon was devoid of air and water, and that the *maria* thought by Galileo to be bodies of water were dry plains, but the notion of lunar life died hard, even among astronomers; as late as 1924, W. H. Pickering was able to convince himself that he had seen dark patches moving near the crater Eratosthenes, which might have been swarms of migratory insects. In that context, nineteenth century inventors of travelers' tales involving the moon were entitled to a little latitude.

When "The Unparalleled Adventure of one Hans Pfaall" was reprinted in 1840, Poe hit back at what he considered to be Locke's plagiarism by adding a brief supplementary essay to the story, laying sarcastic claim to the originality of having been the first writer to produce an account of a lunar voyage that was plausible in the context of the scientific knowledge of the day, and calling for more "verisimilitude" in future endeavors in that vein. Poe was more justified than he probably thought, however, in calling attention to the fact that there really was scope for a more rigorous approach to the business of concocting a traveler's tale that would take a hypothetical traveler outside the earth.

If nothing else, Poe inspired other American writers to be even more straight-faced in future satires, as in J. L. Riddell's pamphlet *Orrin Lindsay's Plan of Aerial Navigation* (1847), which begins with a set of engineering specifications for the construction of a spaceship, and his mini-essay was presumably known in France both to Jules Verne and to Achille Eyraud, whose *Voyage à Venus* (1865; tr. as *Voyage to Venus*) includes a long seemingly-earnest description of the construction of a spacecraft and of the observations made by its pilot while in flight.

In Britain too, similar care began to be taken in works desirous of claiming the reader's sympathy, most obviously in *A Voyage to the Moon* (1864) "edited" by "Chrysostom Trueman," which describes the development of an "antigravity" technology with some care, although the travelers' discussions and the ideal state they discover on the moon are largely devoted to metaphysical concerns. Percy Greg's *Across the Zodiac: the Story of a Wrecked Record* (1880) also co-opted the idea of antigravity in its account of the discovery of the new force of "apergy," and its application to a voyage to Mars; although that work too clearly belongs to the satirical tradition, its introductory pretentions and ambitious reach entitle it to further consideration in Chapter Three as a significant imminent precursor of generic scientific romance.

Increasing awareness of the "new plausibility" of travel to other worlds was undoubtedly welcome to satirists and writers of adventure stories alike because of a similarly-increasing awareness of the imminent exhaustion of the scope inherent in earthbound travelers' tales. Although the fiction of geographical exploration was still in its heyday, as demonstrated by the enormous popularity of Verne's "extraordinary voyages," that kind of fiction was becoming very obviously naturalistic, and the plausibility of discovering new continents, or even islands, in which utopian societies and exotic flora and fauna might be located was dwindling inexorably. The Moon was suffering plausibility problems of its own in that respect, because it was becoming increasingly obvious that it was a dead world devoid of an atmosphere, but that only meant that the lunar voyage often became a stepping-stone in the cause of further interplanetary exploration, tacitly skipped by Eyraud, Greg and others.

By virtue of that combination of circumstances, the first account of a lunar voyage to strive wholeheartedly for "verisimilitude," Jules Verne's *De la terre à la lune* (1865) and its sequel, *Autour de la lune* (1870) initially translated into English in combination as *From the Earth to the Moon direct in 97 hours 20 minutes, and a Trip Around it*, already seemed a little too realistic for its own good. Verne was not only too scrupulous to populate the moon but too scrupulous even let his travelers land on it, given that he had no plausible means of getting them back again once they had. In that respect, however, other armchair inventors were perfectly happy to equip their lunar travelers with versatile propulsion systems, no matter how implausible they might be, whether their intentions were didactic or purely adventurous. Largely thanks to Verne, the lunar voyage was fully in position from 1870 onwards to become one of the "classic themes of science fiction," and to play a brief but significant role in the first heyday of scientific romance.

* * * *

The satirical tradition of travelers' tales took on an important role in philosophical speculation when that literary strategy became the principal format supporting the design of hypothetical ideal societies—a role than can be seen as a natural extrapolation of the narrative development undertaken by Plato in supplementing the *Republic* with the *Timaeus* and the *Critias*. Many such attempts to envision a perfect society attempt to be wholly earnest, in spite of the handicap of the traveler's tale's inbuilt implausibility, but few of them are entirely free from a satirical element, and the work that came to be seen as archetypal of the project, and gave it a slightly-misleading name, Thomas More's *Utopia* (1516), contains more satirical playfulness than its subsequent reputation suggests.

In fact, earnest attempts to present images of ideal societies often become seemingly-parodic in spite of their intentions, reflecting an ironic consciousness that human beings are ill-fitted for life in a perfect State, and a cynical suspicion that all attempts to build a New Jerusalem might inevitably be frustrated. The road to Utopia is always paved with good intentions, but few writers have ever been convinced that it would be a comfortable route to follow.

The irony seems implicit in the name, which More intended to mean "nowhere," although it is often construed as if it were derived from the Greek *eutopos* (better place) rather than *outopos*—a confusion that has encouraged some modern critics to use the term "eutopian" rather than "utopian" when referring to images of ideal societies rather than simply to non-existence places, whereas others use "Utopian" to stress the relationship with More's vision.

That terminological tangle soon became inextricable once historical studies of Utopian fiction began to be written in some profusion, and became even more so when Frank Manuel, the editor of the anthology *Utopias and Utopian Thought* (1966) complicated the scheme of nomenclature even further by observing that the history of Utopian speculation had featured two crucial historical shifts, which transformed the nature of the tradition.

Manuel observes that at the end of the eighteenth century, static descriptions of other places—which he calls "utopias of calm felicity"—were first supplemented, and then to some extent displaced by dynamic images of the progressive state of the future. The first of these "euchronias," Louis-Sébastien Mercier's *L'An deux mille quatre cent quarante* (1771; tr. as *Memoirs of the Year Two Thousand Five Hundred*) originated in the context of the philosophy of progress in pre-Revolutionary France, and literary euchronias remained closely connected with that philosophy, and with reformist political movements, throughout the nineteenth century. Then, Manuel argues, they gradually gave way in their turn to "psychological and philosophical utopias" or "eupsychias".[12] Given the complex nature of the relevant fiction, however, the awkward profusion and occasional ambiguity of the critical parlance used in talking about it is by no means inappropriate

The shifting of Utopian fantasies into the euchronian mode might seem to take them out of the realm of the traveler's tale, but there is an important sense in which that removal was not immediate, and generated a narrative challenge curiously akin to the one affecting the development of lunar fantasies. When Mercier wrote his account of the much-improved Paris of the future, he had no way of giving his protagonist access to it save for putting him to

---

12   Frank E, Manuel. "Toward a Psychological History of Utopia" in Frank E. Manuel, ed. *Utopias and Utopian Thought*. London: Souvenir Press, 1973. p.71.

sleep and causing him to dream it, and portal fantasy via the gates of dream remained a standard method of euchronian access for the next century.

Even more so than travelers' tales, dream tales came with a built-in implausibility: not merely a tendency to exaggeration but to outright nonsensicality. At the same time, however, they also came equipped with a deep-seated conviction that at least some dream visions were potentially "true," symbolically if not literally. Scholars convinced that anything written down must have a seed of truth in it, if only it could be interpreted properly, were merely following the footsteps of the oneiromancers of old, with the exception that the scholars searched for secrets of the past instead of secrets of the future.

Thus, dream tales came equipped with an innate ambiguity even more profound than that of earthly travelers' tales, with the added proviso that the more manifestly unreal they were, the more likely they were to embody the symbolism of truth. Christian fantasists, who understood the logic of Christ's own methods far better than Biblical literalists, produced some of the most elaborate and elegant dream tales, the cardinal British example being John Bunyan's classic account of *The Pilgrim's Progress from This World to That Which is to Come; delivered under the similitude of a DREAM wherein is discovered the manner of his setting out on his dangerous journey and safe arrival at the desired country* (1678), usually known as *The Pilgrim's Progress*. The title page of the first edition, not content to capitalize the word "dream," set it in a far larger font-size than any of the other parts of the title. The book was by far the biggest English-language best-seller of its era, and it added considerably to the lexicon of symbolism employed across the spectrum of subsequent literary endeavor.

The fact that so many travelers' tales, especially those with pretentions to philosophical speculation, are eventually revealed to be dreams rather than "actual" experiences—to the extent that "and then I/he woke up" became the ultimate terminal cliché—compounds the confusion intrinsic to the scholarly consideration of such stories, and blurs Manuel's useful distinction between eutopian, euchronian and eupsychian endeavors considerably. As Kauffmann pointed out in his brief analytical sketch of *New Atlantis*, there is a sense in which it is a futuristic fantasy, even though the narrative involves no temporal displacement; there is also a sense in which it is a dream fantasy, even though the narrator does not appear to be asleep. Indeed, the fact that a final awakening as a means of concluding a narrative ultimately seemed hackneyed as well as anti-climactic became a strong incentive to compilers of philosophical speculations simply to omit the "and then I woke up," and leave it to the reader's discretion to decide whether the story might have been a dream, knowing—or at least hoping—that the conclusion that it must have been would not deprive it of its potential visionary authority as a suggestion of the future.

Like *The Pilgrim's Progress*, many philosophical travelers' tales attempt to make a virtue of their obvious artificiality, and arguably succeed, in much the same way. The crucial importance of the time machine in the first and foremost of Wells' definitive scientific romances is not that a time machine is a rationally plausible mechanical device, but that it provides an impression of authority that adapts the oneiromantic implications of dream tales to the scientific world-view, exchanging a debased currency of apparent plausibility for one of newly-minted coinage. Many of the precursors of generic scientific romance featured in Chapter Two were groping in the same direction, in search of a similar strategy of "narrative authorization" to secure their warrant of truth, because of their imaginative adventurism rather than in spite of it.

The dream vision is, in a perfectly logical sense, the natural method of the "eupsychian" mode of thought identified by Frank Manuel, but all visionaries intent on arguing that the future really might deliver a better world had an obvious incentive for discovering a more seemingly-concrete method of travel into the future and early eupsychians tended to continue and further elaborate a quest for more plausible methods of displacement that had been forced on euchronians.

Inevitably, euchronians had hit on the notion of sleeping for a long time and "actually" waking up in another time—suspended animation, to dignify it with a more technical term—but that did not really solve the narrative problem, because a sleeper transported in that fashion into the future had no obvious way of getting the information thus gathered back to his own time. Even so, the method was employed in the most successful of all nineteenth-century utopian fictions, in terms of its sales, Edward Bellamy's

Looking Backward, 2000-1887 (1888), which prompted a host of replies in kind, the most prominent British example being William Morris' *News from Nowhere* (1890).

The simpler immersive fantasy device of writing a story from a viewpoint located in the future as if it were the present, and not bothering to provide the reader with an explanation of how the report comes to be mysteriously present in the present, was easy enough to discover, but far from easy to establish as an acceptable narrative device. From its early appearances in the 1860s, in such works as Hippolyte Mettais' *L'An 5865* (1865; tr. as *The Year 5865*), all the way through to the end of the century, such works are invariably supported by elaborate explanatory and apologetic prefaces. Even H. G. Wells did not dare to employ the method without the clumsy preliminary discourse contained in "A Story of the Days to Come." The incentive was, however, sufficiently powerful eventually to add the device to the canon of familiar literary devices when that became practicable; in the fullness of time, it provided an important resource for British scientific romance and a vital one for American science fiction.

* * * *

While dream tales, seen as a subspecies of the traveler's tale, became a useful resource for hopeful Christian fantasies in which metaphorical pilgrims received the moral reinforcement enabling them to reach the Celestial City, it is as well to remember that John Bunyan started his pilgrims off from the City of Destruction and that they made their journey under the perpetual threat of the burden of their sins plunging them not merely into the Slough of Despond but into Tophet (i.e.. Hell). As the *Odyssey* had made a point of reminding its readers, dream gates can lead in very different directions.

Even the exaggeration of petty traveler's tales often has a nightmarish aspect to it. Travelers not only have the habit of representing themselves as having seen wonderful and amusing things, but also of having had hair's-breadth escapes. The most obvious survival of oral tradition in the modern world, apart from jokes, is a class of horror stories nowadays known as "urban legends." Folklore is full of such horrific materials, often juxtaposed with purely decorative substance. Heaven and hell might be polar opposites in conceptual terms, but the eccentric topology of imaginative space routinely makes them near neighbors, sometimes with ill-defined borders.

In view of this circumstance, it is only to be expected that the satirical component of utopian travelers' tales routinely extends from relatively amiable caricature through black comedy to flagrant nightmare: a pattern that is very evident in many of the texts to be considered in Chapter Two, detailing the pioneering of scientific romance. It is not surprising that it was in the context of the gradual development of travelers' tales with strong euchronian implications that designs of ideal societies began to be supplemented by alarming images of horrid possibility, which were inevitably labeled—initially, it seems, by John Stuart Mill—as "dystopias." Although dystopian fears, like eutopian hopes, were often incarnate in castaways' remote imaginary islands as well as explicitly futuristic milieux, it was the threat of dire possibilities to come that sharpened the relevant anxiety dramatically.

The shifting of Utopian speculation into the euchronian mode was closely correlated with a growing consciousness of the connection between a society's technological resources and its social organization. With the Industrial Revolution well under way, it became easy to believe that further developments in mechanical technology would create greater wealth, and the potential for a better life for all—a central tenet of the French philosophy of progress.

The possibilities of purely moral reform and straightforward redistribution of wealth remained a major preoccupation of euchronian writers, as with traditionalist writers of present-bound Utopian traveler's tales, but they not only tended to regard future political change as something made possible by the further development of mechanical production and the transformation of the labor process, but something that could not be avoided. It was the unavoidability in question that led writers anxious about the role played in society by recent technology to develop dystopian fiction, which has always been intimately concerned with the possibilities of technological development, and which thus became a key factor encouraging the development of scientific romance of an anxious stripe.

It is obvious in Suvin's bibliography of Victorian science fiction that anxious quasi-futuristic speculations already outnumbered optimistic euchronian fantasies in the first phase covered therein, beginning in 1848, and the same is true of the previous phase, as documented by I. F. Clarke in his bibliography of explicit examples of the *Tale of the Future from the Beginning to the Present Day* (Third Edition, 1978). The pattern was similar in France, where an early alarmist note was sounded in the form of futuristic dream fantasy in Émile Souvestre's *Le Monde tel qu'il sera* (1846; tr. as *The World as it Shall Be*), and it has now been revealed that Jules Verne's first speculative novel, *Paris au XXe siècle* (written 1863; published 1994; tr. as *Paris in the Twentieth Century*) was of a similar ilk.

That anxiety seems to have achieved dominance earlier in Europe than America, where general attitudes to technology remained much more optimistic—which doubtless helped Edward Bellamy's euchronian *Looking Backward* to become a huge bestseller, although its political contentiousness in espousing socialism was also a factor. After 1890, however, the imbalance became more acute even in America; there was a massive displacement of Utopian images of the future by dystopian ones, led by Ignatius Donnelly's *Caesar's Column* (1891, initially by-lined Edmund Boisgilbert). That swerve was even more exaggerated in Britain, in spite the heroic efforts of H. G. Wells, who fought a determined rearguard action to maintain a fundamental optimism at the heart of scientific romance, but who was always painfully aware of the fact that it was, indeed, a rearguard action attempting to stem a mighty tide

* * * *

Travelers' tales received continual boosts from the fifteenth century onwards by virtue of steady improvement in means of transportation, particularly marine transportation, and the spectacular corollary of the discovery of the Americas by Europeans in 1492. That revelation followed a hundred years of enterprising activity, in which the enormous political significance of exploits in long-distance exploration overseas was gradually realized, largely thanks to the fervent encouragement of Portuguese explorers by Henry the Navigator. Where the Portuguese had led, the Spanish rapidly followed, and then the English and the Dutch, instituting a gradual exploration of the entire globe whose primary purposes were plunder, conquest and colonization.

The initial economic motivation for such voyages was often couched as the search for new trade routes to the "spice islands" known as the East Indies. Christopher Columbus stumbled upon the New World while looking for such a route by going the other way around the world, having unwisely, but luckily, invested his belief in an underestimation of its true circumference—and he seems to have remained stubbornly convinced for some time that he had found what he was looking for rather than a new set of "West Indies."

The contribution made by the New World to real and fictitious travelers' tales was immense, and other projects of a Columbian stripe also made a significant contribution. The sixteenth century saw several significant attempts to discover either a "north-west" passage around the north of the Americas that might supplement the troublesome route to the Pacific via Cape Horn, or a "north-eastern passage" around the north of Russia. The two quests combined to give birth to a new subgenre of Arctic traveler's tales that extended all the way into the twentieth century, helping to make the North Pole a significant magnet for actual explorers and Romantic fantasists alike—a game into which Antarctica was inevitably drawn as a complement.

Of all the new myths manufactured in the wake of this Age of Exploration, one in particular stands out in the history of English literature, and literature in general. *The Life and Strange Surprizing Adventures of Robinson Crusoe of York, Mariner* (1719) by Daniel Defoe became a new archetype, not only making the name of its castaway hero universally familiar but renewing and refurbishing the concept of a "desert island" in a manner that made it a key literary resource, exploited in thousands of subsequent traveler's tales, both ostensibly naturalistic and unashamedly fantastic. *Robinson Crusoe* became one of the foundation stones of Romantic fiction, helping to formulate the distinction between "novels" and "romances" that became a central feature of English literary criticism and the jargon of publishers' advertising. Jean-Jacques Rousseau, the most important philosophical precursor of French Romanticism, recommended it as the only book that a growing child ought to be allowed to read. Robinson Crusoe provided the immediate model for Jonathan Swift's equally archetypal Lemuel Gulliver, and the narrative method that Swift used in chronicling Gulliver's exploits is a pastiche of Defoe's.

Robinson Crusoe is not a satire, and its major affiliation is to the accounts of actual voyages that were beginning to appear in some profusion as the age of exploration went into top gear, following a tradition of enthusiastic reportage founded in the Elizabethan era by Richard Hakluyt. Indeed, its popularity might well have helped serve as an inspiration for subsequent explorers to set forth on voyages of their own. Its other major literary connection was with the developing genre of "spiritual autobiography," in which individuals writing accounts of their lives attempted to dodge the accusation of vanity by asserting, and then trying to demonstrate, that they were writing not to glorify themselves but to explain the important lessons they had learned as a result of enduring trials and tribulations. In purely literary terms, however, the most enormous influence of Defoe's novel was the tremendous boost it gave to the production of imaginary travelers' tales as tales of adventure. The tales of adventure produced in imitation or variation of it were rarely pure, often having hints of satire and frequently reproducing the element of spiritual autobiography, earnestly or sarcastically, but the adventure component of their plots was the principal determinant of their commercial success, just as it had determined *Robinson Crusoe*'s.

Several of the notable adventure stories published in the wake of Crusoe's exploits strayed into fantastic realms that associated them with the ancestry of scientific romance, including the previously-mentioned *The Life and Wonderful Adventures of John Daniel* (1751), in which an orthodox tale of plucky castaways is enlivened by a brief trip to the Moon, and Morris' story is frequently linked in historical surveys with Robert Paltock's exactly contemporary *The Life and Adventures of Peter Wilkins, a Cornish Man* (1751), whose castaway hero discovers a society of winged humans. Later contributions to the same transitional subgenre include a story sequence in Frederick Marryat's *The Pacha of Many Tales* (1835) in which Huckaback, a modern Sinbad, undergoes a series of fanciful adventures, including the discovery of a bizarre civilization living in the middle of the Atlantic, whose members' way of life and technology are based entirely on the capture and exploitation of whales. The enormous popularity of *Robinson Crusoe* in France helped to create the market space that was colonized to such great effect by Jules Verne and his imitators.

Robinson Crusoe was probably not the only important contribution that Daniel Defoe made to the reconstruction of the mythology of the traveler's tale. He is widely reputed to have assisted the pseudonymous Captain Charles Johnson in making his *General History of the Robberies and Murders of the Most Notorious Pyrates* (1724) more readable, and is suspected by some commentators of having written the whole book. Although it does appear to the analytical reader that two authorial hands were involved, and Defoe was probably not responsible for the tediously dry lists of ships, crimes and executions that take up many of the chapters, it seems infinitely more likely that he invented and inserted the more colorful biographies, including those of the female pirates Anne Bonny and Mary Read—which, inevitably, caught the popular imagination much more forcefully. At any rate, the image of the swashbuckling pirate supported by the more extravagant passages in the Johnson *History*, which probably bore very little resemblance to the real thing, also became a staple of the literary traveler's tale thereafter, and laid another foundation stone for adventure fiction in general.

The success of navigation as an instrument of enrichment and conquest inevitably provided a boost to science, primarily because the art of navigation was greatly enhanced by scientific instrumentation, scrupulous measurement and mathematical acumen. Galileo might have made the telescope famous by peering at the stars, but the probability is that it had already been invented and swiftly adapted for naval use, kept secret precisely because it was so useful. Whether or not that was the case, there is no doubt that the manufacture of sextants, compasses and chronometers, guided by the demands of navigation, exercised the predominant pressure on the development of scientific measuring instruments and machine tools, and hence of mechanical ingenuity in general.

The race to improve navigation inevitably led to an interest in new kinds of vessels. James I of England, who inherited the great English tradition of navigation along with the throne from the already-legendary Elizabeth, appointed a court inventor,

Cornelis Drebbel, to push forward the cause of English discovery, and Drebbel's most famous venture was his attempt to develop a viable submarine in the early 1620s for possible military use by the Royal Navy. The King was rumored actually to have undertaken an excursion in one of the later models. The Admiralty remained conscientiously unimpressed, but Britain went on to rule the waves anyway, its dominance greatly enhanced by virtue of its navy being the first to be equipped with copper-bottomed ships in the latter half of the eighteenth century.

In such an intellectual climate, it is not surprising that Francis Bacon's fragmentary account of *New Atlantis*, written during James I's reign, should concentrate heavily on the potential mechanical rewards of the new science whose philosophy he had defined—an endeavor discussed in much greater detail in the next chapter. Nor is it surprising that John Wilkins, whose speculative endeavors took up where Bacon and Cornelis Drebbel left off, followed up his "discovery" of the world of the moon with a substantial treatise on *Mathematical Magic* (1648), dedicated to Charles I, which deals with the practical science of mechanics and includes an account of a whole series of hypothetical devices of exploration, including submarines, land yachts and—the ultimate prize in all exercises of that kind—flying machines.

Aerial travel was already built into much ancient myth and legend, in tales of flying horses, artificial wings, magic carpets and simple levitation; it was a necessary prerequisite not only of imaginary travels to the Moon but any imaginable rapid long-distance transit. The design of hypothetical flying machines had been attempted by numerous other ambitious engineers prior to John Wilkins, most famously Leonardo da Vinci. As might be expected, the fantasy bore fruit some time before an actual lunar journey was accomplished, albeit in a more modest and frustratingly limited fashion, when the Montgolfier brothers demonstrated the first hot-air balloon capable of carrying a human passenger in 1783—instantly provoking a craze of heroic endeavor that rapidly spread from France to other European nations and to America.

The actual utility of balloons was severely limited by the fact that they remained at the mercy of the wind, but that had far less effect on their fictitious utility in literary travelers' tales—which, in any case, found it very easy to anticipate imminent success in the ongoing competition to discover a practicable method of steering that might usher in a new era of dirigible airships. The subgenre of nineteenth-century travelers' tales featuring balloons—often as producers of castaways on desert islands—became one of the principal progenitors of the branch of adventure fiction that developed a crucial scientific element; it provided the launch-pad for Jules Verne's career in *roman scientifique*, in *Cinq semaines en ballon* (1863; tr. as *Five Weeks in a Balloon*).

One of the reasons why romances of navigation were so inherently "Romantic" was that they represented a kind of adventure that was theoretically available to anyone, while still remaining glamorously esoteric. In fact, "going to sea" was not something that attracted so many volunteers that it was unnecessary to stock galleys with convicts or obtain naval recruits by means of press gangs. The mortality rate among sailors, once long-distance voyages into dangerous waters became fashionable, was horrific, and active participation in the age of heroic navigation, at least in a minor role, was something that few men who were not desperate wanted to do. Over time, however, the improvements made to navigation gradually made it safer. Travel in general became safer, although the rich and continually-renewed mythology of bandits and highwaymen also continued to supply fiction with a good deal of its romance.

* * * *

Eventually, as was bound to happen, the technological improvements of travel led, if not to complete safety, at least to a diminution of risk to levels that could be considered everyday. Although the sea continued to serve as a relentless widow-maker even after the development of steamships, while aerial transport and submarine transport long remained pastimes only fit for lunatics, the nineteenth century saw dramatic improvements in the domestication of travel, spearheaded by the railway locomotive.

The advent of railways and steamships meant that the world was opened up to tourism, and the real tourists who embarked upon Thomas Cook's famous excursions were only marginally preceded by the imaginary tourists of Jules Verne's novels. Verne had the advantage over Cook that he could invent a host of new vehicles to take his characters into parts of the world unreachable by conventional means, but the inconveniences featured in nineteenth-century literary travelers' tales were soon supplemented by the awful danger of expending tremendous efforts getting to remote areas, only to be interrupted by crass tourists not long after arrival.

The first archetypal character that Verne added to the ever-increasing stock of new myths was Captain Nemo, the constructor and owner of the submarine *Nautilus* featured in *Vingt millie lieues sous les mers* (1870; tr. as *Twenty Thousand Leagues Under the Sea*), but the second was Phileas Fogg in *Le Tour du monde en quatre-vingts jours* (1873; tr. as *Around the World in Eighty Days*), although his journey was not that much faster than the itinerary for such a trip that Cook had already published, and the challenge posed by the novel's title to would be emulators was very soon met; the American reporter "Nellie Bly" (Elizabeth Cochrane), commissioned by the New York *World*, managed it in 72 days in 1889, at the age of 25, dropping in to see Verne as she passed through France on her way.

Nellie Bly's feat symbolized the extent to which the age of heroic navigation was now a thing of the past, having given way to a new era of travel, which needed the exaggeration and elaboration of travelers' tales to make it anything more than banal. Although it was the heroic age that produced the raw materials carried forward into fantastic romances, it was the banality of contemporary travel that created much of the pressure on the development of fantastic devices in the nineteenth century. Many of Robinson Crusoe's followers during the first hundred and fifty years were simple mariners, like him, who ended up on run-of-the-mill desert islands, but by the end of the nineteenth century, they had to be more than that, or to find something more than that, if their tales were to be truly Romantic.

The reason why Jules Verne was such an important exemplary figure in the tradition of modern adventure fiction was not just that his characters were able to use submarines and balloons as well as ordinary means of transport, but that he carefully and ingeniously struck a new balance between the realism and romance of imaginary voyages. He not only paid scrupulous attention to the means by which his characters traveled, whether those means were real or fictitious, but he was earnest and conscientious in constructing the sensations, delights and discomforts attendant on their hypothetical experience, cultivating a seeming naturalism that ballasted the essential romance of their exploits. That kind of scrupulous ambivalence was to become crucial to the subsequent evolution of *roman scientifique* and scientific romance.

The advent of such endeavors did not, of course, put an end to satirical and purely fanciful traveler's tales, but it did make them seem oddly quaint. Such Swiftian "Gulliveriana" as continued to appear in the later decades of the nineteenth century tended to be self-consciously old-fashioned. A notable example is Thomas Lee's *Falsivir's Travels* (1886), in which the crew of a trip trapped in the Arctic ice decide to make a bid to reach the Pole when the ice melts; the narrator attempts to carry out reconnaissance by means of a collapsible balloon, and is sucked into a deep hole that gives access to a subterranean world illuminated by a miniature sun, where relationships between exotic humans of ordinary dimensions and their giant subjects are maintained by ingenious religious propaganda and cunning social engineering. The entire story is possessed by a kind of flamboyant quaintness.

As previously noted, H. G. Wells became sufficiently tired of the comparison to begin denying any real literary kinship between himself and Verne, and Verne similarly denied any real kinship with Wells, but both writers were being a little too jealous in guarding their originality. Not only did both of them strive to locate their imaginary inventions securely within the scientific world-view, irrespective of any technicalities that might render them impossible, but they both strove to make their imaginary travelers react and respond in plausible ways to their various predicaments, within the limits of everyday exaggeration. Thanks to the examples set by Verne, Wells and their followers, traveler's tales entered a new era when travel itself did so, reflecting the technological progress of the Age of Steam.

3. TAINTED REPUTATIONS

Philosophical speculation and the traveler's tale are manifestly types of fiction, the latter seemingly springing from a kind of fundamental storytelling impulse and the former from a desire to exploit the utility of the fact that stories routinely carry meanings that reach far beyond vulgar literality. In examining the ancient roots of scientific romance, however, it is necessary to pay attention to the roots of science as well as those of storytelling. It might appear that that could be adequately done in one section—the next—rather than two, but there is a good reason for dividing the consideration, and for taking the odder strand first. One cannot fully understand the evolution of fictional considerations of science, and perhaps even the evolution of science itself, without paying due attention to the peculiar but undeniable fact that successful scientific endeavor has always given rise to strange and dark suspicions on the part of others.

The ambivalence of scientific reputations is evident in the mythologization of the legendary figurehead of Greek mathematics, Pythagoras. Pythagoras appears in the historical record as the first of a significant series of inspirational teachers whose intellectual efforts helped to lay the foundations of natural science, his key ideas being further developed and selectively refined by Plato and Aristotle. The most important contribution to the development of science attributed to Pythagoras was the empirical discovery that strings of lengths related by simple fractions produce chords that are musically related. That discovery became an iconic illustration of the general notion that mathematical analysis might provide a key to the comprehension of all the transactions of nature.

The Pythagoreans pursued the quest in various ways, allegedly symbolizing it by means of an emblem known as the "tetractys of the decad": a triangular arrangement of ten dots with four at the base, tapering through rows of three and two to a single dot at the apex. They laid the foundations of the geometry that was subsequently codified by Euclid, although they were probably not responsible for what became known as "Pythagoras' theorem," and they did important early work in arithmetic, although they were reputed to have been horrified by the discovery of "irrational numbers" inexpressible as simple fractions.

The Pythagoreans developed a model of the universe whose fundamental harmonizing principle they described as "the music of the spheres"—a notion echoed in many subsequent cosmological models, from Plato's to John Kepler's. Their insistence on seeking keys to understanding in mathematical relationships laid the foundations for scientific measurement and quantification, and also left a legacy of puzzles and enigmas whose attempted solution was an important driving force in the development of pure and applied mathematics. They also seem to have believed in metempsychosis—the transmigration of souls—although it is unclear how that belief related to their interests in mathematical analysis and symbolization, and might have been purely accidental. Accidental or not, that frankly supernatural component of their beliefs came to be associated with the notion that, as well as the knowledge they published and publicly expressed, they were possessed of a secret knowledge—an arcana—known only to privileged initiates.

Plato, who carried forward many Pythagorean ideas and projects, although he was less interested in mathematics, seems to have been entirely candid in his dealings with the world and the teachings of his Academy, but that did not prevent later followers of his philosophy, and especially its supernatural aspects, from suspecting that Platonism too—or, at least, "neo-Platonism"—had its arcana, only available to privileged initiates. Indeed the "neo-Pythagorean" and "neo-Platonic" schools that began to flourish some three hundred years after Plato's death soon acquired a rather shady reputation with regard to the secrets they were reputed to possess.

To confuse the issue further, the neo-Pythagoreans of the 1st century B.C., who tried to synthesize Pythagorean ideas with both Platonism and Stoicism, were forced by the syncretic nature of their aim to emphasize the analogical correlations between those different schools, which tended to mystify the elements all three traditions. That strategy of mystification, and the resulting elaborations of such disciplines as astrology and numerology, laid important groundwork for the holistic inclinations of subsequent neo-Platonists, and for the subsequent evolution of "occult science."

The term "occult" is derived from a Latin word meaning "hidden," but its significance carries a more general suggestion of mystery and the supernatural. Although the term "occult science" is often used simply as an umbrella term embracing such speculative disciplines as alchemy and astrology, it can also signify a complex network of parallels and analogies between such disciplines, secured by their apparent common descent from neo-Pythagorean and neo-Platonic philosophy. Such analogical connections formed the sinews of Medieval mysticism, and provided a fundamental core linking the philosophies of many writers who wanted to retain a holistic and intimate notion of the universe in the face of its infinite expansion and dispersion by Newtonian science.

One of the principal features of occult science is that it continually rewrites its own history—or, at least, the illusion of its history—in the interests of making it more extensive and more prestigious. Because arcana, by definition, have to be handed down secretly and taken on trust rather than published and proven, their authority rests, to a considerable extent on their presumed antiquity and the prestige of their alleged originator. As with travelers' tales, that circumstance is not merely an invitation to exaggeration but a virtual compulsion.

The scope for such exaggeration is abundant, given that the story of something carefully hidden from the history compounded out of official and everyday documents has to demonstrate not only that the secret consists of worthwhile knowledge, but also that there are powerful reasons requiring it to be kept secret. Although invented occult history inevitably makes much of the significance of secrets never committed to script, the progress of writing inevitably encouraged supplementary reference to "secret documents" authored and possessed by covert elites, whose great rarity made them doubly precious. The earliest employers of the notion of secret doctrine, including the Pythagoreans, had no incentive to imagine "secret documents," but when the literate scholars of the Renaissance reinvented the tradition of occult science wholesale, the notion of secret documents acquired a much greater importance—inevitably resulting in the large-scale faking of such documents, necessarily attributed to prestigious authors.

Whether or not the Pythagoreans invented Pythagoras along with the rest of their arcana is unclear, but there is no doubt at all that the neo-Pythagoreans of the first century B.C. reinvented him, and that the neo-Platonists who followed in their footsteps reinvented him again, along with Plato. Nor is there any doubt that the Christian "gnostics" who came after them revised the entire now-elaborate pseudohistory for their own purposes—and so on, all the way to the nineteenth century. The history of actual documents lent increasing support to the notion of secret documents, and offered subtle hints as to what the secret ones might contain—a process whose presently-detectable seeds seem to have been planted by the neo-Platonists.

The most famous of the neo-Pythagoreans, Apollonius of Tyana, had the dubious distinction of being posthumously promoted as a rival to the Christ of the gospels in a highly fantasized "biography" written by Philostratus in the 3rd century. That attempted elevation inevitably provoked a response, which—equally inevitably—took the form of stigmatizing Apollonius, along with other neo-Pythagorean and neo-Platonist mystics, as Devil-led black magicians. To some extent, that stigmatization was an artifact of circumstance, reflective of Christianity's struggle to rid itself of all religious competition by a strategy of wholesale demonization, but it certainly connected with some deeper psychological suspicion of mathematical and scientific enquiry and knowledge—all of which, from the viewpoint of laymen, tends to seem arcane, and threatening in its seeming incomprehensibility. It seems to be a common, if not invariable, aspect of human psychology that people detest what they cannot understand, and are ever-ready to dismiss it, not merely as nonsense but as something inherently menacing. There is something about the mathematical or scientific mind that many people not possessed of one find profoundly unsettling, and that unsettlement can sometimes produce extraordinarily negative reactions.

The most important neo-Platonic philosopher was Plotinus, whose *Enneads* were assembled for publication by his disciple Porphyry. The fundamental holism of Plotinus' thought is there embodied in the notion that the intelligibility of the world had to be attained by a threefold path—integrating the routes to understanding followed by the Musician, the Lover and the Philosopher—and a key analogy likening and linking the microcosm of the human individual to the macrocosmic motions of the heavens. Those elements have tended to be retained and reconfigured by subsequent revivalists, helping to form a perceptible core around which the supposed secret components are allegedly organized.

Porphyry's chief successor, Iamblichus, attempted to reconcile all forms of religion within a single syncretic system, with the sole exception of Christianity—a response to the Christians' determined exclusivity. That helped to establish a crucial rivalry, the effects of which were long-lasting, permanently coloring Christian attitudes to neo-Platonist ideas and causing acute problems in the Renaissance for philosophers who wanted to recover the legacy of neo-Platonism along with other Classical learning. Although Plotinus and Porphyry escaped the kind of brutal demonization inflicted upon Apollonius of Tyana and Simon Magus, the satanic taint attached to their ideas was a major cause of the care with which the ideas in question were disguised and mystified by scholars, especially within the field of alchemy—to the extent that Mysticism became a significant topic in its own right, sprawling across the boundaries of church doctrine.

Greek scientists who flourished before the rise of Christianity also escaped that kind of stigmatization in large measure, and some had heroic reputations established on their behalf that were only slightly tainted by unease—for which reason they are best left until the next chapter for consideration—but once Christendom had become established in Europe, built on the ruins of the Roman Empire, the assumed diabolism of that taint became a powerful factor, not necessarily in determining how would-be scientists were treated while they were alive, but almost invariably affecting their reputations after they were dead.

* * * *

In Christendom, when science was reborn after the hiatus following the collapse of Roman civilization, it came back into the world of the Renaissance with a diabolical stain of sin implicit within it, which required strong resistance if any progress in science were actually to be achieved, and which certainly impeded that progress considerably. There was not a single important proto-scientist of the Renaissance who did not attract suspicions and accusations of diabolical involvement, and the pattern of that demonization is strikingly clear in the posthumous reputations acquired by, and hence in literary representations of, the three cardinal British examples: Michael Scot, Roger Bacon and John Dee.

Michael Scot (c1175-1232) was an early Renaissance scholar born in Scotland—his "surname" means no more than that—who traveled widely in Italy and Spain, picking up enough Arabic in Toledo to enable him to translate Arabic documents as well as Latin ones, thus adding considerably to the ever-increasing stock of Western intellectual resources. He was one of the first Westerners to make the acquaintance of the writings of the Arab scholars who became known in the West as Avicenna and Averroes, both of whom were important contributors to and popularizers of Arabic science. Scot produced numerous manuscripts of his own, not all of which survive, which dealt with mathematics, astronomy, chemistry and physiology—although his accounts of astronomy and chemistry were, inevitably, dominated by the astrological and alchemical ideas dominant at the time. Much of the work in question appears to have been produced at the specific request of his patron, the Holy Roman Emperor Frederick II.

Scot's interest in astrology, alchemy and occult science was undoubtedly sincere and quite typical of the scholars of his era, and there is no reason to suspect, from what is known of his biography, that he was anything but a virtuous individual liked and respected by his peers and patrons. Once he was dead, however, his reputation worsened considerably; he appears in Dante's *Inferno* in the circle of Hell reserved for sorcerers and false prophets, and Boccaccio's *Decameron* represents him in the same light.

Not everyone agreed with that stigmatization, and Michael Scot was included in Gabriel Naudé's *Apologie pour tous les grands personages faussement soupçonnez de magie* [An Apology for all the Great Individuals Falsely Suspected of Magic] (1625)—an oft-reprinted classic of the Age of Reason, which also strives to exonerate Pythagoras, Socrates and Solomon from the false and intrinsically slanderous suspicion of having been magicians—but that defense, although undoubtedly reasonable, could not prevail against the dire suspicions of Churchmen. Nor could it prevail against the melodramatic demands of Romanticism. Walter Scott, anxious to claim Michael Scot (without any reasonable grounds) as an ancestor, incorporated him into his narrative poem "The Lay of the Last Minstrel" (1805), not as a scholar but as a wizard, whose tomb contains a magic book of ominous import.

Such was Walter Scott's popularity that the image in question became virtually unchallengeable thereafter, extending well into the twentieth century, when the fantasy writer Michael Scott Rohan, similarly anxious to claim "wizard Scot" as an ancestor, made him the central character of his novel *The Lord of Middle Air* (1994).

Although he was an important distributor and advocate of scientific ideas, Michael Scot's personal contribution to the evolution of Medieval science was relatively slight, but the same is not true of Roger Bacon (c1220-1292), who was a significant pioneer of experimental science; among other things, he was the first European to record a recipe for making gunpowder, in 1242. Bacon lectured on Aristotle at the University of Paris before moving to Oxford in 1247 or thereabouts, making contact with Roger de Grosseteste, who shared his interests. He invested a good deal of time and money on building a library of esoteric works, and equipping a laboratory for his experimental studies. He attempted research on the viability of flying machines and other forms of powered vehicular transport, but that quest yielded few practical results, and he had more success in observing the magnifying power of combinations of lenses and constructing a *camera obscura* in order to make astronomical observations of the Sun.

Bacon's career abruptly changed direction in 1257 when he fell ill and joined the Franciscan order. His new superiors immediately attempted to curtail his researches, but he appealed to Pope Clement IV—with whom he was personally acquainted—for sponsorship in the compilation of a new encyclopedia. He did not receive any strong support, but he did obtain carefully qualified permission to go ahead, which forced him to work in secret. Before Clement died in 1268, Bacon was able to write three treatises that preserved his knowledge and thought for later generations, known as *Opus majus, Opus minus* and *Opus tertium*. Three fragments of the projected encyclopedia, *Communia naturalium* [General Principles of Natural Philosophy], *Communia mathematica* [General Principles of Mathematics] and *Compendium philosophiae* [Compendium of Philosophy] were completed, but Bacon was imprisoned on suspicion of heresy in the late 1270s; not only did he disappear from historical view thereafter but his works were suppressed too, although the first three treatises named did survive fugitively.

This combination of circumstances fitted Bacon for eventual representation in the Age of Reason as a heroic scientific visionary, cruelly oppressed and prevented from exercising a progressive influence by blinkered dogmatic authority, but in Renaissance literature he was presented as an alchemist and magician, as in Robert Greene's *Friar Bacon and Friar Bungay* (1592), which associates him with a famous legend of the construction of an oracular Brazen Head, attributed by other writers to Albertus Magnus. He might not have had any reputation at all, however, had his manuscripts not eventually come into the possession of the third of the great British posthumously-reputed wizards, John Dee (1527-1609), who found them to be a gold-mine of inspiration.

Dee was educated at St John's College Cambridge, where he showed great promise in mathematics and began to make detailed astronomical observations. In 1548 he went to study at the University of Louvain, where he became a close friend of the cartographer Gerardus Mercator. He lectured on mathematics at the University of Paris before he returned to England in 1551, bringing back numerous navigational instruments. He entered the service of the Earl of Pembroke, and then obtained the patronage of the Duke of Northumberland, but his career nearly came to an end when his Protestant father, Roland Dee, was arrested after Queen Mary came to the throne in 1553.

Roland Dee was eventually released, but never recovered his assets; his fellow mathematician and astronomer, Leonard Digges, who had collaborated with John Dee in astronomical observations and optical experiments based on Roger Bacon's work, suffered a similar fate, hastening his premature death. Dee then took responsibility for Leonard Digges' son Thomas, with whom he continued the elder Digges' work on the development of optical devices. John Dee's release after his own arrest in 1555 has occasioned speculation that he became an informer for the Catholic regime, but that seems unlikely; he was held in sufficiently high regard by Protestants when Elizabeth succeeded Mary in 1558 to be entrusted with casting a horoscope to determine the most favorable day for her coronation.

Dee's liberation was more likely due to the fact that he had become an adviser on navigational matters to the Muscovy Company formed by Sebastian Cabot, assisting its captains with the search for the north-east passage and instructing its officers in geometry and astronomy; he held that position for 32 years, and undoubtedly made his expertise available to other navigators operating with the blessing of the crown, including Elizabethan privateers. His only work on navigation to have survived was printed in 1577—with a note asserting that it was being issued "24 years after its first publication"—but its earlier versions and parallel texts must have been circulated on a strictly "need to know" basis, given the intense international competition for navigational aids and expertise,

In spite of the respect in which Elizabeth apparently held him, Dee never received any substantial financial support from the crown, and lived with his mother in Mortlake. He wrote prolifically, but relatively few of his works were printed and most of them slipped into obscurity, the most conspicuous exceptions being an introduction to a new edition of Euclid and an ambitious exercise in occult science, *Monas Hieroglyphica* [The Hieroglyphic Monad] (1564). In 1568 Dee presented Elizabeth with a copy of his *Propaedeumata Aphoristica* [approximately, A Concise Introduction to the Elements of Knowledge] and offered to give her lessons in mathematics to help her understand it, but she declined; it contained a comprehensive survey of contemporary physics, mathematics and astronomy—the latter inevitably heavily impregnated with astrological theory—and showed an interest in magic typical of its period, but was less inclined to occult syncretism than its predecessor.

Dee and Thomas Digges made disciplined observations of the "new star" of 1572, their calculations of the comet's movement supplying valuable data to Tycho Brahe. They were already committed Copernicans, and the new star seemed to both of them to be final proof of the heliocentric theory. Digges' *A Perfit Description of the Caelestial Orbes* (1576), which he added to a new edition of his father's almanac, *A Prognostocation Everlasting* (first published in 1553), included a diagrammatic representation of the heliocentric solar system in which the realm of the stars was indicated to be infinite. He also included a brief essay on the variation of the compass and some notes on common errors in navigation, although such work—like his work on optical instruments—had to be kept largely secret because of its military value

In the late 1570s Thomas Digges became a full-time military engineer, specializing in ballistics; he took command of ordnance in the Netherlands until his death in 1595. In March 1582, Dee found a far less suitable collaborator when he met Edward Kelley, a counterfeiter and confidence trickster who claimed that he could communicate with angels via a polished lump of obsidian, and that he knew the secret of the Philosopher's Stone. Initially skeptical,

Dee was seemingly persuaded that Kelley had some genuine ability, and they embarked on a long association, apparently recording their intercourse with the angels in a code they called the Enochian alphabet.

From 1583 to 1589 Dee and Kelley traveled extensively in central Europe, mostly in Poland and Bohemia. When Dee returned to London—leaving Kelley in Prague, where he died in 1593—he found that most of his library had been stolen or confiscated; much of it ended up in the British Museum, along with the magic stone and documents relating to the Enochian code. Retrospective interpretations of the true significance of these materials differ sharply, but those who suppose Dee to have been a spy take the view that his journey to the heart of the Holy Roman Empire was a matter of gathering intelligence, and that his arcane alphabet was a means of transmitting coded messages. Dee's attempts to obtain a position from the crown on his return to London were frustrated, but in 1596 he was appointed Warden of the Collegiate Chapter (Christ's College) in Manchester. When Manchester was hit by the plague in 1605, however, his wife and several of their children died, and Dee returned to London, where he died in his turn.

It was not until fifty years after Dee's death that his reputation as a magician took off, by courtesy of Meric Casaubon's highly fanciful *A true and faithful Relation of what passed between Dr. John Dee and some Spirits; tending, had it succeeded, to a general Alteration of most States and Kingdoms in the World* (1659). This was the source of the more widely-read accounts of Dee contained in John Aubrey's *Brief Lives* (written c1692; published 1813) and Charles Mackay's chapter on "The Alchymists" in *Memoirs of Extraordinary Popular Delusions* (1841; reprinted in *Extraordinary Popular Delusions and the Madness of Crowds*). Dee was widely credited thereafter with all manner of other clandestine magical endeavors, which threw his mathematical and scientific endeavors into the historical shade. The preservation of his magical apparatus in the British Museum, while his navigational endeavors and work on optics went largely unrecorded, ensured that he became a central figure in the retrospectively-constructed tradition of occult endeavor, a key inspiration for fantasists of every stripe.

Dee's posthumous reputation guaranteed him a literary afterlife more extensive and more colorful than any other scientist of his era, although the inevitable price paid for that peculiar celebrity was that his supposed magical follies were magnified to a far greater extent than any of his scientific innovations could ever have contrived. Notable examples of his literary employment as a magician include the depictions of him in W. Harrison Ainsworth's *Guy Fawkes* (1841) and Peter Ackroyd's *The House of Doctor Dee* (1993).

* * * *

The pattern of retrospective suspicion of wizardry was even more obvious in continental Europe and in Britain, where two of its most famous victims were Albertus Magnus and Cornelius Agrippa von Nettesheim, whose study of occult science *De Occulta philosophis* (3 volumes 1531-33) was posthumously supplemented in 1559 with a spurious fourth volume that became one of the most famous guides to summoning demons, and led Agrippa's disciple Johann Weyer to mount a blistering attack on contemporary "sorcerers" while simultaneously ridiculing witch-hunting.

The ongoing great witch-hunt also attracted scathing skeptical attacks in England, including *The Discoverie of Witchcraft* (1584), by Thomas Digges' sometime collaborator on military engineering projects Reginald Scott (or Scot, as the title-page of the book has it), which James I ordered to be burned but was nevertheless widely read. Ironically, and perhaps unfortunately, the book's most evident influence was on dramatists, who mined its detailed account of spells, potions and rituals—which Scot had cited in order to demonstrate their ludicrousness—for supernatural apparatus to add to their melodramas. The formulae employed by the three witches in Shakespeare's *Macbeth* are the best-known example.

In terms of relevance to English literature, however, the most significant of the continental scholars whose reputations were tainted by demonization was Theophrastus Bombastus von Hohenheim, better known as Paracelsus. No scholar in the list has retained such an ambiguous reputation as Paracelsus, partly because he, far more than any of the others, pandered to the suspicions of his contemporaries with regard to the occult aspects of his works. His attempts to bring about a reformation in alchemy are now recognized as a significant contribution to the gradual transformation of that proto-science into the modern science of chemistry, but it was his parallel attempt to reform the practice of medicine along similar lines that created a storm and a long-lasting legacy. Although the specific chemical remedies he attempted to substitute for the traditional herbal remedies long sanctified by medical orthodoxy, in *Die Grosse Wundartznei* [The Great Book of Surgery] (1536) and its successors, were mostly no more effective and sometimes more dangerous, he did at least succeed in providing a significant challenge that led his followers and sympathizers to begin experimenting, and open up the possibility of more productive reform.

Paracelsian medicine was imported into England by William Bullein, one of the first writers to attempt to produce medical guide-books aimed at lay readers as well as physicians, in *Bulwarke of Defence againste Sicknes, Sorues, etc.* (c1560), in which part one, "The Book of Simples," deals with orthodox herbal treatments while part four, "The Book of Compounds" deals with the chemical medicine pioneered by Paracelsus. Bullein's later works included *A Dialogue bothe pleasaunte and pietifull, wherein is a Goodly Regiment against the Fever Pestilence, with a Consolation and Comfort against Death* (1564) which eventually begins to resemble a proto-novel; it describes a flight from a plague-stricken London, and its initially-tentative tendencies towards symbolism and allegory eventually erupt into a fabulous satirical traveler's tale narrated by one Mendax, which includes accounts of Mandragata, where headless men have eyes in their breasts; Selenetide, inhabited by egg-laying women; the legendary kingdom of Prester John; and the allegedly-ideal state of Nodnol in the land of Taerg Natrib, situated beyond the Americas.

The championship of Paracelsian medicine in England was taken up much more stridently by Thomas Moffet, or Muffet, who obtained his M.D. in 1579 from the University of Basel, then the most important European center of Paracelsian medicine. When he returned to England the following year, however, Moffet immediately came into conflict with the College of Physicians, and was engaged in a fierce ideological battle with its members until he was finally admitted as a fellow in 1588, the year in which he published *Nosomata Hippocreata* (the Paracelsians had renewed interest in the pre-Galenian theories of Hippocrates). Moffet's clients included Sir Philip Sidney and Walter Raleigh, who also became Paracelsians; Sidney's sister, the Countess of Pembroke and dedicatee of his *Arcadia*, became his chief patron. The principal surviving memory of him derives from the fact that his daughter Patience is widely suspected of being the original "Little Miss Muffet" of the nursery rhyme—he had a strong interest in entomology, although he never managed to complete his major study of that subject—but he was famous in his own day, and was among Francis Bacon's many influential acquaintances.

Largely thanks to Moffet, Paracelsus and his theories became a significant topic of interest, not only within British medicine but in British literary culture—an interest that was still persistent, and considerably renewed, in the era of Romanticism, when Robert Browning employed him as the key figure in a long verse drama exploring the philosophical and personal aspects of the quest for knowledge, *Paracelsus* (1835).

* * * *

The demonization of scholarship reached its apogee in England with the posthumous melodramatization of the career of John Dee, and went into decline in the seventeenth century, even before scientific investigation had finally shuffled off its associations with astrology and alchemy; Dee's near-contemporary Francis Bacon, who founded the modern philosophy of science and whose more adventurous writings are the first requiring more detailed consideration in the next chapter, largely avoided any such stigmatization. The hint of devilry was shifted almost entirely into the realm of fiction—but there, as some of the examples cited above clearly illustrate, it continued to thrive, and another of Dee's contemporaries, Christopher Marlowe, was one of the first writers to take up a new archetype of scholarly ambition that had recently been given memorable literary form on the continent: Faust.

The character of Faust was allegedly based on a scholar based at the University of Heidelberg in the early 16th century, after whose death the rumor was spread that he had traded his soul to the Devil in exchange for forbidden knowledge. Whether that is true or not, his career eventually became a parable in which the hunger for knowledge is represented as essentially satanic. The printed version of the legend, which featured Faust's deal with the demon Mephistopheles, allegedly first appeared in 1587, in a pamphlet usually known as the *Faustbuch*, signed by Johann Spies.

An English version of the story appeared as *Faustus: the History of the Damnable Life and Deserved Death of Dr. John Faustus* (1592) by "P. R., Gent." The story was immediately appropriated by Marlowe in *The Tragical History of the Life and Death Dr. Faustus* (written and performed c1592; published 1604). In Marlowe's version Faust has already mastered all extant human knowledge, and in his first soliloquy in Act 1 he deplores the vanity of logic and medicine, wanting access to secrets that only necromancy can reveal; it is for that reason that he makes his pact with the demon Mephistophilis, one of Lucifer's henchmen, who acts as a middleman in negotiating the pact. In this version, however, Faust does not seem to get a great deal out of the pact in return for his damnation.

Stories in which humans make formal pacts with the Devil were not new in the late 16th century; the earliest recorded in writing is a Medieval cautionary tale about a Bishop named Theophilus. The notion had undergone a dramatic repopularization during the previous three centuries, however, when it had been adapted as an important instrument of the politics of persecution. The slander was used by Philippe IV of France to destroy the Knights Templar—a theatrical extravagance that became the seed of numerous secret histories improvised in the twentieth century. The stratagem was copied in other high-profile sorcery trials before becoming a standard instrument of the persecution of alleged witches, who were assumed to have made such pacts and forced by torture to confess to having done so. Faustian pacts, being contracted by males of relatively high social status, in exchange for knowledge rather than vulgar magical powers, were reckoned to be a cut above witch-pacts.

The most famous literary transfiguration of Faust's story after Marlowe's was J. W. Goethe's, published in two widely separated and markedly different parts in 1808 and 1832, which shows a great deal more sympathy for the protagonist and offers a far more complex account of his temptation. Here, a wager between God and the Devil effectively casts Faust as a substitute for Job, and shifts much attention in Part One to the young woman employed by the Devil for his temptation, Marguerite (or, more familiarly, Gretchen). Again, Goethe's Faust begins by despairing of the limitations of human knowledge and lusting after infinite, magical knowledge, so he is not a scientist in any strict sense; nor is it the case that all of the subsequent transfigurations of the story focus on Faust's scientific achievements or ambitions. Nevertheless, whether future fictional Fausts were represented as scientists or not, future fictional scientists were frequently and routinely likened to Faust, and science itself often came to be represented, in symbolic representations, as a Faustian endeavor.

Oswald Spengler's *Der Undertang des Abendlandes* (1918-22; tr. as *The Decline of the West*) went so far as to characterize the entire modern Occidental culture whose life-cycle was allegedly coming to an end as one possessed of a "Faustian Soul"—by contrast with the "Apollinean Soul" of Classical culture and the "Magian Soul" of Arabic culture. For Spengler, whereas the essence of Classical culture had been symbolized by the nude male of Greek statuary and that of Arabic culture by the dome, the essence of Western culture was symbolized by the infinite space that Faust had desired to grasp and master. Spengler's supposition was that the attempt had always been damned to failure, and had, in fact, failed—although Isaac Newton and Albert Einstein might both have disagreed.

* * * *

The revivification and mystification of the Pythagorean and neo-Platonic traditions in Renaissance Europe continued the syncretizing efforts of Iamblichus by incorporating another holistic and mystical tradition that similarly claimed descent from antiquity: the Jewish Kabbalah. The new synthesis eventually came to be called the Hermetic tradition, because of its alleged origins in the works of the legendary Hermes Trismegistus. Faked documents relating to this supposed tradition began to circulate in manuscript in the 15th century, most importantly the so-called *Corpus Hermeticum*. The idea of the Hermetic tradition was remarkably flexible—an elasticity seized upon by inventive occultists bent on usurping ancient authority and claiming its nebulous weight for their own ideas.

The *Corpus Hermeticum* was exposed as a fraud in 1614 by Isaac Casaubon, who traced many of its sources and identified some of its anachronisms, but skepticism, even accompanied by proofs, has never been effective against the posturings of occultists.

Events had, in any case, moved on; that same year saw the emergence of a new and spectacularly successful mystical mythology cast in the Paracelsian mould. The new occult philosophy made its debut in a pamphlet generally known as the *Fama Fraternitatis* (1614) which offered a brief biography of a magician named Christian Rosenkreutz; it was followed by the *Confessio Frateritas* (1615), which described his magical initiation, and then by the allegorical *Chymische Hochzeit Christiani Rosenkreuz* (1616; tr. as *The Heretick Romance; or, the Chymical Wedding*). The third of these items was signed by Johann Valentin Andreae—who was later to publish the Utopian romance *Christianopolis* (1619)—and who might well have written all three.

The Rosicrucian pamphlets excited an enormous amount of attention, as would-be members searched high and low for the mysterious Brotherhood of the Rosy Cross. The English philosopher Robert Fludd published two apologias for the Brotherhood before setting out to compile his own encyclopedia of the macrocosm and the microcosm in 1617. He engaged in fierce arguments with John Kepler, who criticized his anthropocentric cosmology in *Harmonies mundi*. Fludd's account of the macrocosm fused the Aristotelian cosmology of the Church with neo-Platonic ideas and infusions from the Kabbalah, while his incomplete account of the human microcosm was a grandiose synthesis of contemporary anatomy, mystical interpretations of the body's proportions, astrological linkages between various organs and the signs of the zodiac, neo-Pythagorean theories of musical harmony, and so on. He went on to develop new theories of medicine, and analyses of "Mosaic philosophy" that laid the groundwork for Isaac Newton's Biblical studies.

The Newtonian revolution could not sweep away the mystical geocentrism of men like Fludd, but it did sweep it under the carpet of orthodoxy, into an esoteric niche to which it was well-adapted. Geocentrism was not, however, an essential component of mysticism, whose microcosmic and macrocosmic analogies could easily be reformulated in a heliocentric mould. Once the Rosicrucian renewal of the Hermetic tradition had itself grown old enough to become murkily mysterious, it played a considerable role in the development of literary fantasy, culminating in the Gothic novels associated with the Romantic Movement. William Godwin's *St.*

Leon (1799) makes use of Rosicrucian mythology, and so does Percy Shelley's early Gothic novella developing the same themes, *St. Irvyne; or, The Rosicrucian* (1811). It was, therefore, entirely natural that Edward Bulwer—who was acquainted with the Shelleys before he attached his mother's maiden name, Lytton, to his own—should follow the same track in his classic occult romance *Zanoni* (1842), which made a considerable contribution to the "occult revival" of the second half of the nineteenth century.

It was, however, inherent in the nature of the Rosicrucian legend that it should give rise to rivals, and it did. One of the best-known was the Order of the Illuminati founded by Adam Weishaupt at the University of Ingolstadt, the seat of learning in which the fictional Victor Frankenstein pursues his studies. As an organization, the Bavarian Illuminati never really got off the ground, although the Order did attract sympathizers and ideological fellow-travelers, including Goethe, but its legend was always far more powerful than its reality, leading to its official suppression in 1777 when the oversensitive king of Bavaria, Karl Theodor, banned all secret societies in his realm. Convincing others that one is in possession of precious secrets can be a handicap as well as a useful enticement. In any case, by far and away the most successful of the eighteenth century's neo-occultists, in terms of gathering recruits, was one who did not represent himself as a custodian of secret lore, but one who set out to publish his syncretic system as a new revelation allegedly constituting a crucial synthesis of science and religion: Emmanuel Swedenborg.

Born Emmanuel Swedberg in 1688, Swedenborg originally followed a career in science, founding Sweden's first scientific periodical, *Daedalus Hyperboreus*, in 1715. He was appointed as assistant to the prolific inventor Christopher Polhem on the Royal Board of Mines and wrote treatises on such subjects as cosmology, optics and human sensory perception, but he fell victim to a change of regime and published nothing further until a comprehensive three-volume summary of his endeavors in physical science, *Opera Philosophica et Mineralia* (1734), heavily influenced by the work of René Descartes. It includes an early version of the nebular theory of the solar system's origin, subsequently brought to maturity by Immanuel Kant and Pierre Laplace. Swedenborg followed it with *Oeconomia Regni Animalis* (1740-41; tr. as *The Economy of the Animal Kingdom*), which included orthodox studies in anatomy but also attempted to carry forward Descartes' attempts to clarify the relationship between the human body and soul. He set out to extend this work into a 17-volume encyclopedia of human science, but only published three volumes, as *Regnum animale* (1743-44), which introduced a significant preoccupation with the notion of a universal language. The latter fascination was subsequently transformed into a "doctrine of correspondence" based on the notion that there is a natural symmetry between propositions in natural science and propositions related to spiritual matters, determined by an innate symbolic aspect of Creation: a new version of occult holism.

Swedenborg then began to take an intense interest in his dreams, which he began increasingly to consider as visions offering insight into the supposed universal patterns of symbolic correspondence, and soon abandoned his studies in natural philosophy in order to devoted himself to accounts of his visions, interpreted as communications from and with spirits, and to the interpretation of the Bible in the light of his occult theory. He published abundantly, though mostly anonymously, during the remainder of his life, eventually summarizing his theological ideas in *Vera Christiana Religio* (1771; tr. as *True Christian Religion*).

Swedenborg's published visions, considered as works of fiction or speculative non-fiction, are very striking and unprecedentedly far-ranging, offering detailed accounts of expeditions to other planets within and without the solar system, whose descriptions are ingenuously informed by his early scientific training. They include *Arcana coelestia quae in Scriptura sacra seu verbo Domini sunt detecta, etc* (1749-56; tr. in 12 vols. as *Arcana Coelestia; or, Heavenly Mysteries contained in the Sacred Scriptures, etc*)—an obvious predecessor of several nineteenth-century cosmic voyages, including the vision that Humphry Davy recorded in *Consolations in Travel* (1830).

The appropriation of Swedenborg's works by mystics and religious disciples began in the 1780s, when Swedenborgian societies began to form in some profusion; the first significant congregation of the Church of the New Jerusalem was founded in London. His visions and religious ideas became very influential in nineteenth-century literature, especially on the German and English Romantic

Movements; Charles Augustus Tulk, the founder of the English Swedenborg Society, was a close friend of William Blake and Samuel Taylor Coleridge, while Swedenborg's translator and biographer James Garth Wilkinson was a friend of Thomas Carlyle and Robert Browning; the latter's *Paracelsus* is strongly influenced by Swedenborgian ideas. Because such ideas were exoteric rather than esoteric, however, they did not have quite the same charm as the myth of Rosicrucianism, which also offered far more scope for blithe invention.

* * * *

The supernatural world-view sustaining the Faustian motif of Mephistopheles and the diabolical pact survived in post-Goethean fiction primarily as an exercise in symbolism, and maintained an obvious artificiality even in Gothic fiction that pretended to take it literally, but the taint did not die with the fashionability of the world-view. Rosicrucianism and its analogues helped to keep it alive, and the fictitious scientists featured in literary works often retained a tendency to extend their studies into the realms of the occult.

That strange shadow of suspicion was also frequently transmuted into another form of tacit damnation: the curse of insanity. As the notion of madness made the transition from being regarded as a form of divine affliction to a kind of illness, the suspicion that scientists were secretly but inherently bad was gradually and largely replaced by the suspicion that they were secretly but inherently mad. That notion, sly but not entirely covert, is inherent in the original meaning of "scientific romance," and Isaac D'Israeli's elaboration of that notion in *Flim-Flams!* is shot through with the almost-explicit conviction that not only the hypothetical Uncle at the center of the story but all the scientists whose work the author has occasion to cite or discuss are out of their minds. Nor was the conviction new to D'Israeli, or even to Jonathan Swift's earlier account of Gulliver's voyage to Laputa. It only requires a slight shift in perspective to imagine Faust as a deluded madman rather than a sane scholar literally conjuring demons, and in much the same way that the image of the scientist has always been tainted by a hint of wizardry, so the reputation of would-be wizards, both real and fictitious, has always been tainted by a suspicion of madness.

Significantly, the suspicion that scientists are inherently tainted by madness was widely entertained by writers who—unlike Jonathan Swift or Isaac D'Israeli—were wholeheartedly in favor of scientific endeavors and sincerely admiring of their produce. Their similar conviction that genius is invariably and inherently close to madness—an idea that had originated in Classical Greece but enjoyed a spectacular resurgence in the nineteenth century with the birth of attempts to construct a science of psychology—often caused them to proclaim that the madness concerned was both harmless and glorious, but the typical eccentricity of scientists was nevertheless widely accepted as indubitable.

The presumed eccentricity of scientists is taken for granted in almost all their literary representations, and was built into the first works to be widely described as "scientific romances"—the key works of Jules Verne—apparently automatically. It is very evident in the characterization of Professor Lidenbrock in *Voyage au centre de la Terre* (1864; revised 1867; tr. as *Journey to the Center of the Earth*) and that of Professor Arronax in *Vingt mille lieues sous les mers*, who are by no means the most extreme examples in Verne's canon. In England, although the balance swung in the same direction, the suspicion often cut more deeply than mere eccentricity of harmless delusion—a process encouraged by the production of a further archetypal figure in Mary Shelley's Victor Frankenstein, who, like many Romantic anti-heroes, is not really bad, but is undoubtedly a little mad, and is most definitely dangerous to know.

Such tainted reputations, and the rationale supporting them, played a very considerable part in forming the ideative backcloth against which writers of generic scientific romance eventually had to work. Many such writers were content to endorse it, and it is not easy to find examples of propagandists who struggled hard against it—but the essential point is that anyone who wanted to deny it did, indeed, face a hard struggle. Any writer wanting to represent a scientist as a model of virtue and sanity would have felt compelled to argue for the contention against the assumed skepticism of the addressees of his work. Even the few who did so cannot be said to have done so with any degree of apparent success, in terms of convincing their readers and critics to change their minds, or even any degree of personal conviction.

4. THE ELEMENTS OF SCIENCE

In spite of the tainted reputations of almost everyone who made a significant contribution of scientific progress before Francis Bacon, and quite a few of those who did so afterwards, science did make vast progress, albeit unsteadily. After a promising start in ancient Greece, that progress suffered a definite setback in Western Europe for several centuries, and once progress had been renewed in the eleventh and twelfth centuries it suffered further stutters before the Renaissance built a firmer foundation for continued endeavor, ultimately cemented by the invention of printing.

Because the Greeks had no distinct and integral concept of what we would now think of as "science," its various precursory elements were either considered as separate disciplines or as subsidiary aspects of philosophy. The Greeks had a Goddess of Wisdom, Minerva, and an archetypal divine technologist in Hephaestus, plus a Muse of Astronomy, Urania, but other characters that became symbolic figureheads once the notion of science eventually became clearer were more ambiguous figures. They included the Titan Prometheus—whose theft of the "fire of the gods" on behalf of humankind eventually came to be widely reinterpreted as a symbolic theft of scientific knowledge or technological expertise—and the legendary Daedalus, the builder of the labyrinth and pioneer of human flight.

That list was further supplemented by the elevation of Archimedes, the most famous of the proto-scientists of the era, to quasi-archetypal status, although his actual achievements were evidently considered too slight by the satirist Lucian to warrant such status. Four hundred years after the alleged event, Lucian invented a tale of Archimedes destroying a Roman fleet that had laid siege of Syracuse with some kind of heat ray—a story believed by many subsequent historians, in spite of the fact that Lucian was the most notorious fantasist of his era.

If the triumphs of Greek science continued to bear fruit, it was not without some penalty. Astronomy, by far the most useful of the ancient sciences, in spite of being purely observational, by virtue of its assistance in determining the calendar and regulating time, paid for its predictive successes by being falsely credited with further predictive potential in the development of the pseudoscience of astrology, which kept it company for millennia and still haunts it. Astronomy's attempted extrapolation into cosmology was severely handicapped by the difficulty people had in getting past the seemingly-commonsensical assumption that it was the heavens that rotated around the Earth rather than the Earth whose rotation about its axis created the appearance in question.

Other branches of knowledge fared no better than astronomy. The esthetic assumption that everything ought to be made out of the same fundamental stuff gave rise to four rival theories as to how that ultimate element ought to be characterized, with the paradoxical outcome of a philosophical compromise that eventually accepted all four—earth, water, air and fire—as "elements." The assumption that all chemical reactions and physical phenomena ought to be explicable, somehow, in terms of those four elements cursed chemistry for millennia, while it remained chained to the mystical assumptions of alchemy, and it made effective progress in medicine even more difficult when it gave birth to the analogical doctrine of the four elementary bodily "humors."

The achievement of Christian dominance over the ruins of the Roman Empire did not help in the matter of helping science to overthrow its idols, in that it tended to endow all presupposed knowledge, overtly or covertly, with a dogmatic authority that made intellectual challenge not merely difficult but dangerous. And yet, new knowledge did accumulate, slowly, becoming increasingly secure, and as it accumulated, its overall shape changed, sometimes subtly but sometimes with such sweeping effects as to usher in whole new world-views.

The first great change of the latter sort was, of course the ultimate triumph of the heliocentric model of the solar system over the geocentric one, and the intellectual spinoff to which the changed perspective then gave rise. The battle to establish the revised theory as common belief was a long one, sufficiently hard-fought to produce martyrs and its own legendry, its most important hero-myth being the story of Galileo.

Galileo Galilei was the first person to make extensive and disciplined observations of the sky with the aid of a telescope, and he also made important experimental studies of bodies in motion, which laid the groundwork for Isaac Newton's clarification of the laws of motion. Galileo was born in Pisa, where two of the most famous anecdotes concerning his observations are set. One relates how his observations of a swinging lamp in the cathedral in 1581 inspired his discovery of the regularity of the oscillation of the pendulum, and the potential for its use in clocks; the other—almost certainly apocryphal—relates how he dropped two objects of different weights from the Leaning Tower, to demonstrate that they would hit the ground at the same time. He withdrew from the University of Pisa in 1585 because he was short of money and went to Florence, where he published an account of a hydrostatic balance in 1886, the invention of which won him a wide reputation. He returned to Pisa as a lecturer in 1589, after publishing a treatise on the notion of the centre of gravity, but further financial difficulties led to his seeking a new post at the University of Padua in 1592, where he brought his work on bodies in motion to fruition.

Galileo was convinced that the heliocentric theory of the solar system was true before he began his astronomical observations, but he kept his opinion to himself, with the exception of letters to such like-minded individuals as John Kepler. The early observations he reported in *Sidereus Nuncius* [The Starry Messenger] (1610)—including sunspots, the phases of Venus, the rings of Saturn and the fact that the Milky Way was composed of stars—were mostly uncontroversial. He left Padua to become "first philosopher" to the Grand Duke of Tuscany in 1610, and visited Rome in 1611 to show off his telescope; the welcome he received there encouraged him to propose publicly that the movement of sunspots proved that Copernicus was correct about the Sun being the center of the solar system. A letter written in 1615 to the Grand Duchess, which argued that "experimental truth" is a better beginning in the quest for knowledge than scriptural truth, and ought to be the final arbiter of belief, sparked an ideological dispute with the orthodox academicians, complicated by political wrangles involving Galileo's patron, in which the Inquisition became involved.

The theologian Cardinal Bellarmine responded to this dispute by placing Copernicus on the *Index Librarium Prohibitorum* [Index of Forbidden Books] in 1616, and warning Galileo that he must desist from his assertions. Galileo complied, devoting himself to private research at his house near Florence for the next seven years. He was provoked to reassert his views by a pamphlet on comets by Orazio Grasi that mocked his opinions. The recently elected pope, Urban VIII, was an old friend, to whom Galileo carefully dedicated his reply. In 1624 he went to Rome to ask for the ban on Copernican theory to be lifted; the pope declined, but gave him permission to write a comparison of the Ptolemaic and Copernican systems, on the condition that he came to the conclusion that human intellect is incompetent to decide between them, the responsibility for Creation being God's alone.

Galileo's response to this invitation, *Dialogo sopra i due massimi sistemi del mondo, tolemaico et copernicano* [Dialogue Concerning the Two Principal World Systems, the Ptolemaic and the Copernican] (1632), generated further controversy. While sticking to the letter of his promise, Galileo had taken advantage of irony and the careful characterization of the participants in the dialogue to make a strong case in favor of Copernicanism. He was eventually forced to recant, although legend stubbornly insists that his public pronouncement was supplemented by a covertly muttered "*Eppur si muove*" [But it—i.e., the Earth—does move].

Galileo escaped imprisonment, but submitted to house arrest; that allowed him to complete a further dialogue summarizing and completing his work in mechanics. He went blind in 1638, but continued to correspond with other scientists, suggesting the application of the pendulum in clocks that Christiaan Huygens eventually put into practice in 1656. His persecution probably had at least as much to do with politics as religious doctrine, but it ensured him an unparalleled reputation as a heroic champion of science against superstition. The range of his work, his ability to make complex deductions from primitive astronomical observations, the rhetorical flair of his first dialogue, his deployment of the notion of force in the second, and his conception of experiment as *cimento* [ordeal]—i.e., as a means of putting hypothetical propositions to the proof—certainly entitle him to that status. Huygens completed a Copernican dramatization of his own in the visionary *Cosmotheoros*, but prudently left it unpublished while he was alive; it was issued posthumously in 1695.

Galileo's aesthetic conviction that the planetary orbits had to be circular prevented him from acknowledging John Kepler's laws of planetary motion, and he shied away from a theory of gravity because he could not abide the idea of action at a distance, but he played a greater part than any of his contemporaries in smashing the conceptual barrier dividing the Earth from the Heavens, setting their various phenomena firmly within a single conceptual framework. The literary influence of his work was quick to take effect, and long-lasting. John Donne must have read *Sidereus Nuncius* in the year of its publication, as it is mentioned in his satire on the Jesuits, *Ignatius His Conclave* (1611); *An Anatomy of the World*, published the same year, written for the anniversary of the death of his patron's daughter, represents her as a microcosm whose untimely death mirrors the destruction of old beliefs by the new philosophy that "calls all in doubt."

Galileo appears as a character in Giambattista Marino's cosmological epic *L'Adone* (1622), which praises his work with the telescope. John Milton visited Galileo in 1638 or thereabouts, and mentions him in *Paradise Lost* (1667), in which Satan flies through infinite space "amongst innumerable stars." His name gave rise to an inevitable pun—the "Galilean gospel"—which recurred frequently in seventeenth century literature, applied both approvingly and pejoratively. His status as a hero of science gave his name an iconic status that lasted into the twentieth century, celebrated in such fervently polemical works as Bertolt Brecht's *Leben des Galilei* (1938; pub. 1955; tr. as *The Life of Galileo in Seven Plays*) and Barrie Stavis' *Lamp at Midnight* (1947).

The geometry of the heliocentric theory was completed by Kepler, who became obsessed with the notion of accommodating the Copernican model of the solar system to a mathematical description that would relate the orbits of the planets to the five "Platonic solids"—the only forms whose angles could be fitted to the surface of a sphere. He failed, but a copy of the book on the subject he published in 1596, sent to Tycho Brahe—who was soon to be appointed Imperial Mathematician of the Holy Roman Empire—won him an invitation to join Tycho on the staff at his observatory, and Kepler succeeded him as Imperial Mathematician when he died in 1601. In that year he published *De Fundamentis Astrologiae Certioribus* [The Reliable Foundations of Astrology], which rejected the idea that the stars control or guide the lives of human beings, but asserted instead that the harmony of the universe ensured a reflective correspondence between the movements of the heavens and human lives, thus cementing the foundations of modern astrological "theory."

Kepler's obsession with discovering some underlying logic to the planetary orbits finally bore unexpected fruit when he made the conceptual breakthrough that allowed him to realize that the orbits were not circular at all, but elliptical—a discovery he published, along with two laws of planetary motion, in *Astronomia Nova* in 1609, further elaborating his discovery with a third law in *Harmonies Mundi* [The Harmony of the Universe] (1619). Kepler had to leave Prague for fear of religious persecution when a new emperor came to power, but published his definitive account of the Copernican cosmology, *Epitome Astronomiae Copernicanae* (1618-21) shortly thereafter. He had written another book in 1609, attempting to make his Copernican arguments more accessible and convincing by describing the astronomical observations of Earth that might be made by an observer on the moon, but had not published it and had lost the manuscript in 1611, apparently to theft. The narrative was represented as a dream, but the dreamer's trip to the moon was facilitated by a "daimon" (a favorite term of neo-Platonists, derived from the Greek word for knowledge), and this might have been misconstrued as "demon" by someone who read the manuscript.

It is unclear whether the theft of the *Somnium* had anything to do with the fact that Kepler's mother was charged with witchcraft in 1620, but he defended her successfully, saving her from torture and execution; although he had rewritten his dream story by then, he never published it. It appeared posthumously in 1634 as *Somnium*, attracting little attention in the chaos of the Thirty Years' War (1618-48), although it can be seen retrospectively as a truly remarkable work, not least because the concluding phase of the visionary voyage offers an account of the way in which lunar life might be adapted to the long cycle of day and night.

* * * *

Kepler's three laws of planetary motion provided the keystone of Isaac Newton's final triumphant refinement of the heliocentric theory, with its integration into a theory of universal gravitation. The enormous scope of that theory, which bound earthly and cosmological phenomena together into a seamless theoretical whole, won Newton a reputation as the ultimate scientific genius of his own era, and perhaps of any era. Nor was that his only achievement; he became the central figure of a veritable scientific revolution, which founded the Age of Reason, *Philosophiae Naturalis Principia Mathematica* [Mathematical Principles of Natural Philosophy] (1687) becoming *the* pivotal work in the history of science.

Newton's father had died before he was born, in 1642, and his mother abandoned him upon her remarriage in 1644 to the care of his grandmother, prompting an extreme resentment that permanently colored his character. When his mother was widowed again in 1653 she recruited him to help manage the property she had inherited, but his neglect of this commission was so blatant that he was swiftly packed off to school. He moved on to Trinity College, Cambridge in 1661, having developed a considerable prowess in the construction of machines. Traditional Aristotelianism was still being taught at Cambridge, but Newton's discovery of the work of René Descartes showed him a new direction of rebellion. He also read Pierre Gassendi's new version of atomic theory, Robert Boyle's reformist endeavors in chemistry and Henry More's neo-Platonist analyses of the occult Hermetic tradition, all of which he attempted to carry forward in his own work.

Newton's first manifest achievement was an extrapolation of Descartes' algebraic geometry, circulated in a privately-circulated manuscript in 1669; his discovery of what he subsequently called the method of fluxions—differential calculus, in modern terminology—won him a select reputation, but he did not publish it. While the university was closed in 1665-67 because of an epidemic of the plague he had also carried out experiments with prisms and lenses, which were to provide the foundations of his *Opticks*, but he did not publish his essay "On Colours" either.

Newton was elected to a fellowship at Trinity in 1667 and was recommended by one of the few men acquainted with his work, Isaac Barrow, to succeed him as Lucasian professor of mathematics in 1669. He continued to develop his theory of optics in the context of an annual lecture course, and eventually presented a paper on the subject to the Royal Society in 1672. One of the Society's leading members, Robert Hooke, who considered himself an expert in the subject, wrote a condescending critique of the paper, which so enraged Newton that he became a virtual recluse until 1675, when he heard what he took to be a recantation by Hooke, and presented a second paper on refraction, which became the basis for the second volume of *Opticks*. He was, however, soon embroiled in a new dispute with Hooke, who accused him of stealing the ideas he had incorporated in a further paper on the underlying physics of light.

Newton controlled his anger for a while, but was tipped over the edge again when a group of Jesuits in Liege contended that his experiments were invalid. He suffered what would nowadays be called a "nervous breakdown" in 1678; his correspondence with others ceased, although he continued to work in isolation on all the problems that intrigued him. It was not until Edmund Halley visited him in 1684 that Newton revealed that he had solved the problem of orbital dynamics and reluctantly promised to show Halley the proof. The paper Newton sent to the astronomer did not contain the three laws of motion or the law of universal gravitation, but all of them were subsequently incorporated into the expanded version that he published as the *Principia*.

On seeing the manuscript of the *Principia*, Hooke again charged Newton with plagiarism; Newton reacted by cutting almost all the references to Hooke from the book; the famous anecdote relating how the idea of gravity occurred to Newton when an apple fell on his head as a boy was invented as an element of his defensive strategy against Hooke's allegation. Newton decided not to publish *Opticks*, and swore that he would never accept the presidency of the Royal Society while Hooke was alive.

The international reputation won by the *Principia* made Newton by far the most prominent scientist in England, and he took advantage of his fame to make a political career for himself in London, eventually becoming Warden of the Royal Mint in 1696. The new friends he made in London, who included John Locke and Samuel Pepys, thought it likely that Newton would go mad in 1693, when his relationship with the young mathematician Nicholas Fatio de Duillier came to an end, but he seemed to recover. His principal intellectual labors were devoted thereafter to studies of the text of the Bible based in ideas taken from occult science, but he never published anything of that sort.

Newton accepted the Presidency of the Royal Society in 1703, when Hooke was safely buried, and was knighted in 1705. Again he became embroiled in fierce disputes, with the astronomer John Flamsteed and the philosopher Gottfried Leibniz, but he now had sufficient authority to support his wrath, and that might have protected him from the possibility of another breakdown. He finally prepared *Opticks* for publication in 1704, but he augmented the text twice, in the Latin edition of 1706 and a second English edition of 1717-18, incorporating new material derived from his general physical theories. He imported similar new material into a second edition of the *Principia* in 1713. The final versions of his two key works completed the definitive edition of his model of the universe. Some of his esoteric studies were posthumously published as *The Chronology of Ancient Kingdoms Amended* (1728) and *Observations Upon the Prophecies of Daniel and the Apocalypse of St. John* (1733).

* * * *

From the viewpoint of those convinced by his arguments, Newton became the man who had completed the heliocentric theory, by adding it into a much vaster and more comprehensive vision of the universe, supported by mathematical proofs that might be difficult to understand—the differential calculus, became the new *pons asinorum* for many students of mathematics, the intellectual bridge that mere asses could not cross—but were nevertheless brilliant and irrefutable. He integrated Kepler's individual laws of planetary motion into a general theory of universal gravitation, whose handful of central laws became the scientific equivalent of divine commandments.

For Newton himself, that was no mere metaphor. Intensely devout, he represented and justified his scientific endeavors as a means of increasing human insight into the working methods of the divinity: a matter of gaining a greater inside into the mysterious workings of the divine mind. That philosophy, eventually characterized as "natural theology," became the foundation-stone of a concerted attempt to reconcile scientific endeavor with religion and heal the apparent rift that had developed in the unfortunate trial of Galileo.

Many religious believers felt that they had little alternative but to stop denying the truth of the heliocentric theory, given the overwhelming evidence that piled up, but found compensation of a sort in the idea that Newtonian physics could be represented as a means getting to know God a little better, and that the awesome scope of the Newtonian model of the universe might be usefully combined with the awe that ought to be attached to the notion of the Creator. After all, the creator of a tiny solar system in which the stars were mere cosmic wallpaper seemed a trifle paltry by comparison with the creator of an infinite universe of stars regulated with an iron hand by equations that were striking, and perhaps beautiful, in their simplicity.

Newton became the primary symbol of the New Science among litterateurs. When he died Allan Ramsay wrote an "Ode" in his memory and Alexander Pope wrote an epitaph for him: "Nature and Nature's laws lay hid in night;/God said, Let Newton be! and all was light!" William Wordsworth characterized him in "The Prelude" (1805) as "Newton with his prism and silent face,/The marble index of a mind for ever/Voyaging through strange seas of thought, alone," while James Thomson—who also wrote "A Poem Sacred to the Memory of Sir Isaac Newton" (1727)—described him in "The Seasons" (1726-30; rev. 1744) as "Newton, pure intelligence, whom God/To mortals lent to trace his boundless works." Other tributes included Richard Glover's "A Poem on Newton," which was printed in Henry Pemberton's *A View of Sir Isaac Newton's Philosophy* (1728).

A more profound philosophical influence of Newton's achievements can been seen in several long poems using his ideas as the foundation of a new epic mythology. Richard Blackmore's *Creation: A Philosophical Poem Demonstrating the Existence and Providence of God* (1712) presents the theory of gravity as a striking and conclusive manifestation of divine omnipotence. Henry Baker's "The Universe" (1734), which includes a detailed account of the solar system, including comets and recently-discovered minor planets, and also an elaborate account of "animalcules" discovered by microscopy, similarly takes it for granted that Newton's discovery of physical laws necessarily implies a divine law-maker.

Henry Brooke's "Universal Beauty" (1735) is similar to Baker's poem in its scope, but its method is more elaborate and fanciful, beginning with an invocation of "Tritonia! Goddess of the new born skies"[13] and "Venus Urania." The poem includes footnotes to explain the symbolism of such classical references with reference

13   Henry Brooke. "Universal Beauty" in *Poetical Works*. Dublin, for the Editor, 1792. p.3.

to modern scientific ideas—a method subsequently echoed and greatly elaborated by Erasmus Darwin, who must have been familiar with the poem, which was still in print and well-known in the late eighteenth and early nineteenth centuries. In Brooke's account, again, gravity becomes God's "Secret Hand" operating the universal mechanism.

All three of these weighty poems attempt to employ Newtonian cosmology as a supposed proof of the falsity and futility of atheism—but not everyone saw Newton's achievements in the same way, and the fervent assertiveness of the three items is a tacit recognition of the fact that some people interpreted the Newtonian revelation as a proof that God was now redundant, unnecessary as an explanation of universal order. The contest between geocentrism and heliocentrism continued, within the Church—still reeling from the schismatic effects of the Reformation—as well as within the growing ensemble of scholars who were now forming the nucleus of a "scientific community." Galileo's battle was still being fought a century after the publication of his famous dialogue, with literary methods as well as every other kind of rhetorical strategy.

One of the most important rounds in that contest was fought, and spectacularly won, by Bernard Le Bovier de Fontenelle's *Entretiens sur la pluralité des mondes* [Conversations on the Plurality of Worlds] (1686), which was rapidly translated into English in several different versions, and became as influential in Britain as in France, remaining popular long after its propagandistic work was largely done. Blackmore claimed, albeit unconvincingly, that he had adopted a conversational style in *Creation* in imitation of it.

As the title of his work indicates, Fontenelle substituted for Galileo's essentially combative dialogue a series of amiable, witty conversations, whose light style gave them a persuasive charm far beyond the aggressive dialectics typical of philosophical dialogues. There is a sense, of course, in which offering what is essentially a series of lectures to an avidly curious listener is loading the dice, reducing any objection raised against the case being made to the status of puzzlement merely requiring clarification—but no one could seriously contend that anyone since Plato had ever designed their dialogues without loading the dice surreptitiously.

Because of its format, Fontenelle's *Conversations* became a foundation text of what was later to become known as "the popularization of science": the project of making the seeming arcana of the new scientific knowledge generally accessible to laymen. That task was becoming increasingly difficult, precisely because of the success of men like Isaac Newton in employing esoteric mathematics to pry open the mysteries of the universe—and because post-Newtonian science did seem so very difficult to comprehend, the task of simplifying it, even if that involved selecting out its more comprehensible aspects and glossing over the fluxions, came to seem all the more necessary to the champions of the new knowledge.

In order to justify the lightness of tone and spice up the wit of his conversations, Fontenelle had given the role of the pupil, eager to learn from the informed philosopher, to a young woman, a marquise. In so doing he was, to some extent, reflecting the increasing role that highly intelligent and educated women were beginning to play in French aristocratic society, hosting salons and soirées that became a significant feature of the long reign of the Sun King, Louis XIV, from 1653 to 1715. The battle for general female education still had a very long way to go, and the role of salon-keepers remained ostentatiously marginalized and somewhat disparaged in France throughout the eighteenth and nineteenth centuries, but it set important precedents nevertheless.

There was only the feeblest echo of that social evolution in England at the time, and to the extent that salon society did get off the ground in London, it was generally much less interested in literary and scientific endeavor, but when the battle to obtain the education of women did begin in Britain, as the eighteenth century approached its end, the question of scientific education became an important element within it; the gathering crusade for the popularization of science, although it was aimed at all the ignorant, had a particularly powerful thrust in the context of feminism—a thrust that played a significant role in the work of more than one of the writers who paved the way for the development of scientific romance. The struggle lasted a long time, and cannot be said to have been convincingly won until well into the twentieth century, but the fact that it began in the eighteenth century, and was ongoing from then on, had a significant influence on ideas and representations of progress.

* * * *

Precisely because he became such a heroic legendary figure to the champions of science, for those hostile to the produce of the scientific revolution, Isaac Newton became the great antagonist. A famous illustration by William Blake shows him crouched in a craven pose, equipped with measuring dividers similar to those employed by the Creator, of whom Blake also disapproved. Blake bracketed Newton with Francis Bacon and John Locke as leading enemies of "vision;" he allegedly offered up the regular prayer "May God us Keep From Single vision and Newton sleep" and complained in one of his notebooks that "The Atoms of Democritus/And Newton's particles of Light/Are sands upon the Red sea shore,/Where Israel's tents do shine so bright."

The artist Benjamin Haydon recalled Charles Lamb abusing Blake for putting Newton's head into a picture, and calling on John Keats to support his allegation that Newtonian analysis had destroyed the poetry of the rainbow—support that Keats was allegedly glad to lend. The Romantic poets were by no means all of one mind on the issue—Samuel Taylor Coleridge complimented Newton's "serener eye" in *Religious Musings*—but the antagonistic clamor proved to be more easily audible in literary society than it did in the burgeoning scientific community, and helped to drive an initial wedge between literary and scientific culture, which contrived an ever increasing gap throughout the nineteenth and twentieth centuries, ultimately resulting in the two separate and antagonistic cultures identified and deplored by C. P. Snow.

Blake's argument was not new; before Newton had published either of his masterworks, Margaret Cavendish, Duchess of Newcastle, had written *Observations Upon Experimental Philosophy* (1666) in response to Robert Hooke's *Micrographia*, appending to it a "romantical" and "fantastical" Utopian romance, *The Description of A New World, Called the Blazing World*, which expressed the anxiety that the wonderful discoveries of the Enlightenment might obscure a broader vision based in occult philosophy. As a woman, however, Margaret Cavendish was not allowed to be a member of the Royal Society, and her views went unheeded, although her account of the "Blazing World" is one of the more remarkable traveler's tales of its era, dazzling in its inventiveness and monumental eccentricity. In the interim between her and Blake, such opposition as there was to Newton's legend was muted and largely ineffectual.

The same is not true of Newton's most vocal supporters. Voltaire saw Newton as a welcome flood of common sense cleansing philosophy's Augean stables of undesirable detritus; he popularized Newtonian ideas in *Éléments de la philosophie de Newton* (1738), after his brilliant patroness, Émilie du Châtelet, had performed the Herculean task of translating the *Principia* into French; he also imported them into his *contes philosophiques*, especially *Micromégas*. Voltaire had his detractors too, including contemporaries who adopted the *conte philosophique* as a method in order to oppose him more effectively—most strikingly Charles-François Tiphaigne de la Roche, whose *Amilec* (1753) and *Giphantie* (1760) are more strikingly extravagant than Voltaire's imaginative fictions—but they were far more concerned to oppose his politics than his cosmology. No matter how much allegiance French philosophers maintained, in a nationalistic spirit, to the priority of René Descartes as a natural philosopher and precursor of calculus, they could not be led by that to any opposition to Newtonian physics.

The difficulty of opposing Newton's triumphant conclusions, however, did not prevent his reputation from developing a certain tarnish, for which his surly behavior provided abundant support. David Brewster's *Life of Sir Isaac Newton* (1831) popularized an anecdote about Newton's dog, Diamond, upsetting a candle in 1692 and destroying several years' work, threatening the ever-delicate balance of his mind—a balance that came under increasing retrospective scrutiny as the science of psychology evolved.

Newton seemed to some proto-psychologists to be a perfect illustration of the alleged link between genius and madness, and the retrospective analysis of his personality provided fertile ground for speculative psychoanalysts. His biography provided abundant evidence of fragility, paranoia, obsessive compulsion and a wizard-like tendency to secrecy, in stark contrast to the general desire of scientists to publish their work. As a potential antidote to the tainted reputation of scientific genius, he was a manifest non-starter, but as a stimulus to cosmic ambition in the English poetic imagination, he was second to none in the scientific arena, all the more so because the stimulation he provided could easily be reflected in a slightly ambivalent fashion.

* * * *

The next "scientific revolution" to come along did not have the same apparent sweep as Newton's nor was it so closely identifiable with one man, who could thus become its great hero. It was, in fact, a slow and fragmented affair—as perhaps befits a revolution whose ultimate effect was to split up a system of four "elements" that was already three too many into a series that soon stretched into the eighties and was eventually to extend beyond a hundred. In terms of the mythological reflection of science, the revolution in chemistry was not so obvious in what it achieved, the emblematic status of the periodic table being compromised by its complexity, but it was much more evident in the obliteration of what it overtook: the delusory infections of alchemy, all too easily summed up emblematically in the Philosopher's Stone.

The new taxonomy of the elements eventually achieved a preliminary summary of sorts in John Dalton's *A New System of Chemical Philosophy* (1808), but the hard work had been done in the late eighteenth century, a crucial stage being reached with the realization that water was actually a compound divisible into two elements, and that air was a mixture of two major elements, one significant compound, and various trace elements. The eventual production of Dmitri Mendeleev's periodic table of the elements, published in 1869, was the work of an entire century of slow but steady scientific revolution. The explanation of the pattern revealed by the periodic table wrought a crucial connection between chemistry and the underlying science of physics and opened up a whole new wonderland of subatomic analysis.

Significant foundations for the transformation of alchemy into chemistry had been laid long before that, beginning in the 12th and 13th centuries when a Medieval "industrial revolution" prompted an increase in mining that gave rise to considerable interest in metallurgy. The investigations thus prompted—summarized in Rodolphus Agricola's *De re metallica* (1556)—revealed the woeful inadequacy of the alchemical theory of metals; that was one of the breaches allowing Paracelsus' reformist theories to flourish. The process was supplemented by investigations connected with the gradual development of the most significant early chemical technology: the manufacture of dyes for use in the textile industry. The gradual but marked increase of the range of exploitable substances and the transitions that could be contrived their chemical manipulation was summarized by Robert Boyle in *The Scyptical Chymist* (1661).

The first attempt to produce a general theory of chemistry incorporating that slow progress was, alas, little better than its alchemical predecessors, and was eventually to become a by-word for scientific folly: the ill-fated phlogiston theory advanced by Georg Ernst Stahl in 1697. Phlogiston was a substance allegedly contained in all substances, in proportion to their readiness to be transformed by heat, and liberated therefrom by combustion. The esthetic appeal of phlogiston theory maintained its popularity for a while in the face of such inconvenient facts as the gain in weight sustained by heated metals, until Joseph Priestley's *Experiments and Observations on Air* (1777) assisted Antoine Lavoisier to invert the phlogiston theorists' account of combustion as a kind of dissociation and reimagine it as a kind of combination. "Dephlogisticated air" was then reconceived as an element that combined with others in combustion—oxygen—and combustion was redefined as rapid oxidation, routinely producing the emission of "carbonic acid gas" (carbon dioxide).

The rapid progress of experimental chemistry following the abandonment of phlogiston theory and the discovery of the atmospheric gases, assisted by Dalton's refinement of atomic theory, paved the way for a heroic era of chemistry, although none of its heroes achieved the unique status of a Galileo or a Newton. Its leading figures included Humphry Davy, who was, like Joseph Priestley, a close friend of several of the leaders of the British Romantic Movement. Davy's adventures in electrolysis allowed him to discover several new elements and to pave the way for Michael Faraday's far-ranging revision of the theory of electricity.

* * * *

While the revolution in chemistry was gradually unfolding, aided by electrical methods of decomposition, the development of electrical theory and technology had a more immediate impact on the public imagination—and, in consequence, on the literary imagination.

The adjective "electric" had been coined in the sixteenth century to refer to attractive forces generated by friction, and the noun "electricity" might have been used for the first time by Sir Thomas Browne; the phenomena of "static electricity," which was usually attributed to a "fluid" or "humor" associated with a kind of "aura," were extensively studied by seventeenth-century experimenters because of their intriguing nature, but did not lead to any significant theoretical insights or technological developments until Stephen Gray discovered the electric current in 1729.

Even then, further experimentation was slow to yield results, although it did give rise to one of the most spectacular legends of scientific endeavor when Benjamin Franklin set out to attract lightning by means of a key suspended from a kite, in support of his thesis that the positive and negative components of electricity—which governed its attractive and repulsive abilities and caused the flow of the electric current—always sought to equilibrate their balance. Franklin prompted Joseph Priestley, who published a *History of Electricity* (1767), to enhance the analogy between electrical and gravitational attraction by demonstrating that the former was also obedient to an inverse square law of intensity.

The oddity and somewhat spectacular nature of electrical phenomena—especially the generation of sparks and electric shocks, for which various new items of equipment were devised—also increasingly captured the public imagination, to the extent that some late-eighteenth-century experimenters began putting on "demonstrations" that were essentially "magic shows." Inevitably, this had a spinoff in charlatanry. In Britain James Graham promoted the notion that electric shocks had therapeutic vale in a series of Temples of Health and Hygiene established in Bath, Britsol and London, which made him temporarily famous, while Anton Memser followed a similar path in France.

The notion that electricity might provide the key to the "secret of life" and might be the "vital force" of animation became very popular, greatly encouraged by Luigi Galvani's discovery, made in 1780 and published in 1792, that electric stimulation could provoke the leg muscles of a dead frog to twitch violently—a trick incorporated into many public demonstrations.

Galvani's observations on the electrical effects correlated with moist surfaces assisted Alessandro Volta to develop the Voltaic pile, the first great leap forward in electrical technology, which enabled Humphry Davy to conduct experiments in electrochemistry that led to the discovery of several new elements and greatly assisted the ongoing revolution in chemistry. One of Davy's principal rivals as a pioneering English electrical experimenter, Andrew Crosse, became convinced that he had generated invertebrate life-forms by electrical stimulation, but that proved to be a mistake.

In 1820 Hans Christian Oersted published his observations on the effect of electrical currents on compass needles, promoting André Ampère to produce an early version of the mathematical principles of the interaction between electricity and magnetism. Combined with the results on Georg Simon Ohm's work of the conductivity and resistance of different substances, this work was further extrapolated by Humphry Davy's protégé, Michael Faraday, whose discovery of electromagnetic induction in 1834 laid the foundations for a new technological revolution. That revolution had already got under way in the form of intensive attempts to develop practical electric telegraphy—a technology that made rapid progress in the 1830s and became part and parcel of the revolution in transportation brought about by steam locomotives.

The electrical revolution in technology was, in the fullness of time, to be far more sweeping and far-reaching than the revolution brought about by the steam engine, but the relative slowness of its development and its partial masking by the sheer scale of steam-powered machinery limited its imaginative horizons, and literary responses to and dramatization of the electrical revolution tended to concentrate far more heavily on supposed philosophical implications and alleged connections with the nature of life. The role played by electricity in such deliberate endeavors in scientific romance as the mock-epic poems of Erasmus Darwin can easily seem in retrospect to be short-sighted as well as somewhat misdirected, but it was nevertheless a key aspect of the literary work that now warrants consideration in the context of the origins of scientific romance.

Because the heroic age of chemistry and electrical experimentation coincided with the rapid evolution of the novel, while the succeeding development of organic chemistry implied a radical revision of human perceptions of the order of Nature, the chemist, especially the chemist making use of Voltaic piles, provided one of the two principal 19th-century archetypes of literary images of scientists, alongside the astronomer. Whereas astronomers merely observed, chemists were far more active, routinely getting their hands dirty and causing sparks, shocks and explosions. The chemist provided the archetypal image of the experimental scientist at work, as reflected in the protagonist of D'Israeli's *Flim-Flams!*

The chemist's laboratory, especially when its traditional vessels and furnaces were augmented with Voltaic piles, provided the definitive stage-setting for "scientific work," and the fact that much of the typical apparatus in contained had been invented and used by alchemists became an important aspect of imaginative and representative continuity. The quintessential symbols of alchemy had, however, been the retort and the crucible, the former used for the distillations in the alchemists incessantly indulged in the hope of refining something special and magical, and the latter being the focal point of their attempts to manufacture gold. In the chemist's laboratory—even after its extensive supplementation by electrical gadgetry—the central symbol of the new endeavor was the test-tube, in which disparate substances were mixed and prepared to undergo some manifestly transformative reaction, supplemented by various kinds of apparatus used to hasten or provoke reactions by heating, ultimately to be symbolically represented by the adjustable gas-powered Bunsen burner.

* * * *

The late-eighteenth-century revolution in chemistry was further augmented in the early nineteenth century by rapid progress in organic chemistry. It had long been assumed, even before the initial sophistication of electrical theory, that the substances making up living bodies had to governed by some kind of "vital principle" or "life force," which rendered them unsynthesizable by vulgar means, but this assumption broke down conclusively in 1828 when urea was synthesized from ammonium cyanate. Justus von Liebig's *Die Organische Chemie in Anwendung auf Agrikultur und Physiologie* (1840; tr. as *Organic Chemistry in its Application to Agriculture*) founded agricultural chemistry, prompting a boom in artificial fertilization, while the same author's *Tierchemie* (1842;

tr. as *Animal Chemistry; or, Organic Chemistry in its Relations to Physiology and Pathology*) began the clarification of the metabolic processes of biochemistry. The inordinately complex chemistry of carbon was further rationalized with the aid of Edward Frankland's theory of valency, developed in the 1850s.

Even before the revolution in chemistry was linked to biology by the advent of organic chemistry, however, and long before it reached any kind of climax, another revolution in biological science was in the making, which would make more impact on public consciousness because its implications were more intimate—and also because they seemed to provide the kind of frank contradiction of religious dogma that had been credited to Galileo, and which chemistry had avoided almost completely. Although it was part of a much broader revolution in biology, the hottest debating point that reached the threshold of public consciousness was narrowly focused on the idea of that all living species were related by descent, and that all extant species, including human beings, were derived from more primitive ancestors.

The idea long preceded the adoption of a word to describe it. The term "evolution" is defined in Samuel Johnson's *Dictionary of the English Language* (1755) as the act of unrolling, and the term was initially adapted to a scientific context in order to describe the process of embryonic development. The word did not acquire the meaning it has today until its French equivalent was adopted by Étienne Geoffroy Saint-Hilaire in 1831 to describe the process by which new species arise—which Geoffroy, inevitably, saw in Lamarckian terms as the progressive development of "the tree of life." By that time, the mutability of species had been an issue of considerable controversy for a century, and the idea that all life on Earth shared a common biological heredity had been around for even longer; although the participants in the debate had not used the term before, the historical convenience of gathering them together as "evolutionists" eventually became too tempting to resist.

The development of the idea that different species were related by descent had, however, been severely impeded by powerful opposing prejudices—not merely by the notion that God had created all Earthly life-forms independently, and that suggesting otherwise was insulting to his creative prowess, but by the conviction that he had done so according to a particular timetable. That timetable—calculated on the basis of data relating to the posterity of Adam in *Genesis*, and refined by Archbishop James Ussher's famous calculation, published in 1650, that the Earth had been created in October 4004 B.C.—had been accepted as dogma by many branches of the Church; Ussher's dates were added as glosses to many printed versions of the English Bible, giving them a quasi-scriptural status in the minds of many Bible-readers, especially Protestants who prided themselves on a direct relationship with the holy book.

Although the Ussher chronology seemed to many scientists convinced of the Earth's greater antiquity to be an entirely unnecessary sticking-point as well as an utterly absurd one, it became a flag around which some religious diehards, bloodied and defeated by the unsuccessful war to keep heliocentricity at bay, decided to make their last stand against the corrosions of science. It was still being defended at the end of the twentieth century, with an astonishing fervor and stubbornness, all the greater for the extremism of its intellectual ineptitude. By then, "Creationism" had come to seem the most blatantly dishonest of all scholarly fantasies, but in the eighteenth and early nineteenth centuries, when the balance of power was the other way around, it was what was still known, if it had any label at all, as the "transformist" thesis that was most stridently criticized as "scientific romance" in the sense of the term understood by James Ibbetson, Isaac D'Israeli and Gerald Griffin.

As the eighteenth century began, the early development of classification systems in botany and zoology had already emphasized the obvious relatedness of many natural species, but such works as John Ray's *General History of Plants* (1686-1704) dutifully attempted to account for that relatedness in terms of trivial and accidental variations on fundamental divine designs. The endeavors of Carolus Linnaeus (Carl von Linné) in *Systema Naturae* (1735-1758) called attention to the complexity and subtlety of degrees of similarity, and to the manner in which variant species were adapted to different environments, but Linnaeus did not represent his organization of species into genera, families, classes and orders as a "family tree," after the modern fashion, preferring an aggregation of circles of various sizes, supposedly representative of the pattern of divine determinism. Although Linnaeus did believe in the biological descendancy of species, he was careful not to say so in print, reserving the opinion for his private correspondence, for fear of provoking hostile criticism, and perhaps hostile action. That was by no means a needless anxiety.

Benoît de Maillet, a French diplomat and amateur geologist, had deduced from the observations he made during his various consular postings that the Earth must be far older than six thousand years—his own estimate was two billion years—that the face of the Earth had changed considerably as waters had retreated from the surface of the present continents, and that life on the continents must have evolved as plants and animals had adapted gradually to those changing circumstances. Maillet set out these ideas painstakingly in a long philosophical dialogue called *Telliamed*, written between 1722 and 1732, but it was only published posthumously, in 1748, in a version severely censored by a priest named Mascrier, who had tried to remove, or at least reduce, its contradictions with Catholic dogma.

An edition of *Telliamed* that restored some of Maillet's text and removed some of Mascrier's contradictory intrusions was published in 1755, but the full text was not restored until 1968. Only then was it realized that Maillet's conjectures regarding the possible means by which animals had adapted and evolved to the retreat of the continental waters not only foreshadowed Lamarck's theory of adaptive evolution, but also Darwin's theory of natural selection. Even so, his book seemed sensational enough to many readers, and the much more modest subsequent suggestion by Jean-Baptiste Delisle de Sales that the Earth might be 140,000 years old, with tentative corollary remarks about the possibility of organic evolution, in *De la philosophie de la nature* (1770), resulted in Delisle being brought before a judge. He was heavily fined—he could not pay, and had to obtain subsidies from his friends, including Voltaire—and imprisoned in the Châtelet; then he was banished from France, while his book was burned.

Some of Maillet's contemporaries, however, had ideas similar to his. The notion that species were not fixed had previously been advanced by the Baron de Montesquieu in 1721, reflecting on the recent discovery of a "winged monkey" (the colugo, *Galaeopithecus*), and it was given more detailed consideration by Pierre-Louis de Maupertuis, who suggested in 1751 that there might be a mechanism of variation involving the "elementary particles" transmitted in sperm. The Encyclopedist Denis Diderot supported the notion, but the leading naturalists of the day were half-hearted.

The Comte de Buffon, whose massive *Histoire naturelle* (36 volumes, 1749-1788) was a calculated rival to Linnaeus' *Systema Naturae*, was bolder than his predecessor in openly drawing the conclusion that species must be biologically related, and he was prepared to assert that all the world's quadrupeds must have descended from an original stock of some 38 species, but he stopped short of arguing that the entire pattern of species might reflect a single branching chain of descent. Even so, he had to yield to demands from the clergy that he publicly recant his heretical views. Buffon's ideas were, however, combined with those of Diderot for adventurous literary exploration by the aggressively skeptical Nicolas Restif de la Bretonne, whose *La Découverte Australe par un homme volant* [The Discovery of the Austral Continent by a Flying Man] (1781) includes a detailed allegory of evolutionary development.

The general question of biological relationship had one particularly thorny point, by virtue of the fact that one of the most obvious patterns of resemblance among animals was the one linking humankind to the great apes. Linnaeus and Buffon both observed the similarity when trying to classify the great apes, but the data on which their classification was based was still very sketchy, and Buffon made a complete mess of the classification by confusing sketchy reports of Indonesian "ourang-outangs" with those of African chimpanzees. Linnaeus did not make that mistake, and even took daring so far as to suggest that the orangutan might be assigned to the genus *Homo* along with *Homo sapiens*, but he also attempted to find room in his classification for other marginally-human species described in traveler's tales, including "tailed men."

In Britain, the same confusions and fanciful tales preoccupied James Burnett, Lord Monboddo, who speculated extensively about the relationship between humans and apes in his massive study *Of the Origin and Progress of Language* (6 volumes 1773-1792)—a contention to which Isaac D'Israeli paid particular attention in his satirization of evolutionary ideas, and which also provided a particular inspiration to Thomas Love Peacock in *Melincourt* (1817).

The Comte de Buffon's account of the past distinguished six "Epochs of Nature," designed to accommodate various kinds of fossil organisms discovered in the eighteenth century, but the status of fossils was still in doubt while he was writing, many observers refusing to recognize them as remnants of living organisms. The denial became increasingly difficult as more and more of them turned up, with ever-increasing variety, but Buffon's successor Georges Cuvier was still content to account for vanished vertebrate species by means of a theory of multiple creations in *Ossements fossiles* (1812), even though he recognized the obvious kinship of various sets of extinct and extant mammalian species. By that time, however, the idea had been adopted in Britain by one of the pioneers of scientific romance, Erasmus Darwin, who employed his literary work to popularize it once he had plucked up the courage to do so, and it will be more appropriate to take up the story in the discussion of his work and its aftermath, in the next chapter.

CHAPTER TWO

THE DISCOVERY OF NEW ATLANTIS

1. THE PROSPECTS OF SCIENCE

Although it is not the only starting point for which an argument might be made, it seems entirely appropriate to begin the narrative history of British scientific romance with the writer who did more than any other, at least in England, to found a new philosophy of enquiry and knowledge, which helped to lay the foundations of the way we now conceive science, and the writer whom Moritz Kauffmann credited with being the first to pen a scientific romance: Francis Bacon.

Francis Bacon was born in the Elizabethan Era and formed by it, although his career as statesman and a scholar also spanned the reign of James I. His political career won him the titles Viscount St Albans and Baron Verulam, although it ended badly in 1621, by which time he had risen to the influential position of Lord Chancellor, after he got into acute financial difficulties and was charged with corruption as a result of his understandably-eager acceptance of gifts from those soliciting his favor. He was guilty, but had probably done nothing that the statesmen of the era, including his judges in the House of Lords, did not consider routine, and he was doubtless a victim of political rivalry and opportunism. His subsequent imprisonment did not last long, and he was also let off the heavy fine imposed by the court (which he could not afford to pay), but he was banned from holding any further political office. That might have been a fortunate outcome, from the viewpoint of the history of science, in that it enabled him to put all his subsequent effort into his scholarly work, which had inevitably suffered some neglect while he was busy with other things, but he did not survive long enough to make very much use of the opportunity.

Bacon had conceived a plan early in his scholarly career—echoing one formulated by his namesake Roger Bacon—to produce a vast critical encyclopedia, which would provide a thoroughgoing revision of traditional wisdom in the light of modern discoveries. He called it *Instauratio Magna* [The Great Instauration], thus representing it as a kind of completion of the Renaissance of Classical wisdom, and he published a prospectus of sorts as *The Advancement of Learning* (1605; rev. in Latin as *De Augmentis Scientiarum*, 1623), before writing numerous drafts of a more substantial preface, which was eventually published as *Novum Organum Scientiarum* [A New System of Science] (1620).

These were key works in the development of the philosophy of modern science, stressing the importance of empirical observation and experimentation. They are particularly notable for their urgent warning regarding the hazards of *idola* [idols]: false preconceptions that inhibit enquiry by inducing fatal prejudices. The prospectus had its limitations—Bacon was dismissive of the importance of mathematical analysis and reluctant to acknowledge the significance of such contemporary discoveries as the circulation of the blood—but the arguments he put forward were vital to the progress of science.

Bacon divided the "idols" that stood in the way of progress in thought into four categories. The "idols of the tribe" are fundamental fallacies of human psychology, including a tendency to seek and perceive more order in nature than is actually present therein, which confers psychological plausibility on many notions that turn out, when observations are rationally analyzed, to be devoid of real foundation. The "idols of the cave" are errors produce by a particular individual's sensory and psychological preferences, including convictions based on esthetic judgments. The "idols of the marketplace" are errors induced by the limitations of language and carelessness in its use. The "idols of the theater" are incorrect ways of thinking instilled by received ideas—the products of deceptive rhetoric and baseless dogma.

The basic assumption of this argument is that if all these idols could be toppled and broken, intellectual vision would be clarified, and the accumulation of knowledge would become a straightforward matter of collecting sufficient observations for the general causal principles inherent therein to become manifest, by the process of "induction." Bacon saw experimentation as an open-ended extension of empirical enquiry—a kind of active observation—rather than as a means of putting hypotheses to the proof, and in that regard his philosophy of science was eventually superseded, but his description of the scientific attitude of mind was a definitive summation of a decisive shift, which demoted arguments from authority from their previously-privileged position, and established empirical observations and reasoning therefrom as the sole bedrock of knowledge.

* * * *

Bacon's early works also included *De Sapientia Veterum* (1609; tr. as *The Wisdom of the Ancients*), which offers new versions of a series of tales adapted from Greek myths, adding "explanations" that convert them ingeniously into philosophical allegories—a literary stratagem that is very unusual, and thus seems highly eccentric, but which is nevertheless interesting, and more significant than it might seem at first glance to the present history. In Bacon's scheme, science itself is given a new emblematic figurehead in the monstrous mountain-dwelling Sphinx, which lay in wait for passers-by in the highways around Thebes, confronting them with riddles—supposedly supplied by the Muses in this version—tearing them to pieces if they could not answer, before finally being thwarted and killed by Oedipus.

"This is an elegant fable," Bacon comments, "and seems invented to represent science, especially as joined with practice. For science may, without absurdity, be called a monster, being strangely gazed at and admired by the ignorant and unskillful. Her figure and form is various, by reason of the vast variety of subjects that science considers; her voice and countenance are represented female, by reason of her gay appearance and volubility of speech; wings are added because the sciences and their inventions run and fly about in a moment, for knowledge, like light communicated from one torch to another, is presently caught and copiously diffused; sharp and hooked talons are elegantly attributed to her, because the axioms and arguments of science enter the mind, lay hold of it, fix it down, and keep it from moving or slipping away…. Again, all science seems placed on high, as it were on the tops of mountains that are hard to climb; for science is justly imagined a sublime and lofty thing, looking down upon ignorance from an eminence, and at the same time taking an extensive view on all sides.... Science is said to beset the highways, because through all the journeys and peregrinations of human life there is matter and occasion offered of contemplation....

"Science has no more than two kinds of riddles, one relating to the nature of things, the other to the nature of man; and correspondent to these, the prizes of the solution are two kinds of empire, the empire over nature and the empire over man, For the true and ultimate end of natural philosophy is dominion over natural things, natural bodies, remedies, machines, and numberless other particulars, though the schools, contented with what spontaneously offers, and swollen with their own discourses, neglect, and in a manner despise, both things and works...."[14]

Bacon was attempting to compliment science in making this quirky summary of its attributes, but he also represented science as monstrous, fearsome and murderous—not much of an advertisement for a cause to which he was deeply committed. Perhaps he was simply recognizing that the new science, whose principal champion he was to become, frightened a lot of people, and was trying to persuade them that the fear, although understandable, was unnecessary; at a distance, however, the strategy seems suspect, to say the least.

Most of the other sections in the book deal with philosophical matters other than science, but special mention might also be made of the interpretation of Cupid in terms of "the Corpuscular Philosophy," in which the god of Love is construed as an Atom, youthful, naked, blind and capable of action at a distance. Philosophy is general is, however, credited to Orpheus, whose music is capable, on the one hand, of appeasing "the infernal power" (natural philosophy—another dubious demonization) and on the other, of charming wild beasts (moral philosophy). One further account that eventually achieved a considerable importance in the development of scientific romance, however, is the unusually long and complex essay on "Prometheus, or the State of Man," in which the Titan is held to allegorize "Over-Ruling Providence and...Human Nature."

---

14 Francis Bacon. *The Wisdom of the Ancients* [1609], chapter XXVIII.

The earliest version of the story of Prometheus that has survived is the brief one contained in Hesiod's poem *Theogony* and repeated, in a slightly more elaborate form, in the same poet's *Works and Days*. *Theogony* relates that, when gods and men had a dispute, Prometheus, "the most glorious of all lords" was called upon to carve up an ox and divide its meat. For some undisclosed reason, Prometheus tried to fool Zeus into accepting the bones and fat for the gods while leaving the meat, disguised with the hide, for men—but Zeus saw through the ruse and punished Prometheus by binding him with chains and setting an eagle on him to devour his incessantly-regenerated liver, although he eventually permitted Heracles to free the Titan from his bondage. Also in reprisal, Zeus refused the power of "unwearying fire" to the humans of Earth—but Prometheus, once freed, stole its gleam in a fennel stalk and gave it to them. Zeus then took a further revenge by sending a beautiful woman to Earth, the progenitor of the "deadly race" of women and the source of all evil. The second part of the story is further elaborated in *Works and Days*, where the woman is named Pandora and carries evils in a jar rather than transmitting them through her progeny.

Hesiod's versions of the story probably contain a certain amount of literary decoration in addition to traditional folklore. On the other hand, it is possible that some of the further embellishments added to the story by subsequent poets and dramatists had folkloristic precedents as well as adding purely literary innovations. At any rate, the story was greatly embroidered and reconfigured by other Classical writers, most famously in a version usually credited, perhaps mistakenly, to the playwright Aeschylus, in a trilogy of which only one volume and fragments of a second survive.

In the surviving play, *Prometheus Bound*, Prometheus reveals that fire was not his only gift to humankind, but that he also taught humans the arts of agriculture, writing, medicine, mathematics, astronomy, metallurgy and architecture—thus being, in effect, the father of science. In this version his punishment comes after the theft of fire, not before it, and is intensified because he claims to know a secret that will lead to Zeus' downfall, but refuses to reveal it in order that Zeus might take action to avoid his fate. Although the other plays have not survived, references to the trilogy in near-contemporary sources suggest that in this story, Prometheus does eventually surrender the secret, permitting Zeus to avoid the prophesied misfortune and bringing about a reconciliation between the two of them.

Bacon takes aboard some of the further embellishments of the story, including the notion that it was Prometheus, rather than Zeus—explicitly credited as the creator of humans in Hesiod—who first forged humans out of clay. Bacon, however, suggests that the alleged formation was defective, because Prometheus mixed "particles taken from different animals" with the clay, and suggests that the Titan's attempt to improve his workmanship by stealing fire for the usage of his creations also went badly awry for all concerned. In Bacon's account, ungrateful humans denounce Prometheus to "Jupiter"—for which treachery Jupiter rewards humans with the gift of eternal youth as well, although the gift is unfortunately lost. Prometheus, angry with Jupiter, attempts the deception of the ox, prompting Jupiter to punish humankind by sending Pandora to curse them "all mischiefs and calamities," and then to bind Prometheus to a rock, sending the eagle to devour his continually-regenerated liver.

Bacon's interpretation contends that:

"Prometheus clearly and expressly signifies Providence: and the one thing singled out by the ancients as the special and peculiar work of Providence was the creation and constitution of Man.... The chief aim of the parable appears to be, that Man, if we look to final causes, may be regarded as the centre of the world; insomuch that if Man were taken away from the world, the rest would seem to be all astray, without aim or purpose...and to be leading to nothing. For the whole world works together in the service of man; and there is nothing from which he does not derive use and fruit."[15]

The essay then summarizes all the accomplishments of humankind in the exploitation of nature, from the employment of the stars to the calculation of the seasons through agriculture and the construction of shelters to all manner of productive and locomotive technology, supporting the notion that human being became a microcosm reflecting in miniature the whole of the macrocosm. "Nevertheless," Bacon adds, "we see that man in the first phase of his existence is a naked and defenceless thing, slow to help himself

---

15   Ibid. chapter XXVI.

and full of wants. Therefore Prometheus applied himself in all haste to the invention of fire, which in all human necessities and business is the great minister of relief and hope; insomuch that if the soul be the form of forms and the hand the instrument of instruments, fire may rightly be called the help of helps and the means of means. For through it most operations are effected, through it the arts mechanical and the sciences themselves are furthered in an infinite variety of ways."

This analysis of Prometheus as the symbol and progenitor of human science is given an extra twist in Bacon's account by the subsequent betrayal of Prometheus by ingrate humans to Jupiter, and Jupiter's rewarding of that treachery. Bacon makes this an allegory condemning human satisfaction with acquired knowledge and wealth, and praises the dissatisfaction that causes them to strive for further progress. Further details of the story are recruited one by one to the same cause, as exhortations not merely to human effort in general but specifically to effort in the improvement of the technical arts, counseling persistence when experiments initially fail. According to Bacon, the story goes on to evaluate religion, and then the morality of everyday life. His interpretation of Prometheus' punishment suggests that it exposes the dark side of the "forethought" signified by the name itself:

"The school of Prometheus on the other hand, that is the wise and fore-thoughtful class of men, do indeed by their caution decline and remove out of their way many evils and misfortunes; but with that good there is this evil joined, that they stint themselves of many pleasures and of the various agreeablenesses of life, and cross their genius, and (what is far worse) torment and wear themselves away with cares and solicitude and inward fears. For being bound to the column of Necessity, they are troubled with innumerable thoughts (which because of their flightiness are represented by the eagle), thoughts which prick and gnaw and corrode the liver: and if at intervals, as in the night, they obtain some little relaxation and quiet of mind, yet new fears and anxieties return presently with the morning."

This image of the "fore-thoughtful class of men" was to be transferred in full to many later images of scientists and inventors, bound by their vocation as if to a rock and tormented as if by an eagle. Bacon follows it up, after some further elaboration, by connecting it to the allegation made in his own version of the story that the punishment of having his entrails continually torn out is specifically linked to the accusation that Prometheus had attempted to ravish Minerva. "The crime alluded to," he remarks, "appears to be no other than that into which men not infrequently fall when puffed up with arts and much knowledge—of trying to bring the divine wisdom itself under the dominion of sense and reason: from which attempt inevitably follows laceration of the mind and vexation without end or rest. And therefore men must soberly and modestly distinguish between things divine and human, between the oracles of sense and of faith; unless they mean to have at once a heretical religion and a fabulous philosophy."

That cautionary note must already have seemed urgent to Bacon, and the relevance of the Baconian metaphor of Prometheus being accused—rightly or wrongly—of ravishing Minerva was to increase dramatically in the early days of "scientific romance."

There are several items in Bacon's account of the story of Prometheus that do not match up with the traditional sources, although they do not give the impression of being added to it simply to support subsequent interpretations within the allegorical reading, and they serve to add to the inventiveness of the essay, which must have seemed spectacular to its readers even by comparison with the eccentricity of some of the other interpretative suggestions. That the essay stimulated imagination is indubitable, as it was widely cited by the pioneers of scientific romance in a later era, and they felt free not only to improvise new interpretations of the story, but also to make up new versions of it to interpret in a similar fashion. The Prometheus that Bacon handed down to his successors was a remarkable elastic and versatile symbol, well-suited to very various analyses of the role that science and technology ought to play in human society, and the likely rewards and penalties that might ensure from its pursuit.

* * * *

It was probably shortly after writing *The Wisdom of the Ancients* that Bacon began a Utopian romance, *New Atlantis*, although Kauffmann claims that he did not begin it until 1624, two years before his death. Either way, he did not complete it, setting it aside for unknown reasons and leaving it among his papers for posthumous publication. Even in its abridged form it is a strikingly original work; although solidly set in the tradition of images of ideal society descended from Thomas More's original, it offers a radically different view of the whole prospect of social transformation, stressing the potential contribution to be made to such transformation by science and technology.

The imaginary state in question is located in the "South Sea," the narrator's ship having set off from Peru aiming for China and Japan, but having been driven northwards by a terrible storm. The strayed sailors find themselves in a Christian country whose inhabitants call it Bensalem, their ancestors having been converted by a miraculous revelation some twenty years after Christ's death, receiving the scriptures and the gift of tongues at the same time. The island had once participated in a great age of navigation, involving numerous kingdoms in the Americas and ill-fated Atlantis, which had been terminated by the sinking of the latter realm.

Much of the text consists of a catalogue of new technologies developed by the scientists of "Salomon's House," whose Father is a Scientist-Priest supervising the social and technological applications of a highly-sophisticated science. These include, among others: biotechnologies for the creation of new kinds of plants, the elaborate transformation of animals, and the development of special foods that increase the strength and solidity of the human body; new technologies for producing heat and manipulating light; "sound-houses" and "perfume-houses" for producing effects perceptible to other senses; "engine-houses" whose mechanical products include guns, explosives, aircraft, submarines and perpetual motion machines; and "houses of deceits of the senses," where all manner of illusions can be produced, and hence revealed for what they are.

The text goes on to list various specialist employments associated with gathering information for Salomon's House, but its account of the internal organization of the institution remains incomplete, and almost nothing is said about its relationship with other institutions within the state and the lives of its citizens. The narrative is suspended before the narrator can actually visit Salomon's House and see these wonders in action. The work remains, in essence, a collection of hints, a rough sketch for a book that might have been but never was—perhaps a book that was impossible to write at the time, and impossible to publish if it had been written, but whose future possibility as nevertheless a significant endeavor to glimpse, and to which to raise a hopeful signpost.

From the modern viewpoint, the list of technological possibilities summarized above might seem to be the most interesting aspect of *New Atlantis*—unsurprisingly, given that it takes up almost all of the extant text apart from the contextualizing set-up. Even from the viewpoint of hunters for correct anticipations, however, it is regrettable that the text does not go on to indicate how these devices function in the daily lives of the inhabitants of Bensalem, and how much they have improved that quotidian existence. Without that kind of description, the list remains simply a catalogue of ideas left floating in a nebulous cloud.

There is, however, a second aspect of the prospectus set out in *New Atlantis* that deserves attention in terms of its anticipatory intelligence, which is to do with the integration of Salomon's House into the political apparatus of the state. In a sense, the list of inventions is merely a hypothetical advertisement for the spinoff might be achieved if science, as a both a philosophical and practical discipline, were abundantly funded and encouraged by the state, and organized in such a way as to maximize its progress.

New Atlantis was not the first Utopian novel to credit a hypothetical ideal state with advanced technology or to credit it with institutions designed to foster the further development of science and its practical spinoff—its most notable predecessor in that regard was Tommaso Campanella's *Civitas Solis* (written 1602, revised 1612, published 1623; tr. as *The City of the Sun*), of whose existence Bacon was surely unaware when he wrote his own account—but Bacon went much further than his contemporary, and brought his topic into much narrower focus.

When Bacon resumed scholarly work after his fall from grace, he conceded that the *Instauratio Magna* was now beyond his scope; he planned a modest six-volume series of scientific texts in its stead, but only *Historia Ventorum* [An Account of the Winds] (1622) and *Historia Vitae et Mortis* [An Account of Life and Death] (1623) were completed. A draft of what would have been a third volume, *Sylva Sylvarum* [A Forest of Forests], was issued posthumously in 1627, with *New Atlantis* appended to it (in

English; the Latin version printed in some later editions of *Sylva Sylvarum* is a translation).

* * * *

A continuation of *New Atlantis* was published in 1660, signed "R. H., Esquire," which does offer some details of what happens in Salomon's House, but is more concerned with Bensalem's peerage and honors system than its technology. An essay by Joseph Glanvill published in 1680, "Antifanatickal Religion and Free Philosophy," also claimed in its subtitle to be a "Continuation of the *New Atlantis*" but is nothing of the sort, merely disguising the Cambridge Platonists who influenced Isaac Newton as "Academicians" in the tradition of Salomon's House in order to attack their views without naming them. The anonymous poem *The New Atlantis*, published in 1687, has no connection at all with Bacon's text; nor has Mrs. Manley's scandalous satire *The New Atalantis* (1709). The account of Salomon's House thus went without any manifest elaboration, and the ideas embraced by the depiction lay virtually fallow, in literary terms, for the remainder of the seventeenth century.

In spite of the sparseness of any direct response, *New Atlantis* was undoubtedly widely read. Its influence during the century after its publication is difficult to measure, however, and it is also difficult to estimate the extent to which it extrapolates ideas that were current in the milieu in which Bacon was operating. James I's court inventor Cornelis Drebbel appears to have been working very much in the spirit of Salomon's House, and his most significant endeavors and discoveries all became manifest in the early 1620s. It was in that period that Drebbel invented an improved compound microscope and an improved thermometer, published a treatise on chemistry that included an account of a new explosive nowadays known as mercury fulminate, began experimenting with submarines, and attempted to develop an air-conditioning system for buildings. Bacon and Drebbel were acquainted, and must presumably have talked about the notions contained in *New Atlantis*, but whether those notions served as inspiration in either direction or merely revealed a similarity of ideas, there is no way of knowing.

Drebbel's exploits must have encouraged Bacon in his conviction that the plan for Salomon's House was a good one, and that some such institution might be able to deliver on the promises he made on its behalf, and they might have helped other members of James I's court to think likewise, but there must also have been skeptics convinced that it would all come to nothing; in the wider balance of opinion, the latter party evidently won out, at least in the short term.

James I was a considerable intellectual himself—probably the only monarch England ever had about whom that could be said in all seriousness—but his own writings were mostly political, centrally concerned with supporting the divine right of kings, and the only ones that had any lasting influence were an attack on tobacco and a book fervently asserting the reality of witchcraft, *Daemonologie* (1597). It is, however, possible that James' accession to the English throne modified his views on the latter subject; he certainly took an interest in several English witch-trials, but seems to have taken a skeptical view in almost every case, presumably retaining his fundamental belief while formally deciding that the individual cases in question were not instances of it. His ideas might well have become more Baconian once he was exposed to Bacon's benign influence.

Another book roughly contemporary with *New Atlantis* that shows some evidence of Baconian's philosophy and method, albeit in a fashion very different from Drebbel's practical endeavors, is Robert Burton's *The Anatomy of Melancholy* (1621), which also has something in common with *The Wisdom of the Ancients* in the author's adoption of the pseudonym Democritus Junior and extravagant use of myth and folklore as a source of presumed insights into the psychological pathology of melancholia. The book's fundamental plan is organized in a spirit of methodical observation and analysis that is at least mock-Baconian, and probably more sincere and earnest than the author's irrepressible wit and dexterity of thought sometimes makes it seem.

Bacon's contemporaries also included Bishop Francis Godwin, and Godwin's Utopian satire *The Man in the Moone*, posthumously published in 1638 under the by-line of its protagonist, Domingo Gonsales, might owe something to Baconian inspiration; some commentators of the text have suggested that Godwin borrowed Gonsales' method of flying to the moon in a chariot harnessed to a flock of geese from a flippant remark in *Sylva Sylvarum*, although no one knows when Godwin actually wrote his satire, and it might date from considerably earlier than 1627. The novel's description of a lunar pastoral paradise contrasts markedly with Bacon's Bensalem, however, and the story's significance in the context of the evolution of scientific ideas has much more to do with its artful support for the heliocentric theory than any strictly Baconian ideas; the eventually-widespread influence of Godwin's text owes far more to the elegance of its humor than to its underlying philosophy.

* * * *

It is not easy to find many other signs of activity or thought following up the ideas expressed in *New Atlantis* in the generation following Bacon's death. The most obvious reiteration of the accomplishments of Salomon's House is in the works of John Wilkins, especially *Mathematicall Magick* (1648), which follows up a summary of existing mechanical devices with a remarkable catalogue of potential inventions that might be expected to flow from future developments in technology. In the literary arena, where it might have been expected to have had most impact, if it were to have any, *New Atlantis* seems to have had very little. Subsequent designers of ideal states mostly ignored its argument that the institutional organization of scientific and technological endeavor might help bring about considerable improvements in society. The best-known British Utopia published in the remainder of the seventeenth century, James Harrington's *The Commonwealth of Oceana* (1656)—dedicated to Oliver Cromwell, who was initially inclined to suppress its publication—is entirely concerned with desirable political reforms involving land tenure and democratic elections.

One Utopia that appeared to be intent on continuing Bacon's train of thought but flattered only to deceive was *A Voyage into Tartary* (1689), which bore the by-line "Heliogenes de L'Epy" but was undoubtedly written by an Englishman. The author's explicit aim is to describe a society strictly based on Reason, which rejects religious revelation and is essentially democratic. Its focal point is the circular city of Heliopolis, strongly reminiscent of Campanella's City of the Sun, but it has no equivalent of Salomon's House. Instead—and rather mysteriously—all the technological inventions made by its citizens in the past, including firearms, flying machines, enormously powerful telescopes and microscopes, and accurate chronometers, have been consigned to a museum, along with the printing press, having been rigorously excluded from everyday use.

Presumably, throughout the seventeenth century, Bacon's conviction regarding the scope of the technology that might be spun off from the advancement of scientific knowledge was considered implausible in England, in spite of Drebbel's exemplars—or, at least, far less relevant to the immediate prospects of social progress than political reforms that were not dependent on as-yet-undiscovered principles and processes. A hundred and fifty years were to pass before the advent of "euchronian fiction" obliged the employers of that procedural method to consider seriously the question of what future advances in science and technology might be possible, and to what extent they might contribute to the sum of human happiness. In fact, it is not obvious exactly what differences they have made to everyday life in Bensalem. Bacon's spokesman for Salomon's House proclaims that the island's inhabitants are very happy, and those whom the narrator meets endorse the view, but the truncated narrative never shows the reader that supposed felicity in action, so the contribution made to it by the listed technological wonders is not dramatized, and hence not obvious.

The suggestion has been made that Bacon's intention in writing *New Atlantis* was not so much to dramatize his ideas about the scope and potential of science conducted according to his principles as to provide a prospectus for an actual institution that he wanted James I to endow: an English equivalent of Salomon's House. Whether that is true or not, the fact that the king—no fan of governmental bureaucracy—did not oblige would surely not have been altered had Bacon finished and published the book in 1609. Its publication in 1627, however, did encourage some observers to link the eventual foundation of the Royal Society of London by Charles II, in 1660, to the plan of Salomon's House laid out in *New Atlantis*. John Wilkins was one of the early propagandists for the Society.

The Royal Society initially included poets among its members as well as scientists, and two of the most renowned paid homage to Bacon as one of the key contributors to English science. John

Dryden's "Epistle the Third, To my Honoured Friend, Dr. Charleton" (1663) places Bacon at the head of a triumphant list that goes on to cite William Gilbert, Robert Boyle and William Harvey:

> *Among the asserters of free reason's claim.*
> *Our nation's not the least in worth or fame.*
> *The world to Bacon does not only owe*
> *Its present knowledge, but its future too.*[16]

In a similar vein, Abraham Cowley's "Ode to the Royal Society" (1667) celebrates Baconian iconoclasm, and the manner in which it opened the way to the Tree of Knowledge:

> *The orchard's open now, and free;*
> *Bacon has broke the scare-crow deity;*
> *Come, enter, all that will,*
> *Behold the ripen'd fruit, come gather now your fill!*[17]

It is certainly arguable that the Royal Society did eventually make a significant contribution to the promotion of scientific endeavor in Britain, as the enthusiasm echoed by Dryden and Cowley expected, but it did not bear its "ripen'd fruit" rapidly or prolifically.

It is possible, but by no means certain, that the Society played a slight, if ironic, role in helping Britain to take the lead in the technological surge of the Industrial Revolution, as the Huguenot refugee Denis Papin addressed the society in 1679 on the subject of his work on steam power, which he was not able to develop himself because religious persecution in his homeland robbed him of the necessary developmental support. Further papers of Papin's were read to the Society, apparently without his permission, in 1707 and 1712, the latter being the year in which Thomas Newcomen demonstrated his first successful steam engine. A direct causal connection is, however, difficult to establish. Newcomen was not a member of the Society and might have been completely ignorant of that fact that Papin had informed it of the principles of the steam engine before he actually built one—in which case, the fact

16 John Dryden. *The Collected Works*. Edinburgh: Constable, 1821. p. 15.
17 Abraham Cowley. *The Works*, Vol. I. London: Kearsley, 1806. p.153.

that Newcomen had to do the work from scratch, a long way from London, might count as an example of the Society's inefficiency, and perhaps impotence, in actually putting science to work in society, and drawing the kind of benefits therefrom that Bacon had promised.

It is not obvious, therefore, in spite of the active involvement in the Royal Society of such evident luminaries as Isaac Newton, that it made any substantial contribution in the first century of its existence to the fulfillment of the aims and achievements of Salomon's House, and it was not difficult for its dissenters to support the view that it was a mere talking shop, little different from any other gentlemen's club, which produced a certain amount of hot air and a great deal of tedious reportage, without giving rise to any practical results at all. Although the satirization of the Society in Jonathan Swift's account of the Academy of Lagado was vicious in its exaggeration, it has to be admitted that it does not seem entirely unjustified.

The Wisdom of the Ancients was at least as widely read as *New Atlantis*, but it was even less influential in any direct sense, probably by virtue by virtue of its eccentricity. It went largely unappreciated as well as unimitated, but it did foreshadow certain future adventures in literary method. If its image of science as a cruel sphinx was less than flattering, it can nevertheless be read as an allegory in its own right, of the manner in which the tainted reputation of science was represented in many subsequent cautionary fables, and Bacon's rather uncharitable interpretation of Prometheus was to be echoed with a certain irony in several Romantic works, including Mary Shelley's account of the unlucky Victor Frankenstein as "the New Prometheus."

On the whole, however, it is from the modern viewpoint that Bacon now seems to have made a crucial contribution both to the philosophy of science and the development of literary methods of exploring scientific thought and scientific possibility. His contributions to the art of scientific romance were far ahead of the time when such endeavors could be fully appreciated, and he was disconnected from anything even faintly resembling a coherent tradition by an entire century. Nevertheless, his eventual contribution to that tradition is worthy of complimentary recognition.

* * * *

It must also be noted that there is another way of interpreting *New Atlantis* and Salomon's House than as a prospectus for something akin to the Royal Society. In *The Rosicrucian Enlightenment* (1972), Frances A. Yates suggests that there is evidence in *The Advancement of Learning* that Bacon was aware of the Brotherhood of the Rose Cross before the publication of the three Rosicrucian pamphlets, and argues that Salomon's House in *New Atlantis* is a representation of that Brotherhood. Yates suggests that Bacon's avoidance of mathematical science in his philosophical writing stems from a determination to distance himself, in the eyes of James I, from John Dee, who had allegedly tainted mathematics irredeemably with magic, and of whom James seems to have disapproved. In this thesis, it is Bacon rather than Robert Fludd who becomes the principal figure in British Rosicrucianism, and *New Atlantis* becomes an allegory of the same kind, referring to the same occult truth, as the *Fama Fraternitatis*.

This might conceivably be true, if there ever really was an actual Brotherhood of the Rose Cross rather than a purely imaginary organization. Even if it is not true, however, and the entire narrative of *The Rosicrucian Enlightenment* is a scholarly fantasy—which seems more likely—the allegation is interesting as a further example of the confused reputations that have routinely been credited to natural philosophers, and emphasizes the fact that the birth of science as we now understand it carried a hereditary stain of suspicion. It also functions as an invitation to further alternative decodings of *New Atlantis*.

The more familiar notion that the work was a prospectus for an actual institution of learning and research is taken very seriously by Paul R. Josephson in *New Atlantis Revisited: Akademgorodok, the Siberian City of Science* (1997), which suggests that where James I failed to come through, Nikita Khrushchev did, modeling a new city carved out of the Siberian forest in 1958 specifically on New Atlantis, in the hope that it would deliver on the promises of Salomon's House and help the U.S.S.R. surpass the West technologically.

Perhaps *New Atlantis* does have some hidden meaning relevant to the narrative history of occult science. Perhaps, too, it really was intended as a prospectus for an actual institution that Bacon wanted James I to endow, and which Nikita Khrushchev did create. In retrospect, however, it is also evident that it provided a prospectus of sorts for a new kind of philosophical speculation in fictional form: for "scientific romance."

If the Brotherhood of the Rose Cross ever did exist, it remained—and perhaps still remains—invisible to history. The existence of Akademgorodok was a state secret at the time, and its failure to live up to the hopes invested in it eventually reduced it to irrelevance. Scientific romance had its troubles too, but while it lasted, it had a much higher profile than either of its putative rivals as Bacon's true imaginative heritage, and it is arguable that of all the potential functions that *New Atlantis* might have fulfilled, its role as an inspiration for and exemplar of scientific romance was eventually, if temporarily, the most successful.

The elaboration of the brief description of New Atlantis provided by Francis Bacon into a generic gazetteer did not happen rapidly, but it did happen. An entire collaborative endeavor grew up, dedicated not to treating the produce of Salomon's House as a potential reality, but to exploring the possible social consequences of the items In its catalogue if ever they were to become real, and also to mapping the remoter areas of the imaginary continent and its surrounding waters—where, as ancient maps were quaintly wont to put it "here be monsters."

Perhaps that endeavor was corrupted from the very start by hints of occultism, which it never escaped, but it is at least arguable that they served to make it more rather than less interesting, and perhaps even more rather than less truthful. At any rate, generic scientific romance was the progeny of *New Atlantis* in more ways than one, not only taking a strong dose of direct inspiration from it, but also echoing its ambitions, its scope, and its dubious secrets.

* * * *

It was, in fact, ninety-nine years, rather than a round hundred, that elapsed between the publication of Bacon's *New Atlantis* and that of the next work of crucial relevance to the initial stock-in-trade of scientific romance—and the work in question echoed *New Atlantis* only to put the boot into its claims in no uncertain terms. In the meantime, science had made great strides: the Newtonian revelation had completed the victory of the heliocentric revolution, and the telescope and the microscope had expanded the horizons of human vision into the celestial realm and the biological microcosm; but the technological revolution hopefully anticipated by Francis Bacon had not occurred, and the technologies sketched out as the material rewards of Salomon's House remained beyond the range of practical endeavor.

We can now see that skepticism and cynicism with regard to the promises of Salomon's House were ultimately unjustified, but no one considering the case in 1726 could be criticized overmuch for thinking the opposite. The attitude to science and technology delineated with great skill and tremendous rhetorical incision by Jonathan Swift, in very striking contrast to Bacon's, must have seemed painfully apt at the time.

Swift was born in Dublin in Ireland in 1667, his father, who did not live long enough to see him born, having gone there to seek his fortune after being ruined by the Civil War. His mother returned to England and left him in the charge of his uncle, Godwin Swift. Jonathan Swift's great-grandmother had been the sister of Francis Godwin, author of what was by then recognized as the most interesting of lunar utopian satires, *The Man in the Moone*, and he was also distantly related to John Dryden and, by marriage, to Walter Raleigh.

Swift's uncle sent him back to Ireland to complete his education at Kilkenny College and Trinity College, Dublin, but the political troubles consequent on the accession to the English throne of William of Orange forced him back to England again. He became the personal assistant of the diplomat Sir William Temple, and the tutor of an eight-year-old girl who was the daughter of a friend of Temple's sister, whom he nicknamed Stella, and with whom he maintained a relationship for the rest of her life—she died in 1727—which some commentators have thought suspicious.

Swift returned to Ireland again and took holy orders, but he found the remote parish to which he was assigned direly uncongenial, and went back to work for Temple again. He wrote the satire *The Battle of the Books* in reply to one of Temple's works, but diplomatically left it unpublished until Temple was dead. After editing Temple's memoirs he returned to Ireland and clerical duties again. He published the first of his many political pamphlets in 1701, anonymously; he never signed any of his works with his own name.

Swift's first long satire, *A Tale of a Tub*, appeared in 1704, in the same year as *The Battle of the Books*. He wrote steadily from then on, but his pamphleteering did not move into top gear until the 1720s, when his more acerbic works appeared, culminating with the classic *A Modest Proposal* (1729), which suggested sarcastically that Ireland's two main problems—the overproduction of children and lack of food—might be mutually soluble, with only a little moral ingenuity. It was during the same period that he wrote *Travels into Several Remote Nations of the World, in Four Parts by Lemuel Gulliver, first a surgeon, and then a captain of several ships*, first published in 1726.

* * * *

Lemuel Gulliver's first two voyages, to the land of Lilliput, where he is a giant relative to the inhabitants, and to the land of Brobdingnag, where the inhabitants are giants relative to him, are certainly not without interest to the subsequent history of romance—including scientific romance, in which Lilliputians sometimes make guest appearances—but such relative variations in size had been a common theme of folklore for a long time, and all Swift added to consideration of the theme was a sophisticated ironic perspective and a specific satirical reduction of England to Lilliputian dimensions. It is Gulliver's third voyage, in particular, that bears directly upon the general theme of the treatment of science and scientists in scientific romance, and it features one particular image that was to re-emerge frequently in scientific romance, with the burden of Swift's version of the argument bound to it like a ball and chain to a convict.

Gulliver's account of his third voyage initially takes him to Tonquin (Tonkin) and swiftly moves to an account of a pirate attack, which results in his being set adrift in a small canoe, left to explore a small group of islands, which turn out to be on the edge of a continent filling much of the north Pacific Ocean. He is rescued from his plight by inhabitants of the flying island of Laputa. Having been hauled up to the island he finds himself among individuals whose heads are tilted in such a way that one of their eyes is turned inward while the other is directed to the zenith, while their garments are adorned with the images of moons and stars interspersed with those of musical instruments.

The aristocrats of Laputa employ "flappers": servants equipped with bladders on sticks, who use that instrument to touch the mouths or ears of their masters in order to bid them speak or listen, because "the minds of these people are so taken up with intense speculations, that they can neither speak, nor attend to the discourses of others, without being roused by some external taction"[18]—in other words, they are natural philosophers very apt to lose themselves in flights of speculation. The character-trait of distraction had become very obvious by 1727 in mathematicians and natural philosophers; whatever else it had failed to achieve, the Royal Society had certainly provided an opportunity to study such individuals in a collectivity and to suggest some of the difficulties that an entire society of their like might experience.

Gulliver soon learns the language of Laputa, the phraseology of which is heavily dependent on the terminology of geometry and music, although their emphasis on theoretical rather than practical geometry results in their clothing being very ill-fitting and their houses very irregular in construction. The language lacks words for imagination and invention, which are concepts unknown to the Laputans, and they are as clumsy as they are lacking in common sense; the principal employment of their mathematical acumen seems to be in political matters, in which Gulliver is understandably skeptical of its competence. They live in perpetual dread of cosmic disasters and experience despair at the idea of the ultimate expiration of the sun.

The flying island owes its suspension and maneuverability to a massive "loadstone" kept at its center, in the "astronomer's cave." Its guardians and manipulators spend most of their time in astronomical observations, which have allowed them to compile a vast star catalogue and not only to detect the two moons of Mars but to prove them obedient to Newtonian law. Mars' two moons were still undiscovered at the time, although—as Voltaire subsequently took the trouble to point out in *Micromégas*—the argument had been bandied around that the planet "ought" to have two, in order

---

18   Jonathan Swift. *The Works of Jonathan Swift: Gulliver's Travels*. London: Walter Scott, 1814. p.204

to fit a brief numerical sequence, Venus having none, Earth one and Jupiter being thought at the time to have four.

Gulliver leaves the island in order to tour the continent over which it routinely flies, Balnibarbi, beginning with the capital city of Lagado. There, unfortunately, people who have visited Laputa have embarked on schemes for a complete revision on arts, sciences, languages and mechanics, along vaguely Baconian lines, and have founded a series of academies for that purpose, where great projects of social improvement are planned, although none ever comes to fruition.

Gulliver visits the central Academy in the capital and observes the projects in progress (or, in fact, making no progress at all), including the oft-quoted attempt to extract sunbeams from cucumbers, a project to reconstitute food from excrement, another to "calcine ice into gunpowder," one to build houses from the roof down instead of from the foundations up, one to use spiders fed on colored insects to spin silken webs in no need of dyeing, and so on. The syllabus and teaching methods of the Academy of Lagado are as preposterous as the research projects of its faculty, especially those bearing upon political and economic matters. The chapter in question is, to some extent, a pastiche of a passage in François Rabelais's *Cinquième livre de Pantagruel* (c1564) describing the *royaulme de la Quinte Essence*; Quinte means folly, although the name is rendered in most English translations as Queen Whim, sacrificing the pun on "quintessence." The quintessential folly assailed by Rabelais in his depiction of the realm in question is the alchemical quest for the philosopher's stone, but the sick are cured there by means of song, and various other absurd projects of a vaguely technological nature are also featured.

After Lagado, Gulliver visits Glubbdubdrib, an island governed by magicians, whose necromantic skills enable them to employ the shades of the dead as servants. The governor kindly employs this ability to summon a series of historical notabilities for his guest's benefit, beginning with Alexander the Great, Hannibal and Julius Caesar, but eventually moving on to Homer and Aristotle, at the head of the legions of their commentators. Gulliver takes the trouble to introduce Aristotle to Gassendi and Descartes, so that he can be instructed as to their modern system of thought, but Aristotle is unimpressed, and suggests that even Newton's theory of universal gravitation will only enjoy a temporary vogue. The survey of the shades leads Gulliver to become thoroughly disgusted with modern history, the sight of whose recent actors gives him an exceedingly low opinion of their merits and virtues.

Gulliver then heads westwards to the island of Luggnagg, where his most striking educative experience is the description he is given of the unluckily immortal struldbrugs, born to extreme longevity but, like the mythical Tithonus, not gifted with eternal youth. Their consequent existential plight is described at some length, in dismal terms. The prospect of human immortality has always had a rather bad press in literary examinations of the notion, many writers choosing to represent it as a worthless acquisition, perhaps in the spirit of Aesop's fox contemplating the tempting but unobtainable grapes. Swift's demolition proved particularly memorable, however, and the struldbrugs were rarely left unmentioned by subsequent attempts to examine the notion with a supposedly clinical eye. From Luggnagg Gulliver is able to reach Japan, and eventually to obtain a passage back to England.

The commencement of Gulliver's fourth voyage follows much the same pattern of piratical treachery, resulting in him being marooned on an unknown island, of whose location he has no idea, having keen kept prisoner for a long time. There he encounters the disgusting humanoid Yahoos and the intelligent, culturally superior horses known as Houyhnhnms, who initially mistake him for a Yahoo, and who persist in finding symptoms of Yahoodom in his observed inclinations and his long account of his own world, which he eventually comes to observe for himself, while his disgust for the Yahoos grows apace.

When his Houyhnhnm host has given him a complementary account of Houyhnhnm life, Gulliver comes to see the situation of the Houyhnhnms and the Yahoos not as an inversion of a supposedly natural order but as an ideal of which his own world falls far short. In consequence, he wants to stay, but is forbidden to do so; although his host is prepared to make allowances for him, the other Houyhnhnms are not, and want him gone. After further tribulations, he eventually arrives home, much the wiser for the sum of his experiences, and eventually becomes able—not without difficulty—to tolerate the proximity of the seeming Yahoos of his own family again.

Even more so than the struldbrugs, the Yahoos provided an image that was to recur frequently in literary parlance, by no means confined to the annals of scientific romance. It was not merely Gulliver who was taught to see his contemporaries in those terms and to find distressing symptoms of the same brutality and obscenity in his own urges and inclinations, but many of his readers.

Following the publication of *A Modest Proposal* in 1729, Swift's career went into something of a decline, and he suffered numerous personal troubles, some of his closest friends dying. Those that remained eventually had him certified as being of unsound mind in 1741, but opinions vary as to whether he really had gone mad, rather than merely suffering after-effects of a minor stroke, preliminary to a more serious one that robbed him of the power of speech the following year. Some subsequent critics—notably J. B. Priestley in *Literature and Western Man* (1960)—cite the conclusion of Gulliver's story as evidence of incipient madness, but, given the extent to which so many later commentators took up the thread of Gulliver's dark view of human Yahoodom, it seems just as reasonable to interpret it as evidence of penetrative sanity. Swift eventually died in 1745, a year after his last remaining close friend and colleague in satire, Alexander Pope.

* * * *

Swift's account of Gulliver's travels eventually gave rise of a whole subgenre of "Gulliveriana," including numerous sequels in which the intrepid traveler returned to sea again and again. There was, however, something of a hiatus in the production of such works after the immediate supplementation of the lunar satires *A Voyage to Cacklogallinia* (1727) by Samuel Brunt and *A Trip to the Moon* (1728) by Murtagh McDermot, and both of those titles might also owe a debt to one of the few lunar voyages published between Francis Godwin's and their own that might have been influenced by Francis Bacon: Daniel Defoe's *The Consolidator; or Memoirs of Sundry Transactions from the World in the Moon* (1705), which makes elaborate use of imaginary machines as allegories of human ambition and inclination. It would probably be fair to say, however, that no satirical imaginary voyage published in Britain after 1726 escaped Swift's influence entirely, and many can be seen as evident homages to it. Its influence spread far and wide throughout Europe and America.

The advent of generic scientific romance prompted numerous direct and obvious responses to *Gulliver's Travels*, testifying eloquently to the book's importance as a precursor. Several belated sequels followed in the footsteps of Mortimer Collins' *Squire Silchester's Will* (1873), in which a record is found of Gulliver's visit to Amazonia. In Walter Copland Perry's *The Revolt of the Horses* (1898) the Houyhnhnms invade England with genocidal intent. *Laputa Revisited by Gulliver Redivivus* (1905) by Theo B. Hyslop puts Gulliver into suspended animation in order for him to discover the contemporary decadence of the Laputans. The title story of Barry Pain's *The New Gulliver and Other Stories* (1913) appears to be a fragment of an aborted novel, but is long enough to offer a striking account of the bizarre land of Ultima Thule. In Louis Herrman's *In the Sealed Cave* (1935) Gulliver discovers surviving Neanderthal humans.

Perhaps the most significant early work following up on ideas contained in the account of Gulliver's third voyage, albeit obliquely, was *The Prince of Abissinia, A Tale* (1759) by Samuel Johnson, better known as *Rasselas*. Although it is primarily a boisterously skeptical philosophical enquiry into the possibility of human happiness—and hence a significant complement to the most famous of Voltaire's satires, *Candide*, similarly published in 1759—it contains a remarkable account of the intercourse between the eponymous prince's guide to the world outside his Happy Valley, Imlac, and an astronomer.

Consulted as to the merits of his choice of life, the astronomer offers a bleak judgment of the psychology of the career scientist:

"I have passed my time in study without experience: in the attainment of sciences which can, for the most part, be but remotely useful to mankind. I have purchased knowledge at the expense of all the common comforts of life: I have missed the endearing elegance of female friendship, and the happy commerce of domestic tenderness. If I have obtained any prerogatives above other students, they have been accompanied with fear, disquiet, and scrupulosity; but even of these prerogatives, whatever they were, I have, since my thoughts have been diversified by more intercourse with the world, begun to question the reality. When I have been for a few days lost in pleasing dissipation, I am always tempted to think that my enquiries have ended in error, and that I have suffered much, and suffered in vain."[19]

This passage, echoing Francis Bacon's interpretation of the punishment of Prometheus as an allegory of the scourge of the scientific mind, is a particularly eloquent summary of what was subsequently supposed by many others to be the typical existential fate of any man who devoted his life to science. *Rasselas* was a story generally considered to be uncannily accurate in its description of certain psychological syndromes—the book was compulsory reading for many years for students at Johns Hopkins Medical School in Baltimore—and this capsule analysis was echoed in many future literary representations of scientists and analyses of their characteristics. *Rasselas* was one of the two favorite texts enjoyed in his youth by Tertius Lydgate, the luckless would-be medical researcher in George Eliot's *Middlemarch*, who is ultimately pressured into a preference for female friendship and domestic tenderness, and is thus obliged to abandon his scientific quest. Lydgate's other favorite text, equally ominously, was *Gulliver's Travels*.

Many critical accounts of *Rasselas* refer to the character quoted above as "the mad astronomer," automatically associating him with the tainted reputation of scholars with scientific interests, and appointing him as an archetype of a significant motif in all subsequent fiction depicting scientists. The second-hand description of him given by Imlac, while stressing the astronomer's great integrity and benevolence, does indeed reveal him to be subject to a terrible delusion. By virtue of long observation of the heavens, and knowing the correlations of their movements with the cycle of the seasons, the astronomer has become convinced that he is in control of that cycle, and that, in consequence, he has the ability to bring about meteorological variations on the Earth's surface. Well aware of the difficulty of demonstrating this ability, and even suspecting himself of madness because he believes that he has it, the astronomer nevertheless cannot dispel the feeling, and excuses his failure to make more use of the power by pointing out that altering the relative positions of the Earth and Sun in order to favor

---

19   Samuel Johnson. *The History of Rasselas, Prince of Abissinia*. Boston: J. Belcher, 1811. p.142

one region of the surface would inevitably work to the detriment of another, which would cancel out the benevolent intention.

This revelation on the astronomer's part leads Imlac to undertake a discourse on intellectual disorders, stressing the dangers of the imagination—whose effects, he fears, are so widespread and insidious that no one can be considered to be entirely sane, although people who combine a powerful imagination with the combustible fuel of knowledge are likely to be markedly less sane than others. It is not so much the practice of science that is condemned by his inference, therefore, as the baleful combination of science and imagination: or, in other words, "scientific romance" in its original meaning as a kind of scholarly fantasy.

Similar observations and similar judgments were to be made by so many other writers depicting the lives of real and imaginary scientists that this characterization of their psychology qualifies as one of the fundamental assumptions of scientific romance: an assumption that seems, with an entirely appropriate paradoxicality, fatal to any ambition that the genre might have to rationality. If the madness of scientists originates from their tendency to romance, then any romance of science, whether expressed as reportage, popularization, poetry or fiction, is condemned from the outset as evidence of insanity. Many observers have, indeed, felt that this is the case, and it is hardly surprising that some of the earliest literary texts taking aboard the concept of "scientific romance" are so direly hostile to it. The argument was not, however, one-sided, and the early theorists of British Romanticism were very much aware of that opposition.

2. THE PLEASURE AND PERILS OF THE IMAGINATION

When Samuel Johnson penned Imlac's cautionary speech about the dangers of the imagination he was undoubtedly aware of the existence of Mark Akenside's long didactic poem *The Pleasures of Imagination* (1744), which was issued after its publisher, hesitant to meet Akenside's exorbitant demand for a payment of £120, had sent the manuscript to Alexander Pope for a expert opinion as to its worth. Johnson was aware of the poem's authorship, although it was issued anonymously, and he was by no means entirely averse to it as a work of art, complimenting its blank verse in *Lives of the Poets* (1783); he also commented acerbically on Akenside's early reformist politics, however, saying that he had "an impetuous eagerness to subvert and confound with very little care what shall be established." Akenside also attracted the disapproval of a rival author-physician, Tobias Smollett, who included a caricature of him in *The Adventures of Peregrine Pickle* (1751).

Akenside had been born in 1721 into a family of fervent Dissenters, and was lame all his life because of an injury received from a cleaver wielded by his father, a butcher. He was sent to study in Edinburgh with a view to making him a minister, but he quit theology, becoming a Voltairean deist, and studied medicine instead, although he always had ambitions to make a career as a writer. He seems initially to have regarded the practice of medicine as a "day job" and a distraction, although he eventually devoted himself to it more wholeheartedly, becoming chief physician at Christ's Hospital before a surprising political conversion to Toryism allowed him to obtain a position as the queen's physician during the reign of George III. His political career also took off at that point, and he held important positions in the Treasury before becoming a privy councilor in 1774. In the meantime *The Pleasures of Imagination* was thoroughly revised and a new version, bearing the subtly different title *The Pleasures of the Imagination*, was published in 1757.

Both versions of the poem begin with an analytical preface separating the pleasures in question into various categories, corresponding to the various sections of the poem, making similar points in somewhat different terms—the clearer and more economical version in *The Pleasures of the Imagination* identifies the first "book" of the poem as considering the pleasures obtainable from natural objects, and proceeding from "our natural inclination to greatness and beauty."[20] The second part proceeds to an analysis of the pleasures received from the "elegant arts," in which more varied reactions stem from representations vice and virtue, of objects stimulating laughter, and measures calculated to "Excite... pity, fear, and the other passions." The third section is an addendum to the second, while the fourth considers pleasures more limited in their attainment because they require greater intelligence and a

---

20   Mark Akenside. *The Pleasures of the Imagination and Other Poems*. New York: R. & W. A. Bartow, 1819. p.3.

more philosophical turn of mind. Certain men, the author argues are possessed of an imagination "endowed with powers," who are, in consequence, men of genius.

The last point is vital, because the role credited to imagination in the apprehension of various kinds of beauty is "not alike to every mortal eye." People possessed of different slants of imagination perceive different kinds of beauty in the natural world. Thus:

> *To some she taught the fabric of the sphere.*
> *The changeful moon, the circuit of the stars,*
> *The golden zones of heaven. To some she gave*
> *To search the story of eternal thought;*
> *Of space and time; of thought's unbroken chain,*
> *And will's quick movement."*[21]

In Akenside's view, imagination is no mere inventive fancy, but a kind of mental penetration, which seeks and grasps the "vast, the stable [and] the sublime" within "the transient and minute." Although it can see things in terms of the vocabulary of mythology, it is, or at least ought to be, aware of the symbolic quality of such contrivance. Although the poem makes elaborate use of Classical imagery, therefore, it routinely moves on to stress that such imaginative endeavor is a means to an end, because "the various charms of life and sense adjoined" are "pledges of a state entire/ Where native order reigns," and beauty is the "lovely ministress of truth and good/In this dark world. For truth and good are one./And beauty dwells in them, and they in her."

The identity of truth and beauty were later to be asserted, more famously, by John Keats, but what Keats meant to assert by that alleged equivalence is that the beautiful is always, in some sense "true," while Akenside is approaching from the opposite direction, convinced that the truth is the ultimate source and vindication of beauty, and that a privileged understanding of the natural world—science—is not merely one of the pleasures of the imagination but the key to them all.

---

21   Ibid p.11. The only differences from the earlier version of the poem are the substitution of "search" for "weigh" and "movement" for "impulse."

This view is expressed more explicitly in Akenside's "Hymn to Science," which summons Science to "bless my labouring mind," and adds;

> *But first with thy restless light,*
> *Disperse those phantoms from my sight*
>   *Those mimic shades of thee:*
> *The scholiast's learning, sophist's cant.*
> *The visionary bigot's rant,*
>   *The monks' philosophy.*[22]

The poet asks to be taken "Where reason points the way" to "learn each secret cause" in mathematics and motion, and then to approach the human mind in the same way, in order to:

> *Say from what simple springs began*
> *The vast ambitious thoughts of man,*
>   *Which range beyond control,*
> *Which seek eternity to trace,*
> *Dive through the infinity of space.*
>   *And strain to grasp the whole.*[23]

In all probability, Samuel Johnson would have had no quarrel with the ambition of that quest, although he might well have been skeptical about the prospects of its success, and fearful, with Imlac, of the possibility that the sheer scope of the ambition might lead the scientific imagination to overshoot its target and stray into the realms of delusion.

In its mode as well as its message, Akenside's account of "The Pleasures of the Imagination" was very much in the spirit of emerging Romanticism; by virtue of that, it echoed something of the method of Francis Bacon's reinterpretative approach to *The Wisdom of the Ancients* and laid considerable groundwork for Erasmus Darwin's account of *The Loves of the Plants*. There is no enmity in Akenside's work between the imagination's use of mythological imagery and its search for truth by scientific methods and means—quite the reverse; they can function as aspects of the

---

22 Mark Akenside. *The Poems of Mark Akenside*. M.D. Chiswick: Whittingham, 1822. p.212.
23 Ibid p.213.

same endeavor, provided that they cast off the burdens and idols of authority in order to open the mind.

* * * *

Akenside's second attempt to describe and evaluate the capacities and pleasures of the imagination, thus to reconstruct the esthetics of sensory perception and intellectual evaluation thereof, was published in the same year as Edmund Burke's *A Philosophical Enquiry into the Origin of Our Ideas of the Sublime and the Beautiful* (1757), which makes an interesting contrast with it.

Whereas Akenside subsumes the idea of the sublime within the imagination's quest for truth via beauty, Burke separates the two. Adopting the Aristotelian division of causality into formal, material, efficient and final causes, Burke finds the formal cause of beauty in the emotion of love, as materially caused by various objects whose efficient causality works through soothing of the nerves, the final cause being left—as is perhaps only polite—to God's providence.

More interest has inevitably focused on the other part of the enquiry, but Burke's analysis of beauty is similarly original, sharply contradicting recent attempts to locate beauty within quasi-mathematical aspects of proportion and teleological theories of perfection, and seeking to locate it instead in terms of passionate physiological response—not merely in the eye of the beholder but the entire nervous system.

Burke's account of the sublime runs parallel, locating its formal cause in fear, its material cause in vastness and the suggestion of the infinite, working through the efficient causes of nervous tension, the final cause here being abandoned, not to Satan *per se*, but to an echo of God's heroic battle with Satan, as depicted in John Milton's *Paradise Lost*. Burke thus helped pave the way for, although he would not have approved of, the attempt made by Percy Shelley to argue that, if one reads the poem objectively, the sublime Satan is the true hero of *Paradise Lost*, and that, although the battle between God and Satan had inevitably been won by omnipotence, the might of omnipotence did not make it right.

"Whatever is fitted in any sort to excite the ideas of pain and danger," Burke writes, in defining the sublime, "that is to say, whatever is in any way terrible, or is conversant about terrible objects, or operates in a manner analogous to terror, is a source of the sublime; that is, it is productive of the strongest emotion which the mind is capable of feeling."[24]

This passage, and others like it, was widely construed as an esthetic justification of the Romantic poets' use of extreme and extravagant imagery, and, more specifically, of the excesses of the Gothic novel, whose practitioners attempted to use the narrative techniques developed by novelists to communicate a sense of verisimilitude in order to excite sensations of terror or horror, sometimes with the mere appearance of the supernatural and sometimes going the whole hog and deploying the entire panoply of supernatural armaments, including Satan in person. Most such authors sided unequivocally with virtue, but such was the nature of their work that it was easy to suspect some of them of being of the devil's party, even if they were not fully aware of it. No one in England went as far as the Marquis de Sade did in France, in taking up the temptation to revel in Gothic horrors wholeheartedly, but the search for thrills and the inevitable effects of melodramatic inflation pushed them gradually toward more sadistic refinements of the threats they featured and the fates they doled out.

Burke's sweeping and original arguments generated a great deal of discussion—more so, it seems, than Akenside's celebration of the pleasures of the imagination. At least to some of the participants in that discussion, they made imaginative pleasures seem even more attractive in making them perilous, not because of the threat of delusion, but because of the supposedly terrible aspects of the satanic seductions of the sublime. Burke's sharp contrast between the psychology underlying the esthetics of the sublime and that underlying the esthetics of beauty was not endorsed by everyone, but in the context of Romantic literature and its use of fantastic motifs he did seem to have hit on something. Nathan Drake's *Literary Hours* (1800) includes an essay on "the Gothic," as well as an exemplary tale intended to illustrate and prove his point, in which Drake splits the "vulgar gothic" into two, in much the same way that Burke had divided esthetic experience, employing the figureheads of "the awful administrations of the Spectre [and] the

---

24   Edmund Burke. *A Philosophical Inquiry into the Origin of Our Ideas of the Sublime and the Beautiful.* New Edition. Basle: J. J. Tourneisen, 1892. p.46.

innocent gambols of the Fairy,"[25] to distinguish two distinct "terrible" and "sportive" species of superstition and art.

Drake's emphasis on "superstition" reflects the fact that Gothic fiction, and Romantic literature in general, were almost exclusively supernatural in suggestion and manifestation, and thus easily contrastable with the produce of the scientific imagination, but Akenside had made the sublime an integral feature of the scientific imagination and Burke had not disagreed, in placing vastness and infinity—key aspects of cosmology—at the heart of the material causes of the relevant emotional and esthetic response.

Akenside might well have dissented from the view that the ideas of vastness and infinity intrinsic to the scientific view of the universe of stars were intimately connected with fear and terror, but he could not have dismissed it out of hand, and it is undeniable that a certain element of terror was creeping into the perceptions of scientific truth glimpsed by many laymen. That element of terror had long been familiar in a religious context, although it was notionally defused in the apparent amelioration of God's awesome vastness by the comforting humanization of Christ: something that the scientific world-view, while not necessarily lacking—as Bacon had emphasized in making Bensalem a devoutly Christian nation—at least tended to de-emphasize.

Samuel Johnson's Imlac had stressed that the astronomer in *Rasselas* was an utterly benevolent individual who meant no harm to anyone, and the exposure to sublimity that had driven him to delusion and depression had not altered that disposition; Swift's Laputan astronomers were also broadly benevolent—but it was not obvious that the same must be true of all their kind. Anyone who agreed with Burke was therefore entitled to wonder whether the imagination of scientists, in tending to the sublimity of the scientific imagination in the contemplation of the vastness of space and time, might have its terrible aspects—and hence, perhaps, the potential for terrible consequences.

* * * *

Many scientists, not unnaturally, were disinclined to agree with Burke that the vastness of the perspectives cultivated by

---

25   Nathan Drake. *Literary Hours; or, Sketches Critical and Narrative*. Second Edition. Volume I. London: Cadell & Davies, 1800. p.139.

post-Newtonian science was necessarily inductive of fear and terror in cultivating a sensation of sublimity. They preferred Akenside's opinion that the sublime was merely a subcategory of the beautiful, and that the wonder induced by the vast Newtonian universe was a thing of beauty. They approached the pleasures of the imagination from a different direction, and were keen to argue that fear was unnecessary on the part of those who found the notions of modern science difficult to grasp. That determination did not, however, prevent scientists from taking part in the Romantic Movement, or from seeming to those opposed to the movement to be particularly dangerous in their support.

To some extent, the association of scientists with Romanticism seemed to the movement's opponents to be a coincidence of political ideals. Romanticism was revolutionary in its aims, not merely within the literary context but a political content as well; many of the leading Romantic poets were supporters of the French Revolution and lent succor to English agitators, and their friends in the scientific community tended to have been drawn into that alliance by similar sympathies. There was, however, more to the sympathy than mere coincidence, just as it was more than mere coincidence that had made Francis Bacon the philosopher of science the utopian author of *New Atlantis*. Science did, indeed, seem inherently democratic, scientific truth being exactly the same for everyone, while anti-democratic institutions and prejudices seemed to be reflected in an endorsed by the Church, in spite of the Christian teachings the Church claimed to embody.

The paragon of Romantic science in Britain as the century drew to a close, in terms of his status as a figurehead if not his actual achievements, was Erasmus Darwin. Erasmus Darwin is nowadays primarily remembered as the grandfather of the more famous Charles, but he played a key role of his own in the development of British perceptions of science. His detractors could, and still can, claim with some justification that his discoveries were slight, his inventions trivial and his commentaries open to ridicule, but, partly because of the last-cited circumstance, he attracted enormous attention.

Darwin was the host and leading figure of the Lunar Society, a talking shop for scientists and technologists that seemed something of an absurdity itself in being based in Lichfield, and in selecting its name not because of any particular interest in lunar astronomy but because of its suggestion of lunacy. Nevertheless, it was a cabinet of authentic celebrities. In himself, Darwin seemed larger than life, not merely because of his successful publications and awesome bulk—he had his obese chauffeur go ahead of him when making house-calls as a physician, to make sure that the floors could bear his weight—but because of his many offspring, estimated at fourteen in all, including three known illegitimate children. Whatever he was reckoned to be, he was certainly not mediocre.

Darwin was born in 1731 in Nottinghamshire, and educated at Chesterfield Grammar School, St. John's College Cambridge and the University of Edinburgh Medical School, although there does not seem to be any record of his ever having obtained an M.D. He moved to Lichfield after failing to set himself up in Nottingham, and maintained a practice there for fifty years, which won him a considerable reputation, although it is unclear to what extent that success was based on treatments derived from the unorthodox theory of disease set out in his treatise *Zoonomia; or, The Laws of Organic Life* (1794), which we now know to be incorrect. Like some other incorrect theories employed as bases for medical treatment in the eighteenth and early nineteenth centuries, however, Darwin's would have had the benefit of avoiding chemical treatments that did more harm than good—the only possible way, in the golden age of quackery, to become a reasonably successful physician. He gained enough of a reputation to be invited to serve as a Royal Physician alongside Mark Akenside, but he declined, not wanting to leave peaceful Lichfield for the hurly-burly of London.

The members of Darwin's Lunar Society included James Watt, whose crucial improvements to Newcomen's steam engine gave such machines the ability to transform the worlds of labor and transportation; Watt's business partner Matthew Boulton; the chemist and clergyman Joseph Priestley; the potter Josiah Wedgwood, who was to become Charles Darwin's other grandfather; and Samuel Galton, who was to become, along with Erasmus Darwin, the other grandfather of Francis Galton, the pioneer of eugenic theory. Meetings of the Society also entertained such famous occasional guests as Jean-Jacques Rousseau and Samuel Johnson.

Darwin's treatise on physiology was by no means his first publication, although he did not make a rapid start on his literary career, being over fifty when he embarked on it. He began work as a translator, taking seven years to render Linnaeus' *Systema Naturae* into English, in *A System of Vegetables* (1783-85) and *The Families of Plants* (1787). That labor inspired him to dramatize the Linnaean system of classification, based on plant reproductive systems, in a long poem, *The Loves of the Plants* (1789), which was reprinted as "part two" of *The Botanic Garden* (1791). The first part of the latter book is "The Economy of Vegetation," which is introduced as a survey of contemporary botanical science, although its scope is actually considerably greater.

The Loves of the Plants is elaborately footnoted in order to explain its imagery, and also includes prose "interludes" framed as dialogues between the author and a bookseller, in which the former attempts to justify the method of the poem and explain its esthetics, especially its use of "monsters" and nightmarish imagery. Oddly enough, Darwin does not employ one readily-available argument to justify his use of mythological symbolism in describing the reproductive apparatus of plants: that the Linnaean system of classification has no alternative but to borrow many of its generic and specific designations from mythologically-associated terms, thus building the language of myth into scientific terminology at the most elementary level. In addition to Greek myth, however, Darwin also draws upon a fourfold classification of "elemental spirits" that discriminates those of earth (gnomes), air (sylphs), water (nymphs) and fire (salamanders). In his Apology he calls this the "Rosicrucian doctrine." That taxonomy provides the main organizing principle of "The Economy of Vegetation.

"The Economy of Vegetation"—which is even more elaborately footnoted than *The Loves of the Plants*—begins with an invitation to the Goddess of Botany, who descends from the sky in a "blushing car" with wheels entwined with flowers, in a fashion very similar to the eponymous guide in Percy Shelley's *Queen Mab*. The poem then proceeds, by way of a general introduction and background to its botanical subject-matter, with discussion of chemical explosions, steam engines and the "electrical fluid," enthusiastically celebrating recent discoveries and practical achievements of science. "Immortal Franklin" is hailed as a virtual equal of the mythological figures cited, and Joseph Priestley also takes a leading role. The "additional notes"—which take up considerably more than half of the text—include essays on meteors, comets, primary colors, the steam engine, electricity and numerous other topics, including various aspects of geology, metallurgy and meteorology, and an analysis of the imagery of the Portland Vase.

The Botanic Garden is primarily an exercise in the attempted popularization of science, an enterprise in which the Lunar Society had long taken a keen interest; in addition to the scientists and technologists listed above, its members included Richard Lovell Edgeworth, the father of the novelist Maria Edgeworth, who also undertook exercises in the popularization of science, and Thomas Day, the author of the didactic children's book *The History of Sandford and Merton* (1783), which made significant efforts in the same cause. Joseph Priestley was also extremely interested in the cause of education—a vocation as important to him as his clerical one, relative to which his scientific researches were a mere hobby. The Lunar Society's endeavors helped to inspire the production of such works as *Conversations in Chemistry* (1805) by Maria Edgeworth's friend Jane Marcet, Samuel Parkes' *Chemical Catechism for the Use of Young People* (1806) and Jeremiah Joyce's *Scientific Dialogues* (1807),

Because gardening was becoming a popular hobby in England at the time, the title of *The Botanic Garden* helped the book to sell very well, although some of its readers might have felt that they had been slightly misled, and some undoubtedly disagreed strongly with its declarations of support for the French Revolution and calls for the abolition of slavery—inclusions that helped to make it one of the principal identifying texts of the "Jacobin science," against which the editors of the *Anti-Jacobin* protested strongly.

The Anti-Jacobin, or Weekly Examiner was set up by George Canning, John Hookham Frere and others, as a Tory reprisal against the burgeoning radical press. Founded in 1797, it immediately launched a strident campaign against "Jacobin science" and "Jacobin poets," often including parodies of their various works. Robert Southey was a favorite target for poetic travesty, and the assault might have assisted his eventual decision to follow Mark Akenside's example and quit the radical camp for conservatism, but the Lunar Society was also an immediate target. The most memorable and most famous of all the periodical's parodies was a caricature of *The Loves of the Plants*, "The Loves of the Triangles"

(1801). Whether the parody in question caused its target any distress, it is impossible to guess, but it is probable that the publicity it provided merely helped to swell Darwin's bulk as a figurehead.

The Botanic Garden was represented as a tribute to Joseph Banks, who had greatly expanded the scope of the Linnaean classification of plants, having collected many new specimens when he sailed with James Cook's first exploratory expedition. Banks had promoted the extension of such work when he became president of the Royal Society; he commissioned William Bligh to collect the breadfruit from Tahiti that became one of the bones of contention occasioning the mutiny on the *Bounty*. His interest was not purely scientific; Banks recognized the importance of plantations in the project of colonization, and he was interested in breadfruit because he thought that it might become a useful staple crop in Caribbean colonial endeavors. When he eventually took charge of the Royal Gardens at Kew, one of Banks' primary missions was to equip the colonists of Australia with useful crop-plants and herbal medicines. Banks had, however, previously been the dedicatee of James Perry's "Mimosa; or, The Sensitive Plant" (1779), which had taken some inspiration from Linnaeus but far more from the erotic euphemisms of Thomas Stretser's quasi-pornographic *The Natural History of the Frutex Vulvaria, or Flowering Shrub* and *Arbor Vitae; or, The Natural History of the Tree of Life* (both 1732, by-lined Philogynes Clitorides).

The theme and title of *The Loves of the Plants* also called attention to the fact that the Linnaean system of classification is based on the characteristics of their sexual organs—a circumstance that had already given rise to some muted accusations of indecency, although the vast majority of scientists did not regard it as a suitable occasion for suggestive nudges. There was, however, more than puerile prurience at stake: the fact that a logical plant taxonomy had to be based on reproductive systems added further evidence to the supposition that the evident relatedness of species must be based on a common heredity and evolutionary sequence.

Whether Erasmus Darwin had been a convinced evolutionist before setting out to translate Linnaeus or not, he was certainly one thereafter—but the hints of that belief set out in *The Botanic Garden* remained hints, and it was not until 1794, in a single paragraph buried deep in *Zoonomia*'s chapter on the medical relevance of human reproductive physiology, that Darwin felt able to express it explicitly. The paragraph has since become more famous than the rest of the text, but it did not generate overmuch comment or controversy at the time.

"From thus meditating on the great similarity of the structure of the warm-blooded animals," Darwin wrote, "and at the same time of the great changes they undergo both before and after their nativity…would it be too bold to imagine, that in the great length of time since the earth began to exist, perhaps millions of years…that all warm-blooded animals have arisen from one living filament, which THE GREAT FIRST CAUSE endowed with animality… and thus possessing the faculty of continuing to improve by its own inherent activity, and of delivering down those improvements by generation to its posterity, world without end?"[26]

Later, he added: "As the earth and ocean were probably peopled with vegetable productions long before the existence of animals… shall we conjecture that one and the same kind of living filament is and has been the cause of all organic life?"[27]

Zoonomia was not nearly as successful commercially as *The Botanic Garden*, and Darwin's theory of disease never won enough disciples to become a school or occasion a movement. As summed up in the preface to part three of the text, that thesis is that "all diseases originate in the exuberance, deficiency or retrograde action of the faculty of the sensorium, as their proximate cause; and consist in the disordered motions of the fibres of the body, as the proximate effects of the exertions of those disordered faculties."[28] Darwin divided diseases up into four classes, consequent on four different ways in which the sensorium has the ability to affect the "fibrous parts" of the body, the four classes in question being diseases of irritation, sensation, volition and association. Each class of disease, in Darwin's view, requires a different approach to its cure.

Although we now have a much clear idea of the causes of diseases, it is hardly fair to blame Darwin for not having originated or reinvented the germ theory forty years in advance of François

---

26   Erasmus Darwin. *Zoonomia; or, The Laws of Organic Life*. Phildelphia: Edward Earle, 1818. Volume I. p.397.
27   Ibid. p.398.
28   ibid. Volume II. p vi.

Raspail, and he doubtless thought that he had obtained some vindication for his theory in his own observations; if his theory was no better than the most orthodox theory then current—that diseases were caused by airborne "miasmas"—it was surely no worse, and at least Darwin did not suffer the tragic fate of his fellow "Jacobin scientist" Humphry Davy, who wondered whether miasmas might be combated by curative gases, and inhaled chlorine in order to test its effect. In spite of the primitive nature of *Zoonomia*'s account of human physiology, its brief summation of comparative anatomy did indeed lead Darwin to a correct conclusion with regard to the "filament" connecting the descendancy of all life on earth.

One significant corollary of the theory of disease elaborated in *Zoonomia* is the role played by the imagination in both health and disease; among other effects Darwin suggests that, although early embryos are not formed by parental imagination, they are nevertheless susceptible to them in their development, productive of the resemblances of offspring to parents—thus adding, at least potentially, a whole new dimension to the pleasures and perils of the imagination.

Darwin undoubtedly made more impact on his contemporaries with his ideas on educational reform, which he summarized in *A Plan for the Conduct of Female Education in Boarding Schools* (1797), a crucial work in the campaign not merely for the better education of women but for their education in science. In *Anti-Jacobin* abuse, Darwin was routinely bracketed with the radical propagandist and novelist William Godwin, the husband of Mary Wollstonecraft, the feminist who had argued cogently in *A Vindication of the Rights of Women* (1792) that women were not naturally inferior to men, and that it was only their lack of education that made them seem so. Erasmus Darwin's support for her thesis might seem a trifle superfluous today, but it did not seem so in 1797, however unfair it is that his word should have carried so much more apparent weight than hers. Unfortunately, Mary Wollstonecraft died in 1797 giving birth to a daughter, Mary, who was later to elope with Percy Shelley.

Darwin moved on to safer ground with a straightforward championship of hobbyist botany in *Phytologia; or, The Philosophy of Agriculture and Gardening* (1800), but then reverted to work on the epic project begun in *The Botanic Garden*, the final produce of which was the posthumously-published *The Temple of Nature; or, The Origin of Society* (1803), the ultimate summation of his thought and art. Darwin's evolutionism was reiterated there more elaborately, flamboyantly dressed with the symbolism of mythology and poetic verve, and infused with a relentless and typically Romantic optimism based in faith in the idea of progress. The Preface states, with conscientiously deceptive modesty, that:

"The Poem, which is here offered to the Public, does not pretend to instruct by deep researches of reasoning; its aim is simply to amuse, by bringing distinctly to the imagination, the beautiful and sublime images of the operations on Nature, in the order, as the author believes, in which the progressive course of time presented them."[29]

The Poem proceeds by dividing the past into four ages, with a fifth having just begun. The first is described in mythological terms, syncretically, taking in, among other motifs, Adam and Eve, the binding of Proteus, the School of Venus, the Eleusinian Mysteries and Orpheus' Descent into Hell before proceeding dutifully to God's function as the First Cause, prompting the origin of earthly life in the sea with the spontaneous production of minute animals, which then began their evolution from the simple and microscopic toward the complex and ponderous. The mythological imagery does not conclude there, however, being continually reintroduced with various symbolic purposes.

The poem is extensively annotated by footnotes explaining its symbolism and elaborating the evolutionary account, which supportive evidence drawn from a variety of sources, including Linnaeus, Lord Monboddo, Edmund Halley, John Locke, Antoine Lavoisier and—most extensively by far—Darwin's own earlier works.

Reflecting on a passing reference to the cave of Trophonius, Darwin explains the myth and his interpretation of it, very much in the spirit of *The Wisdom of the Ancients*, but decidedly less gloomily than Francis Bacon:

"Plutarch mentions, that prophecies of evil events were uttered from the cave of Trophonius; but the allegorical story, that

---

29   Erasmus Darwin. *The Temple of Nature; or, The Origin of Society*. Baltimore: Bonsal & Niles, 1804. Part one, p.5. [The edition has two sets of pages numbers.]

whoever entered this cavern were never again seen to smile, seems to have been designed to warn the contemplative from studying too much the dark side of nature. Thus an ancient poet is said to have written a poem on the miseries of the world, and to have thence become so unhappy as to destroy himself. When we reflect on the perpetual destruction of organic life, we should also recollect, that it is perpetually renewed in other forms by the same materials, and thus the sum total of the happiness of the world continues undiminished; and that a philosopher may thus smile again on turning his eyes from the coffins of nature to her cradles."[30]

Another arithmetician might have calculated on the basis of the same data that the sum total of the world's misery similarly continues undiminished, and a cynic might have disputed Darwin's fundamental assumption—repeated elsewhere in the poem—of the "happiness of life," but such quibbles did not bother him, if they even occurred to him; in his eyes, the surge and progress of life, reflected in the ambition and adventurism of individual organisms, was intrinsically good, not merely a cause for wonder but for rejoicing.

In describing the crucial emergence of life from water on to land, Darwin's comments echo those of Benoît de Maillet, although he does not cite that author and probably had not read him. The terms in which he describes the adventure however, could equally well have helped to spark the imagination of the Chevalier de Lamarck or his own grandson:

"After islands or continents were raised above the primeval ocean, great numbers of the most simple animals would attempt to seek food at the edges or shores of the new land, and might thence gradually become amphibious.... At the same time new microscopic animalcules would immediately commence wherever there was warmth and moisture, and some organic matter, that might induce putridity. Those situated on dry land, and immersed in dry air, may gradually acquire new powers to preserve their existence; and by innumerable successive reproductions, for some thousands, or perhaps millions of ages, may at length have produced many of the vegetable and animal inhabitants which now people the earth."[31]

---

30   Ibid. Part one, p.18.
31   Ibid. Part one, p.39.

There is, as usual, an extensive set of "additional notes" appended to the poem, which more than double the length of the text, and constitute a series of essays on its various themes and assumptions: the spontaneous generation of the microscopic animals from which more complex life-forms develop; the faculties of the sensorium, and so on. They include accounts of aging, death and reproduction, based on the fundamental theses of *Zoonomia*, and, more adventurously, a chemical theory of electricity and magnetism, based on significant observations made by Humphry Davy, Benjamin Franklin and Luigi Galvani. The additional text includes in its discussion of the sensorium an essay on the origins of the "sensation" of beauty, heartily endorsing Burke's contention that its ultimate basis is love, but repeating from *Zoonomia* the judgment that it "appears to be attached from our cradles to the easy curvature of visible objects, and to have been derived from the form of the female bosom."[32]

All of this speculative theorizing can now be seen to have been, in very large measure if not completely, incorrect. It reaches too far from inadequate data, and when fuller data became available in the course of the next two centuries, its falsified hypotheses were replaced by better ones. The entire exercise is, therefore, a kind of "scientific romance" even if one sets aside the deliberate romanticization of the poem and its symbolic mythological imagery. Given that, it might seem that Darwin fully deserved the satirization to which his work was subjected, to an even greater extent than Francis Bacon's depiction of Salomon's House warranted the parody of the Academy of Lagado.

It does not follow from that argument, however, that Darwin would have done better to stick to the mere accumulation of data, and leave romance out, either in the matter of speculative thesis-building or in the dramatization of his speculative theses in poetic form. We have now progressed beyond Francis Bacon's philosophy of science, and appreciate the fact that it is not sufficient simply to smash the idols of false belief and then collect observations until the truth falls out by a process of induction. We now appreciate the necessity of constructing hypothetical edifices precisely in order to put them to the proof: to subject them to rigorous trial by ordeal.

---

32   Ibid. part two, p.105

Popularization, dramatization and satirization might be regarded as superfluous to that process, from a rigorously scientific viewpoint, irrelevant if not actually pernicious, but that is to set aside not merely the esthetic aspects of scientific endeavor and discovery, but other aspects of its human significance: the manner in which people conceive of themselves, their situation within and relation to the universe, and, in sum, what Erasmus Darwin was determined to consider as the never-diminishing sum of "happiness of life." In that context, both levels of Darwin's scientific romance—his hypothesizing and his poeticizing—might be considered to have all the justification they need, and to represent significant accomplishments even though the hypotheses turned out to be wrong and the poetry, on the whole, not much good.

In spite of—or perhaps because of—the popularity of *The Botanic Garden*, Erasmus Darwin was never taken entirely seriously in Britain, but the German Romantics thought highly of him, and his influence on English Romanticism might have been greater by the indirect route of Samuel Taylor Coleridge's intense interest in German Romanticism than via his own works. He did, however, have a considerable influence on several significant later works embodying an element of scientific romance, as future pages in this chapter will observe.

Darwin's reputation as a poet did not wear well, and he was probably best-known to twentieth-century literature students because excerpts from "The Loves of the Plants" were prominently featured in D. B. Wyndham-Lewis and Charles Lee's showcase anthology of "bad verse," *The Stuffed Owl* (1930), but it is very noticeable that the anthology in question—which also includes samples from the works of the Royal Society poets Dryden and Cowper, and several examples of Romantic poetry celebrating the glories of the steam engine and engineering projects—has a distinct bias against the subject-matter of "scientific romance," reflective of the growing antagonism between C. P. Snow's two cultures, coincident with and represented by the second phase of the Wellsian genre's development.

* * * *

Erasmus Darwin's contemporaries did not wait for the jury of future data or future esthetic appraisal to pass judgment on his endeavors. When the *Anti-Jacobin* eased off, perhaps because the rapid advancement of George Canning's political career left him no time for such frivolities, others took over, including a prolific journalist whose brief essays on *The Curiosities of Literature* (5 vols. 1791-1823) had won him a considerable reputation for wit and erudition: Isaac D'Israeli.

Although D'Israeli was widely read in philosophy, including natural philosophy, it was literature that was his primary interest, and the development of modern science lay somewhat beyond his expertise. That did not stop him from poking fun at science, but he does appear to have been a trifle tentative in his approach and somewhat embarrassed by his achievement. When Benjamin Disraeli wrote a memoir of his father's life for inclusion in later editions of *The Curiosities of Literature*, he did not even mention his satirical novel, which was not only issued under a preposterous pseudonym—"Messieurs Tag, Rag and Bobtail"—but was significantly revised in between its two editions, of 1805 and 1806, the first of which was entitled *Flim-Flams! or the Life and Errors of My Uncle and the Amours of my Aunt*, and the second *Flim-Flams! or the Life and Errors of My Uncle and His friends*.

The phrase "scientific romance" crops up in the elaborate introductory material to the text, when the author introduces the protagonist, sarcastically, as "the Sir Charles Grandison, or the Amadis de Gaul of the world of scientific romance," swiftly adding that "I hold him out as an *example*, he may also be considered as a *warning!* He fell a victim to the *deliramenta doctrinae*: the wild speculations of the learned" and "Mine is a narrative of the sufferings of Science; the disasters of universal Curiosity."[33]

Sir Charles Grandison is the eponymous hero of Samuel Richardson's response to Henry Fielding's parodies of his previous novels, published in 1753, and is designed as a paragon of virtue, although D'Israeli, who appreciated Fielding far more than Richardson, probably thought him sufficiently absurd as to need no further parody. Amadis de Gaul is the hero of the archetype of the sixteenth-century Iberian romances that took over and revitalized the defunct tradition of French romance, and which enjoyed

---

33   [Isaac D'Israeli] *Flim-Flams! or, the Life and Errors of my Uncle, and the Amours of my Aunt*...by Messieurs Tag, Rag, and Bobtail. Volume 1. London: John Murray, 1805, pp.2-3.

a tremendous vogue before being outclassed and outshone, in the eyes of subsequent commentators, by Miguel de Cervantes' devastating parody of their conventions and artifices, *Don Quixote* (1607). *Amadis of Gaul* had been translated into English in 1803 by Robert Southey; D'Israeli presumably thought that it had arrived in nineteenth-century England without any need of further parody, given that *Don Quixote* was already well-known there.

D'Israeli uses the phrase "scientific romance" in much the same way as James Ibbetson, and the purpose of the text's account of the fictitious uncle's eccentricities is to poke fun at many of the ideas that D'Israeli had found in contemporary scientific texts in the course of his reading. The uncle is a chemist whose reputation is said to rest on his enormous patience in repeating experiments hundreds of times and always getting the same result. He is said to have "a particular genius [for the] anti-sublime in science," that being "the science of turning the big into the little."[34]

In the course of the narrative, which mostly deals with the uncle's relationships with other members of a scientific club known as the Constellation or the Pleiades—reflective of the Lunar Society—scathing accounts are offered of craniognomy (what later became known as phrenology), the meteorology of Luke Howard, geological accounts of the shaping of the Earth by volcanic or hydrologic action, recent conflicting accounts of the properties of nitrous oxide—"philosophical brandy"—and so on, in company with abusive dismissals of theorists in general as builders of "magicians' bridges" that only they can cross. Mockery is also directed at female scientists, in the account of the protagonist's wooing of and marriage to a female astronomer who subsequently cuckolds him. The most elaborate and extensive satirical assault is, however, on proto-evolutionism, in the course of which the novel's footnotes—which are even more elaborate than those attached to the poem in *The Temple of Nature*—cite Benoît de Maillet, Lord Monboddo and Delisle de Sales as well as Erasmus Darwin himself.

The serial demolition carried out by *Flim-Flams!* offers a much fuller account of the range of varieties of "scientific romance" than can be found elsewhere in the period, but there was probably no one else in England during the period who read as voluminously

---

34   Ibid. p.74.

and as omnivorously as D'Israeli, at least with such a caustic eye. Because he is attempting to emphasize the absurdities of "scientific romance," D'Israeli is reluctant to indulge in it himself, but in the second edition of the work he simply could not resist the temptation to indulge in a little philosophical speculation of his own.

In terms of its comparison with the substance of generic scientific romance, the most interesting passage in the story is the chapter added to the beginning of volume III of the second version, in which the uncle actually encounters a homunculus: a "miserable fruit of experimental philosophy"[35] grown artificially from a microscopic seed, who has recapitulated in his development the kind of evolutionary sequence described by Darwin in the embryological development and subsequent growth of a single individual—thus constituting an anticipatory literalization of what subsequently came to be known as Haeckel's Law: "ontogeny recapitulates phylogeny." Alas, the finished homunculus is a dwarf, stigmatized by a tail, like the primitive humans envisaged by Lord Monboddo. Partly in consequence, he enjoys no Darwinian "happiness of life," but is a wretched individual regretful of his own perverse existence.

The elaborate introductory material to *Flim-Flams!* begins with a series of fictitious "anticipatory reviews," including one from the *Anti-Jacobin*. The "review" in question dos not express any hostility to the book's assaults on science, but does dismiss the entire exercise as trivial and protests its deceptiveness, evidently but absurdly failing to appreciate its sarcasm—and, indeed, D'Israeli had no real reason to think that the editors of the *Anti-Jacobin* would approve of him. They had no way to know, of course, that he was the father of a future Tory prime minister, but even if they had been able to know that, it is by no means obvious that George Canning would have approved of Benjamin Disraeli in that capacity, all the more so because the younger Disraeli became a novelist and satirist himself, by no means reluctant to use Romantic methods and themes.

Isaac D'Israeli would surely have been regarded, from the *Anti-Jacobin* viewpoint, as warranting a certain amount of guilt by

---

35   [Isaac D'Israeli] *Flim-Flams! or the Life and Errors of My Uncle and His Friends*...by Messieurs Rag, Tag, and Bobtail. Volume 3. London: John Murray, 1806. p.11.

association with the Romantic Movement, despite having no hint of the "Jacobin" about his politics. He was personally acquainted with several Romantic poets and at least one of Britain's "Jacobin scientists" (Humphry Davy). One of the longer journalistic essays collected in *Curiosities of Literature* praises "Romances" as a form of artistic endeavor, and contrasts modern exemplars with novels in a fashion that is by no means entirely to the advantage of the latter.

D'Israeli had practiced what he preached in this regard, publishing a collection of his own *Romances* (1799), which was perhaps enough in itself to identify him as a significant contributor to the British Romantic Movement. It would have been surprising, therefore, if he had not had a little sympathy for "scientific romance," and *Flim-Flams!* is, in fact, a very mild satire, which often betrays an obvious fascination with the ideas that the author cannot quite bring himself to take seriously—and which Tag, Rag and Bobtail do, after all, attribute to a near relative for whom they clearly have a family affection, in spite of his eccentricities.

* * * *

That kind of wry sympathy was not a problem for the author of the other early literary work indexed by the Hathi Trust and Google Books that embraced the term "scientific romance": the Irish Catholic writer Gerald Griffin. Griffin's dogmatically-based opposition to "scientific romance" was far more earnest. His "Tales Illustrative of the Five Senses," first published in the *Christian Apologist* in 1830, were reprinted with supplementary non-fictional material as *The Christian Physiologist* later that year, and reprinted several more times over the next thirty years.

The work in question was evidently inspired as an ideological reply to attempts by proto-psychologists to co-opt the human soul into a mere mechanical adjunct of the senses. Although Griffin makes no specific reference to Erasmus Darwin's *Zoonomia* or *The Temple of Nature*, the theses set out in those two books are, at the very least, significant specimens of the position that Griffin attacks; his method is only dissimilar in that he uses prose fiction in preference to poetry to illustrate his own ideas, and places his non-fictional commentaries before the stories rather than alongside or after them.

Griffin's specific use of the term "scientific romance" is to declare, pompously, and rather optimistically, that "the day of scientific romance is past."[36] As with the *Anti-Jacobin*'s famous parody and D'Israeli's satire, however, the narrative method of his opposition becomes itself a wry foreshadowing of what would later become the literary genre of "scientific romance."

In the Preface to the collection, Griffin observes that "Men seem to have forgotten the experience of all ages, which leaves the world still in the same position with respect to the science of psychology (as it is called); that it presents a set of schools in our own days no less worthy of the derision of the satirist than those which have almost only descended to us in the ridicule of Lucian; while our religion (for even ridicule is not a match for truth) has alone survived."[37]

The first section of the text begins with an account of the anatomy of the eye and the physiology of sight, as known at the time, and then proceeds to an account of "the uses and government of sight" crediting it as the principal agent of the imagination. Griffin compliments the sense of sight on permitting literature, and then invites the reader who wants to "appreciate the excellence of this wonderful organ" simply to look up at the night sky and remember the true size, distance and number of the stars, concluding that it is hardly possible after having done so to imagine and impious astronomer or anatomist. The story illustrating the sense in question is "The Kelp-Gatherer," a brief sentimental account of the restoration of a blind mother's sight by surgical operation on her cataracts.

In the same way, the second story features the restoration of a young deaf mute's recovery of his hearing and his voice. The third part features "the sense of feeling" and the illustrative story, "The Voluptuary Cured" maintains the pattern of sensation lost and found. The author has little to say about the physiology of smell, and "The Self-Consumed" is a very peculiar illustration thereof, being a strange tale whose protagonist encounters a victim of "lycanthropia"—the insanity of believing oneself to be a werewolf—apparently induced by having witnessed a case of

---

36   Gerald Griffin. *The Christian Physiologist: Tales Illustrative of the Five Senses*. London: Edward Bull, 1830 p.149.
37   Gerald Griffin. "Preface" to ibid. p.viii.

spontaneous human combustion in stressful circumstances; the latter phenomenon is explained hypothetically in a footnote by the highly implausible suggestion that it might result from bathing with the aid of ill-chosen cosmetics. Consideration of the sense of taste inevitably brings the censorious Griffin back to consideration of the vices of "voluptuaries," but "The Selfish Crotarie" (a crotarie is a harper) is a historical tale of the ancient Irish fighting against Danish colonists, the relevance of which is distinctly dubious.

The frame-text goes on, however, to discuss the intellect—consciousness and its attributes—in order to conclude that truth must ultimately be obtained by something beyond the scope of the five senses combined with the application of reason. The narrative voice complains about those who claim otherwise, naming no scientists but only "infidel poets," whom he affects to pity: Shelley and Byron. In this section too there is an exemplary tale, and the author abandons naturalism altogether to turn to fantastic allegory, in a manner reminiscent of Erasmus Darwin, although inclining toward a very different moral.

In "A Story of Psyche" the titular character is banished from Eden for having committed a crucial sin, but compensation for her fallen plight is offered by her two children, Judgment and Imagination—a boy and girl respectively, the latter being, in her turn, the parent of Science. Guided by Imagination, Science and the Senses, Psyche is led on a quest for happiness through the gate of knowledge, in spite of the advice of Judgment to cultivate virtue instead, but she occasions evil wherever she goes. When Imagination finally deserts her, she seeks out Judgment again, only to find him metamorphosed into Philosophy, quoting Socrates, Newton and Democritus. All is not lost, however, and she is eventually guided back to the true path of progress by ardent prayer.

For Griffin's Psyche, as for D'Israeli's homunculus, there is no innate "happiness of life," but the misery of the fallen state, from which the only possible escape is piety—a piety that only holds out the remote promise of reward, a heaven undescribed by virtue of being unimaginable. It is not obvious why Griffin or his devout readers—the book must have been popular to have gone through so many editions, although it is forgotten today—felt that this was a preferable outlook to the one embraced by *The Temple of Nature*, but they were not lacking in support in the next century and a half, when there was to be no shortage of people who wished sincerely, if somewhat hopelessly, that the age of "scientific romance" would very soon be past. In fact, in Griffin's own day, it had hardly begun.

3. THE NEW PROMETHEIA

When the Romantic Movement eventually went into full swing in Britain, it produced Gothic fiction in profusion, of both the terrible and sportive varieties; specters undertook their awful administrations, and fairies gamboled in profusion as imagination was given the free rein that previous orthodoxy had attempted to tighten. Science was not left entirely out of account in the exploits of the Romantic poets, however, especially by Percy Shelley, who had been an enthusiastic experimenter in chemistry in his school days at Eton; one of his teachers there, Adam Walker, was keenly interested in contemporary developments in science, and sometimes gave public demonstrations of the wonders of electricity.

Shelley worked very extensively with Classical imagery, casually embellished with supplementary imagery borrowed from the entire lexicon of the "sportive Gothic," and the legacy of the scientific component of his education was fused with or subsumed within that imagery, somewhat unobtrusively. The thrust of his most visionary works was revolutionary in both artistic and political terms, and he became the British Romantics' principal illustration of the dangers of being too explicit in expressing revolutionary zeal. He first ran into trouble when his essay on "The Necessity of Atheism" had him thrown out of Oxford and branded as a troublemaker.

Ostracism by polite society called forth a supportive reaction from sympathizers, but the reputation was not without dangers, because of the possibility of prosecution for "blasphemous libel" if he gave full expression to his atheism in print. It did not matter how elaborately he dressed the ideas in question in poetical imagery; having been branded in advance, he had every reason to suppose that there would be readers anxious to penetrate the veil and strike at the face behind.

Shelley's eventual widow, Mary, the daughter of the radical philosopher William Godwin—with whom he eloped to the continent, running away from an unhappy first marriage, also the result of an impulsive elopement—was later to contend that Shelley's revolutionary spirit had calmed down somewhat over time, that he had eventually decided that political upheaval was inapt and insufficient to further the work of moral progress, and that what was required was a more gradual but more sweeping evolution of an ideal society appropriate to perfected human beings. That might well have been true, but until he died in 1822, a month before his thirtieth birthday, he retained the reputation of being the most extreme Jacobin among the Jacobin poets, and hence the most dangerous. In the most fervently revolutionary of his early works, *Queen Mab*, written in 1813, the future social transformation he envisaged was far more sweeping than anything envisaged by social reformists like William Godwin, tending more to the apocalyptic than the political.

The publishing history of *Queen Mab* was complicated and troubled, by virtue of its insistent, explicit and flamboyant reiteration of Shelley's atheism. Although more than two hundred copies were privately printed when it was completed, Shelley only circulated seventy of them to friends and sympathizers, storing the rest in a bookshop. In 1821, the bookseller, William Clark, or one of his employees, found the unbound pages, which had by then acquired considerable commercial value as Shelley's reputation had soared. They were bound and sold, without consultation with Shelley—who had left the country for good by then, hoping that the milder climate of the Mediterranean countries might be better for his fragile health than England's cold and damp—with the result that a copy fell into the hands of the Society for the Prevention of Vice. Charges were brought and Clark was imprisoned—but other publishers immediately began pirating the work, whose commercial value had only been increased by the attempted suppression, and was further increased by Shelley's death.

When Mary Shelley published a collected edition of Percy's work in 1839, she thought it prudent to remove the passages from *Queen Mab* that had occasioned the prosecution by virtue of their atheism, and when they were restored in the second edition of 1841, the publisher, Edward Moxon, was immediately prosecuted for blasphemous libel. In the 1847 Moxon edition Mary rejoiced in her preface that the "obstacles" that had previously prevented her from making a "perfect" edition of Shelley poems available had at last been removed, but she dutifully refrained from printing the whole of *Queen Mab*, restricting herself to reproducing the opening two cantos, thus eliminating all the contentious material—and it is that truncated version of the poem with which the majority of subsequent readers became acquainted.

* * * *

In the poem, the fairy Queen Mab arrives in a chariot pulled by "celestial coursers" in order to carry away the soul of the sleeping Ianthe. The journey immediately takes them out of the atmosphere and into space, in order that the Earth can be placed in its appropriate cosmic context.

This vision does not produce the surge of piety that Gerald Griffin thought inevitable, but rather an evocation of a "Spirit of Nature" much more in keeping with the environment of Erasmus Darwin's Temple. Having introduced this cosmic perspective, the poem moves on to Mab's realm, and her "Hall of Spells," where the secrets of the future are to be revealed, in the context of a universe moved harmoniously by "Eternal Nature's law" and in which the "faintest thought" within "one human brain…becomes a link in the great chain of nature."[38] In the truncated text, however, the vision only takes in the ruins of the past, insisting that all monuments are doomed to disappear, with the result that the final image of the extract preserved in that version leaves the Spirit standing:

> *High on an isolated pinnacle;*
> *The flood of ages combating below,*
> *The depth of that unbounded universe*
> *Above and all around*
> *Nature's unchanging harmony.*[39]

The full version contained in the pirated text goes on to take far more detailed lessons from that vision of the past, reading within it a "tale of horror" in which the human sufferings obliterated by the passing of the ages are attributed to the actions of oppression, elaborated in the third canto in a vision of an exemplary king, reveling

---

38   *The Poetical Works of Percy Bysshe Shelley*, edited by Mrs. Shelley. London: Edward Moxon, 1847. p.14.
39   Ibid. p.18.

in luxury and vice. The fourth canto broadens that perspective into a wider indictment.

> *Kings, priests and statesmen, blast the human flower*
> *Even in its tender bud; their influence darts*
> *Like subtle poison through the bloodless veins*
> *Of desolate society.*[40]

Continuing the angry rhetoric, the fifth canto expands on the subject of religion's "twin-sister," selfishness, as embodied in commerce and economic oppression, but ends on a brighter note, suggesting that the entire social system in question is "tottering to the grave" and that all its evils are about to be replaced. Even so, the sixth canto reiterates the same lament, mounting a further attack on religion before finding hope again in a vision of the universe entire and "The storm of change, that ceaselessly/Rolls round the eternal universe,"[41] while finding the Spirit of Nature a much kindlier power than "the God of human error," by virtue of a more complex and elaborate version of the vision revealed in Erasmus Darwin's *Temple of Nature*. In this prospect, despite the fact that there is no innate "happiness of life" for human beings, thanks to the depredations of tyrants, there is always hope in the endless sequence of natural renewals.

In the eighth canto, the poem finally rends "time's eternal veil" in order to display "hope...beaming through the mists of fear" over an Earth that is "no longer hell."[42] Indeed, the future Earth is displayed as a literal paradise, in which it is not just human life that is blissful, but in which lions can lie down with kids, because "custom's force" has made their nature lamb-like. Humans are here immortal, free from all the "germs of misery, death, disease, and crime."

> *All things are void of terror: man has lost*
> *His terrible prerogative, and stands*
> *An equal amidst equals: happiness*

---

40   Percy Bysshe Shelley. *Queen Mab*. London: R. Carlile, 1922. p.35-36.
41   Ibid. p.57.
42   Ibid. p.72.

> *And science dawn though late upon the earth....*[43]

The fairy goes on in canto nine to offer a summary of what has gone before and extract a lesson therefrom, before descending to Earth once again to return the soul to Ianthe's body. Like *The Temple of Nature*, however—with which it forms an eccentric pair—this version of the poem is followed by an elaborate set of notes, including supportive quotations from authors such as Pliny, Francis Bacon, Spinoza and—very extensively, albeit in the original French—the atheist philosopher Baron d'Holbach's *Système de la nature* (1781). The first note explains in great detail what the sun would look like seen from outside the atmosphere, and explains the consequences of the finite speed of light. The second emphasizes the immensity of the universe and the plurality of its worlds. Others argue matters of political and economic philosophy, and expand at length on the evil consequences of religion in general and Christianity in particular.

It is in this long section of the text that Shelley occasionally devotes himself to scientific speculation, supplementing a reference to the pole star with the observation that "It is exceedingly probable, from many considerations, that this obliquity [i.e., of the earth's axis] will gradually diminish, until the equator coincides with the ecliptic.... There is no great extravagance in presuming that the progress of the perpendicularity of the poles may be as rapid as the progress of intellect; or that there should be a perfect identity between the moral and physical improvement of the human species."[44]

The notes also contain a transfigured version of the legend of the Wandering Jew, Ahasuerus, who makes a brief appearance in the poem, which the author claims to have found in "some German work" picked up by chance—actually Christian Schubart's "Der Ewige Jude" (1783).

The final, and longest, note begins with a commentary on the story of Prometheus, which, the author contends "although universally admitted to be allegorical, has never been satisfactorily explained."[45] Shelley then offers an interpretation in which the fire

---

43   Ibid. p.79.
44   Ibid. p. 113-114.
45   Ibid. p. 162.

stolen by Prometheus is specifically culinary, and the vulture sent to devour his entrails is symbolic of disease, crediting that decoding to "Mr. Newton's Defence of Vegetable Regimen," and including a brief supportive quote.

* * * *

The latter reference is to John Frank Newton's *The Return to Nature; or A Defence of the Vegetable Regimen*, published in 1811. Shelley had met Newton in 1812, having been introduced to him by William Godwin's son. The version of the story of Prometheus contained in Newton's book begins with an account of Francis Bacon's explanation of the myth, but then proceeds to offer a variant:

"I beg permission of the reader to venture with great humility my own conception of the story of Prometheus, who, it is pretty generally admitted, represents the human race. Making allowance for such transposition of the events of the allegory as time might produce…the drift of the fable appears to be this: Man at his creation was endowed with the gift of perpetual youth; that is, he was not formed to be a sickly suffering creature as we now see him, but to enjoy health, and to sink by slow degrees into the bosom of the parent earth without disease or pain. Prometheus first taught the use of animal food, and of fire with which to render it more digestible and pleasing to the taste…. Thirst, the necessary concomitant of a flesh diet, ensued…and man forfeited the inestimable gift of health which he had received from heaven: he became diseased…"[46]

Newton goes on to recruit Pliny to support this interpretation, translating the relevant passages as "Pyrodes first struck fire from a flint, Prometheus first preserved it in a stick," and "Hyperbius, the son of Mars, first killed an animal, Prometheus first slew an ox." He adds:

"By these passages we become acquainted with two particulars not unimportant in the present discussion; first, the sense in which the theft of fire from the sun's chariot by Prometheus was understood according to the instruction of Pliny's time; and secondly, that it was the same man, Prometheus, who first preserved it for

---

46   John Frank Newton. *The Return to Nature; or, A Defence of the Vegetable Regimen*. London: Cadell & Davies, 1811. pp 8-9.

human uses, and who likewise set an example of slaughtering an ox....

"It may be remarked that the Greeks, who seem to have had a pretty inordinate and superstitious belief in the efficacy of medicine, included Prometheus among the claimants to what they conceived to be the honour of that invention....

"Many ancient writers look with no favorable eye on the great change which Prometheus achieved in the condition of mankind... Hesiod too acquaints us, that before the time of Prometheus, mankind was exempt from all sufferings...."[47]

Newton then goes on to cite the example, also borrowed by Shelley, of the desirability of the Earth's axis being perpendicular to the plane of the ecliptic, except that instead of placing the supposed Age of Plenty associated with that modification in the future, where Shelley locates it, he places it in the distant past. Newton goes on to recruit far more elaborate support for this thesis than the brief argument that Shelley borrowed, citing observations by Michael Adams in the pioneering scientific journal *The Philosophical Magazine*, and also quoting Dryden and Swift. He does not give a full reference to the Adams article, but it must be "Some account of a journey to the frozen sea, and of the discovery of the remains of a mammoth, Translated from the French," in volume 29, issue 114 (1807). Adams was a Scottish botanist then attached to the Russian Academy of Science.

The long essay Newton then presents, in the attempt to prove that humans are really adapted for a vegetarian diet rather than meat-eating, similarly mingles scientific references with literary and Classical ones, in a remarkable syncresis. In this account—ultimately derived from the theories of John Frank Newton's physician, William Lambe, the pioneer of veganism—all disease is explained by carnivorism, and all evil is represented as disease. As a general theory of disease, the one proposed by William Lambe is certainly no better than Erasmus Darwin's, but also no worse, and the method of popularization chosen by John Frank Newton and subsequently appropriated by Shelley is very similar to the one adopted by Darwin.

Prometheus, as the symbolic figurehead of carnivorism, becomes a satanic figure in Newton's decoding. It is not surprising

47   Ibid. pp.11-13.

that Shelley did not want that particular part of *Queen Mab* reprinted, not merely because it asserts dubious dietary opinions that he probably recanted, but because, by 1821, he had produced his own highly distinctive reinterpretation of the myth of Prometheus, which similarly makes him satanic, but in a much more complimentary fashion.

* * * *

Given that Shelley and his widow both undertook to suppress the greater part of *Queen Mab*, it ought perhaps to be admitted that it does little to add to his reputation as a poet, and might be held liable to detract from it, but it is nevertheless highly significant from the viewpoint of the present history, not only in locating Shelley more precisely within the tradition of "scientific romance," but in prompting him to produce his own reinterpretation of the myth of Prometheus.

The only part of the *Prometheia* popularly attributed to Aeschylus that survives intact is *Prometheus Bound*, although the story of the part that follows it, *Prometheus Liberated* or *Prometheus Unbound*, is known from second-hand descriptions. The third part, *Prometheus the Fire-Bringer*, remains stubbornly mysterious, to the extent that scholars have never been entirely certain whether it is the first part of the trilogy, referring to the theft of fire preceding the binding, or the final phase of the story, dealing with Prometheus' subsequent education of humankind in the arts, with or without the story of Pandora's Box. The latter seems more likely.

Shelley's own version of *Prometheus Unbound*, published in 1820, does not follow the plot of that section of the original *Prometheia*, nor does its recapitulation of the events that led to Prometheus being bound correspond exactly to the account in the original *Prometheus Bound*. We can, therefore, be reasonably certain that its account of events following the Titan's release bears no resemblance to the vanished *Prometheus the Fire-Bringer*, although its inclusion does mean that Shelley's poem sketches out an entire three-part *Prometheia* rather than merely the fragment suggested by its title. Significantly, however, the project had an immediate predecessor of its own, in that Shelley began to write it in 1818, the year of publication of Mary's *Frankenstein; or, The Modern Prometheus*, which also employs the myth as an allegorical bedrock, and, in that respect, can also be considered a transfiguration in the chain of manifest influences that began with Francis Bacon and reached the Shelleys via John Frank Newton.

Although *Frankenstein* is undoubtedly Mary's work, and was not, as some critics suspected at the time, written by Percy, there is also no doubt that Percy made a substantial contribution to it while it was in progress. Although there is no record of their verbal discussions, some of Percy's annotations of Mary's drafts survive, and it would, in any case, be ludicrous to imagine that she did not consult with him during the process of its composition; her own subsequent statements freely acknowledged that it was a brainchild with two parents, even though the labor was hers. There is, therefore, good reason to give it some consideration as an intermediate between *The Return to Nature* and *Prometheus Unbound*. It is, of course, many other things as well as that, but that aspect of its identity might help to cast some light on its puzzling features.

Frankenstein is one of those literary characters whose names have entered common parlance; everyone recognizes the name and uses it casually. The recognition and the usage are often slightly uncertain—most people know the name from the film versions, which are significantly different from the book, and some people have to be reminded that Frankenstein is the name of the scientist, not the "monster" that the scientist made—but that uncertainty is not entirely inappropriate to a work whose implication and significance are rather problematic. As Percy Shelley said of the story of the ancient Prometheus, although *Frankenstein* is generally accepted to be allegorical, it is arguable that it has never been satisfactorily explained.

The circumstances of *Frankenstein*'s genesis are also very familiar, thanks to the second preface that Mary added to the revised edition of the novel published in 1831. The stormy night in 1816, on which Lord Byron, the newly-married Shelleys, Mary's stepsister Claire Clairmont, and Byron's doctor John Polidori amused themselves at the Villa Diodati on the shore of Lake Geneva by reading tales from a volume entitled *Fantasmagoriana*, which consisted of horror stories translated from German into French, has acquired a legendary status of its own. The participants in the *soirée* agreed that each of them would write a horrific tale of his or her own, although Polidori was the only one apart from Mary to produce anything substantial, and that was eventually published under circumstances that caused considerable embarrassment to him—and even more to Byron, to whom the anonymously-published work in question, *The Vampyre* (1819), was at first falsely attributed by rumor.

Any attempt to analyze the contents of *Frankenstein* must, however, also take into account the events of Mary's life leading up to that night, beginning with the death of her mother, Mary Wollstonecraft, in giving birth to her. That death did not prevent Mary from becoming intimately acquainted with her mother's works, and she was proud in later life to sign herself Mary Wollstonecraft Shelley, although the first edition of *Frankenstein* was issued anonymously. She detested the stepmother she acquired in 1801, Mary Jane Clairmont, although the marriage saved the family from virtual destitution, at least temporarily—Godwin soon went heavily into debt again, trying to run a publishing company specializing in children's books, and was only saved from debtor's prison by virtue of the charity of his friends.

Mary was brought up by her father in accordance with her mother's principles, and encouraged to read very freely. She undoubtedly read Erasmus Darwin's works and many other early exercises in the popularization of science, including Jane Marcet's best-selling *Conversations on Chemistry, Intended More Especially for the Female Sex* (1806) and Maria Edgeworth's didactic novels. She attended lectures at the recently-founded Royal Institution with her father and with Shelley, presumably hearing both Humphry Davy and his protégé Michael Faraday. She must also have read her father's two moralistic Gothic novels, including *St. Leon* (1799), whose eponymous protagonist comes into possession of the alchemists' philosopher's stone, but is led by his acquisition into misery and alienation. We can only speculate as to whether or not she read *Flim-Flams!*, but if she did, its account of the homunculus, the "miserable fruit of experimental philosophy," might well have made an impression on her.

Mary was at school in Scotland when Shelley first became acquainted with her father, but as soon as she returned to London he fell madly in love with her; she was sixteen when they eloped (Harriet Westbrook had been the same age when Shelley had eloped with her) and Shelley naturally continued her education; they read aloud to one another as they made their way across France to Switzerland, and doubtless continued the habit when they were forced by destitution to return to England. Mary was pregnant by then, but the child, born premature, died. They returned to Switzerland in 1816 at the instigation of Claire Clairmont, who was in love with Byron and used the Shelleys as bait to lure him to Geneva.

Part of the significance of the story's original inspiration to an understanding of *Frankenstein* is that its author was charged from the very beginning with the task of writing a horror story. The particular horror story she settled on grew from a fragment of an actual nightmare she experienced soon afterwards. If Mary's claim in the 1931 preface is to be believed—and there seems no reason to doubt it in essence, although the original experience might well have been embellished in memory to take on some of the features of its transformed version, and the subsequent commentary is definitely a later superimposition of the waking mind—that nightmare displayed to her a creator's first and direly uncomfortable confrontation with his creation:

"I saw—with shut eyes, but acute mental vision—I saw the pale student of the unhallowed arts kneeling beside the thing he had put together. I saw the hideous phantasm of a man stretched out, and then, on the working of some powerful engine, show signs of life, and stir with an uneasy, half-vital motion...."[48]

Thus, Mary did not begin the work of ideative elaboration with the initial premise of her story, but with its crucial image. The beginning and the end of the story are both extrapolations of that single instant, the one constructed in order to explain how it came about and the other to follow it to its implicit conclusion. Both are consistent with that visionary moment, but it is arguable they are not really consistent with one another, at least in the way that they would have been had the author extrapolated an ending from the apparent premises contained in the beginning. Because the fact that the story was to be horrific was accepted as an axiom, much of what was eventually presented as the logic of the story—the "explanation" of how the nightmare confrontation came to take place—was formed by way of ideative apology, not as a set of

---

48   "Preface to the Last London Edition." Mary Shelley. *Frankenstein; or, The Modern Prometheus*. 1869. p. 11.

propositions established from scratch in order to be examined on their own merits.

Given all this, it is not entirely surprising that the logical patchwork leading to the true point of origination is a trifle awkward. Had the author actually started to make up a story about a "modern Prometheus" she might have come up with something very different; that first awakening of a homunculus activated by scientific means might conceivably have been a joyous and triumphant affair, full of Darwinian happiness of life, had its horrific nature not been already determined by the *raison d'être* of the whole exercise. On the other hand, being acquainted via her husband with John Frank Newton's Prometheus, and hence with Francis Bacon's Prometheus, it is perhaps not surprising that she similarly characterized her own as a bungler, whose efforts were always going to lead to disaster. Even so, the preface to the first edition, generally believed to have been written by Percy on his wife's behalf, treads a delicate argumentative line and introduces a cautionary note with regard to Frankenstein's character: "The opinions which naturally spring from the character and situation of the hero are by no means to be conceived as existing always in my own conviction; nor is any inference justly to be drawn from the following pages as prejudicing any philosophical doctrine of whatever kind."[49]

* * * *

The text of *Frankenstein* begins with a series of letters written by the explorer Robert Walton, who has been trying to navigate his ship through the Arctic ice in the hope of finding a warm continent beyond it, akin to the legendary Hyperborea, and perhaps being able to "solve the problem of magnetism" by discovering the magnetic north pole. That might well seems like a fool's errand today, but its foolishness was by no means certain in 1818. Thus, although Walton's situation is clearly symbolic—his entrapment in the ice implies that his ambitions have unfortunately alienated him from the warmth of human companionship—it cannot be taken for granted that Mary Shelley saw him as a lunatic who should have known better.

Victor Frankenstein's story, as regretfully told to Walton, is essentially that of a man who once "had everything" but lost it

---

49   "Preface" in ibid. p.6.

through desiring even more. The "everything" that he had included material goods, but its most precious aspects were friendship and love, embodied in his relationships with his friend Henry Clerval (an enthusiastic fan of Amadis de Gaul) and his cousin Elizabeth. Frankenstein explains that his ambitions had first become further inflated by the grandiose dreams of Cornelius Agrippa—in spite of his father's dismissal of such work as "sad trash"—supplemented by the works of Albertus Magnus and Paracelsus. His discovery of the mysteries of electricity, however, set him on a new path, including a replication of Benjamin Franklin's famous experiment in attracting lighting with a key tied to a kite-string; chemistry then came to seem tedious to him, although he still read natural history, from Pliny to Buffon, with delight.

One of the most significant passages in the novel, from the point of view of its relationship with the science of the day, is the one dealing with Frankenstein's contrasted reaction to two of the teachers he encounters when he goes to study at the university of Ingolstadt: Krempe and Waldman. Krempe, the professor of natural history, is short, thickset and ugly, and the thrust of his science is negative; he dismisses all of Frankenstein's earlier reading as a complete waste of time. The chemistry professor Waldman, however, is much more prepossessing in person, and his ideas are much more seductive. Although he admits that the ancient masters who fascinate Frankenstein produced nothing in spite of promising so much, he argues that their modern successors, while promising far less, have actually achieved far more.

"They ascend into the heavens;" Waldman says "they have discovered how the blood circulates, and the nature of the air we breathe. They have acquired new and almost unlimited powers; they can command the thunders of heaven, mimic the earthquake, and even mock the invisible world with its own shadows."[50]

Waldman is much more sympathetic to Frankenstein's old favorites, as significant pioneers of modern science, and reignites all his enthusiasm, enabling him to obtain valuable instruction from Krempe as well as instruction and inspiration from his own lectures. Significantly, though, it is Krempe rather than Waldman who subsequently forms the higher opinion of Frankenstein's abilities, once the latter has become a true disciple of science. Frankenstein

50   Ibid. p.38.

sums up his own conversion by observing that: "None but those who have experienced them can conceive of the enticements of Science. In other studies you go as far as others have gone before you, and there is nothing more to know; but in a scientific pursuit there is continual food for discovery and wonder."[51]

Frankenstein becomes obsessed by such studies, but his first achievements are modest improvements in instrumentation, which win him admiration from specialists but are incapable of impressing anyone else. Nursing greater ambitions, he turns his attention to the phenomenon of life, initially by studying the phenomena of death and decay—and by that route, although the text does not map his progress in detail, he eventually discovers the secret of "bestowing animation upon lifeless matter." After some hesitation, he begins work on an experimental subject: a homunculus compounded out of parts appropriated from corpses. Finding the smallness of some parts inconvenient, he deliberately selects large ones, thus gradually compounding a giant eight feet tall. This arduous task monopolizes his time and attention for a considerable interval, separating him from those he loves: something he regrets and bitterly laments by the time he tells his tale to Walton.

Frankenstein's social and intellectual isolation makes him ill, but he persists, and his arduous task reaches a frightful climax when the work is finally complete. The "creature" that he has made has only to open a "dull yellow eye" for Frankenstein to be suddenly overcome by repulsion at what he has wrought, and to flee in horror. When he returns, however, it is to find Clerval waiting for him, having come to bring him back to his old life; the creature has gone. Clerval nurses Frankenstein back to health, never knowing, in spite of the patient's ravings, what the "monster" is that is haunting his hallucinations. Frankenstein, gladly reverting to type, renews his relationships with Elizabeth and his family, and resumes his studies, in spite of a new nervousness in confronting his professors.

All seems well until Frankenstein's father writes to tell him that his young brother has been murdered. Frankenstein immediately becomes afraid that his creature is the murderer, but an innocent servant has been framed for the crime, and it is not until he confronts the creature again that his suspicions are confirmed. The

---

51   Ibid. p.39.

creature then explains that he has craved the kind of loving fellowship that has provided a safe psychological refuge for the sick scientist, but that it has been cruelly denied to him. Having been rejected by his creator at the moment of his first awakening, he was subsequently reviled by everyone who caught sight of him; even his desperate attempt to make a home with a blind man came to nothing. It was, the creature claims, the madness born of this rejection that led him to kidnap a child, and the revelation that the child was the brother of his creator that drove him to murderous frenzy. In consequence of all this, the creature demands that a companion be made for him, given that he is too repulsive to be accepted into the community of men.

Frankenstein initially agrees to this request, and sets out to accomplish it on a remote islet in the Orkneys, but he is no longer insulated by obsession, and becomes terrified by the thought that he might engender an entire race of monsters, whose co-existence with mankind will be—to say the least—problematic; this prospect causes him to abandon the work. No immediate repercussions ensue, but the creature eventually sets out to exact his revenge, not upon Frankenstein himself but upon his friends and loved ones. First Clerval is murdered—Frankenstein is charged with the crime but eventually acquitted—and then Elizabeth, on the night of her marriage. Isolated once again by these deprivations, Frankenstein has little difficulty recovering the motive force of obsession; this time, however, his determination is to rid the world of his creation.

All of this is mere hearsay, so far as Robert Walton is concerned, and seems too fantastic to be believable, at first. Frankenstein explains to Walton that the consequent pursuit of the monster has led him into the Arctic wastes; he looks to Walton for aid, but when he learns that his host has already turned back from his own quest, and is now heading out of the ice-field, he realizes that he cannot carry through his purpose. He gives up and dies. The final confrontation with the creature is left to Walton, and might conceivably be interpreted as one more hallucination in a long series, obtained by suggestive contagion. At any rate, Walton finds Frankenstein's adversary every bit as fearful as Frankenstein had led him to expect—but also confused, agonized and contrite.

One of the few books that the creature has had the opportunity to read since he learned the uses of language by secretly observing a family at work and play is Goethe's proto-Romantic classic *The Sorrows of Young Werther* (1774), which waxes lyrical about the propriety of suicide as a solution for those bereft of any meaningful connection with their fellows, and it is hardly surprising that the creature chooses self annihilation himself, by continuing into the wilderness of the Arctic ice. "I am content to suffer alone, while my sufferings shall endure," the creature says, regretfully, "when I die, I am well satisfied that abhorrence and opprobrium should load my memory."[52] His author could not possibly have guessed how prophetic those words would prove to be.

* * * *

As a reinterpretation of the Prometheus myth, *Frankenstein* is obviously very different from Francis Bacon's, John Frank Newton's or Percy Shelley's, but much of the difference follows naturally from the fact that its eponymous character is advertised as a *modern* Prometheus. Like Bacon's Prometheus, Frankenstein is an incompetent; the "clay" into which he imparts the "divine fire" of life is corrupt. In his world, however, there is no Zeus or Jupiter to punish him, whether for his crime of theft or for his subsequent efforts to make good his fault by educating his faulty creation in the technological uses of ordinary fire. Indeed, Frankenstein brings about his own punishment precisely by failing to make good his fault. Instead of accepting responsibility for his creature's education, he rejects him, and, by virtue of his carelessness in the creation, has already condemned the creature to be rejected everywhere else. The modern Prometheus thus manufactures his own "eagle" to tear out his guts, by murdering those he loves; nor can he free himself from that irredeemable binding.

Having set out from the start to write a horror story, Mary's choice of that version of the Prometheus story is entirely appropriate, if not inevitable, but it is worth noting that the creature's final lament indicates a different one, which might have unfolded had Frankenstein not botched his work, or even if he had then tried harder to make amends for his mistake. Had Frankenstein contrived a creature acceptable in the eyes of his fellows, or had he even accepted him as a brother or a friend in spite of having made him a monster, things might have worked out very differently.

52   Ibid. p.175.

Then, the mysterious method of animation discovered by Frankenstein might not have had to be thrown away; it might, instead, have been used to free humankind from the threat of death, to change the parameters of human existence, and perhaps to usher in a new Golden Age, with or without the adjustment of the Earth's axis.

That alternative Promethean tale could not possibly have been as successful as *Frankenstein*, partly because—as Edmund Burke had pointed out—terror is a more powerful emotion than love, and the sublime a more forceful esthetic response than beauty, but partly, too, because it would have seemed far more blasphemous. Although *Frankenstein* is atheistic in the sense of excluding Zeus/Jupiter from the Prometheus story, it nevertheless retains a certain tacit piety with respect to the Christian God. Indeed, one of the most popular allegorical interpretations of the text sees Frankenstein as a victim of hubris, struck down by vengeful fate for daring to usurp the godly privilege of creation. That interpretation has been largely replaced in modern academic discourse by feminist variants that see Frankenstein attempting to usurp the female prerogative of birth, and struck down by the metaphorical fury of woman scorned, but that is probably no better—and no worse, if one takes the view that the whole point of the exercise is that the myth is mere raw material, open to interpretation and reinterpretation however one likes.

At any rate, it was the horror of *Frankenstein* that was communicated to its immediate readers, and to generations of readers to come—not to mention movie-goers, television viewers, comic-book readers and all the other twentieth-century consumers of modern myths—and understandably so, given the awesome force of the text and the perfect sublimity of its theme. Along with that communication, however, came the notion that scientific ambition and scientific method themselves were tainted, along with their individual employer, as something ugly and dangerous.

That was neither a new implication nor, so far as many recipients of the message were concerned, an unwelcome one. The editors of the *Anti-Jacobin* would doubtless have been delighted by it, although Erasmus Darwin would probably have wept, especially in view of his citation in support of the plausibility of the thesis in the very first line of the Preface. That interpretation too is fair play, if the game is a free-for-all, but it was surely not what either of the Shelleys intended.

Isaac Asimov, one of the staunchest advocates of the virtues of science and technology to be recruited to the burgeoning American genre of science fiction, complained bitterly about the effects of the Frankenstein myth on twentieth-century attitudes to science, identifying a "Frankenstein complex" that he felt obliged, in his own work, to fight with all the allegorical armaments at his disposal, like a true Amadis de Gaul of science fiction.[53] He was absolutely right in his diagnosis, but his oppositional quest inevitably seemed to the unsympathetic to be merely Quixotic.

* * * *

Perhaps unfortunately, but understandably, Percy Shelley's response to the Modern Prometheus of *Frankenstein* was not to produce the alternative Modern Prometheus suggested by the monster's lament, but rather to produce a new Ancient Prometheus, still bound in God-cursed world, but who would face the tyrannical oppression of that world heroically, and by his opposition, bring it to an end.

In the plot of the original *Prometheia*, according to secondhand reports, Prometheus eventually buys his freedom from Zeus by betraying the secret of which he claims in *Prometheus Bound* to have become the unlikely custodian. He knows, thanks to a prophetic gift, that if Zeus marries Thetis, as intended, the marriage will produce a child who will bring him down. By releasing this information to Zeus in the original *Prometheus Unbound*, Prometheus enables the latter to avoid that fate, and in exchange, Zeus permits Heracles to set him free—although, in the third part of the trilogy, if it really is the third part that is missing, Zeus would presumably have taken exception to Prometheus' subsequent use of his freedom and sent Pandora to afflict humankind by way of further punishment.

Shelley's alternative Prometheus, in his *Prometheus Unbound*, does not capitulate with his divine torturer. Instead, he holds his tongue until the prophecy is fulfilled, waiting for the eventual release that is bound to come when Jupiter is brought down by the

---

[53] Isaac Asimov. Introduction to *The Rest of the Robots*. Garden City, NY: Doubleday, 1964. p.xiii.

child that remained unborn in the Classical version, Demogorgon. When that has come to pass, worn out by his exceedingly long ordeal, Shelley's Prometheus then retires quietly to a cave, in order to enjoy the fellowship of the loving Asia and her fellow Oceanides, Panthea and Ione, who have kept him company throughout the torment of his terrible binding, offering him moral support and consolation.

Prometheus does not lend humankind any further active educative support, but be does not have to, because the Spirit of the Earth, freed from divine tyranny, takes on the task of her own regeneration, restoring—or perhaps creating for the first time—a Golden Age, initially symbolized by the restoration of life to the Moon. Prometheus is, however, represented in the poem—in a long speech by Asia summarizing his achievements before his binding—as already being the parent of human science, including herbal medicine, love, metallurgy and "speech" (i.e., poetry):

> *Prometheus saw, and waked the legioned hopes*
> *Which sleep within folded Elysian flowers,*
> *Nepenthe, Moly, Amaranth, fadeless blooms,*
> *That they might hide with thin and rainbow wings*
> *The shape of Death; and Love he sent to bind*
> *The disunited tendrils of that vine*
> *Which bears the wine of life, the human heart;*
> *And he tamed fire which, like some beast of prey,*
> *Most terrible but lovely, played beneath*
> *The frown of man; and tortured to his will*
> *Iron and gold, the slaves and signs of power,*
> *And gems and poisons, and all subtlest forms*
> *Hidden beneath the mountains and the waves.*
> *He gave man speech, and speech created thought,*
> *Which is the measure of the universe;*
> *And Science struck the thrones of earth and heaven,*
> *Which shook but fell not; and the harmonious mind*
> *Poured itself forth in all-prophetic song....*[54]

All of that bounty, however, has been spoiled by God (this phase of the poem does not bother with euphemism) and cannot resume

---

54   Shelley (*op. cit.* Moxon, 1847) pp.318-319.

its proper effect until God is brought down—which Demogorgon, who hears Asia's speech, undertakes to do, thus completing an apocalyptic liberation at a stroke. The liberation is question seems magical, although it is not—but the manner of the triumphant flourish enables the roles played therein by science, technology, medicine, and even by "speech" and love, to be easily overlooked.

Had *Prometheus Unbound* been annotated in the fashion of the full version of *Queen Mab*, that part of its implication would probably have been much clearer, especially if Shelley had taken the trouble to explain his cosmological imagery and the manner of the moon's transformation into a living world, but it was not. All it has by way of supplementation is a preface provided by the author, in which he argues that his Prometheus is a better hero than Milton's Satan, because he does not have Satan's faults, and a note provided by Mary, alleging that Shelley had planned to write "prose metaphysical essays on the nature of Man, which would have served to explain much of what is obscure in his poetry"[55] but had been prevented from doing so by his premature death.

Because of this lack of authorial commentary, it is perfectly possible to read *Prometheus Unbound* without quite realizing that it is an item of futuristic fiction, supposing that the apocalypse it describes takes place in some sort of "alternative mythological past." Unlike *Queen Mab*, the poem does not insist that what it is presenting, in allegorical terms, is a vision of the liberation of contemporary humankind from Godly tyranny, nor does it give Prometheus' long binding a chronological framework that would allow Demogorgon's triumph to be located in the nineteenth century, and the greening of the moon to take place some time thereafter. It *is*, however, a futuristic fantasy, which looks forward, exactly as *Queen Mab* had, to the possible establishment of an actual paradise on, and at least slightly beyond, Earth.

The cave to which Prometheus and his Oceanides retreat is, in essence, the depository of all ancient myth, retired from active involvement with the world in order to leave human science and speech a disenchanted world in which to work—a symbolism grasped by later British Romantic fantasists who took up that particular motif, in such poignant fantasies as John Sterling's "Cydon" (1829) and Richard Garnett's "The Twilight of the Gods" (1888),

55   Ibid. p.372.

although the point might have been missed by John Edmund Reade, whose derivative drama *A Record of the Pyramids* (1842) shifts Prometheus' cave to ancient Egypt and has him emerge therefrom to pit him against Pharaonic rather than Jovian oppression.

In the context of futuristic fantasies, *Queen Mab* and *Prometheus Unbound* are both highly distinctive, their euchronian philosophy going far beyond the sedate exercises that followed more narrowly in the footsteps of Louis-Sébastien Mercier's pioneering endeavor, but they do help to reflect one aspect of a significant shift in the nineteenth-century imagery of the future, which will be discussed in more detail in the next section.

* * * *

Perhaps, in other circumstances, Mary Shelley could have produced a more detailed annotation of "Prometheus Unbound" herself, or at least continued the Prometheian project that she and her husband had begun together, and of which it formed a part. That was not possible, however, in view of the precarious social and economic circumstances in which she found herself after Percy's death, supported in a rather meager fashion by Shelley's father, Sir Timothy Shelley, and unable any longer to resist the pressures of oppressive opinion with the same Promethean heroism that Percy had barely been able to maintain himself. Mary never wrote anything else as remotely venturesome or controversial as *Frankenstein*, and she promoted the legacy of her husband's work at the expense of doing everything possible to take the sting out his atheism and his radicalism. Like Victor Frankenstein, she had been punished by having her metaphorical heart ripped out, without even having committed any moral failure potentially deserving of it, but merely by virtue of the cruelty of hazard.

Mary Shelley did go on to write an apocalyptic fantasy of her own, in *The Last Man* (1826), but it is the complete opposite of the kind of hopeful apocalypse described in *Prometheus Unbound*, being a description of the total destruction of human society by a great plague—which seems to be an allegorical transformation of her own experiences, culminating in the devastation of Shelley's death and the effective end of her personal world. Her historical novelette "The Mortal Immortal" (1834) is an account of a student of Cornelius Agrippa who drinks an elixir of life, but finds, like

William Godwin's Reginald de St. Leon, that its effects are utterly spoiled by the fact that his condition alienates him from his fellows and denies him the reward of lasting love. Among the manuscripts she left unpublished at her death in 1851 was the fragmentary "Valerius: The Re-animated Roman" (published 1976), in which an ancient Roman mysteriously alive in the nineteenth century is similarly embittered, and probably similarly immune to the possibility of redemption by love.

The legacy of *Frankenstein* of which Isaac Asimov was later to complain did not show up very rapidly, in spite of the continuing reprinting of the text. The novel does not seem to have been much imitated during the fifty years after its publication, or even significantly echoed in other allegories of a similar stripe. The one novel often linked to it in modern histories, *The Mummy! A Tale of the Twenty-Second Century* (1827) is bracketed with it as much because it was also produced by a surprisingly young woman as because of the similarities of its theme. Its author was Jane Webb, born in 1807, who subsequently became Mrs. Loudon when she married a landscape gardener, and dedicated most of her subsequent literary efforts to endeavors in the horticultural vein of Erasmus Darwin's work rather than his bolder scientific speculations.

Like *Frankenstein*, *The Mummy!* features the reanimation of the dead, apparently by means of electricity, applied to the mummy of Cheops—discovered in the great pyramid—rather than a patchwork of corpse-parts. Like Victor Frankenstein, too, Edric Montague, the user of the method, collapses in terror when he sees the result of his action and loses track of his patient, but the similarity does not extend much further than that. Although an object of dread to the characters in the plot, the mummy turns out to be innocuous, save to the wickedly ambitious, whom he tempts to defeat, and the story is nowadays more interesting by virtue of its notions of technological advancement and its earnest feminism than by virtue of any allegorical interpretation. Its depictions of advanced steam engines and dirigible balloons are understandably primitive, but by no means inept or unadventurous by the standards of the day, and are broadly representative of the futuristic expectations of the time with respect to those manifestly-evolving technologies—ideas that Jane Webb might well have acquired from her one-time mentor, the painter and technological enthusiast John Martin.

A more obvious partner for *Frankenstein* from a modern viewpoint, even before the association was cemented by cinematic adaptations that gathered both stories into the genre of "monster movies," is Robert Louis Stevenson's *Strange Case of Dr. Jekyll and Mr. Hyde* (1886), which is similarly allegorical and was also written around an image experienced in a nightmare. Although the publication of the two works was separated by more than half a century, it was immediately possible to link them via the interpretation of *Frankenstein* that represented it as an account of punishment for hubris, damning science itself along with its practitioner and his project.

It is not at all certain that that is the correct way to decode the allegory of Jekyll and Hyde, but if the two novels are bracketed, the parallels to be drawn between the two ambitious scientists and their respective *doppelgängers* become very seductive. The circumstance of the well-intentioned but naïve Dr. Jekyll not merely making a monster, but making a monster out of himself, added a highly effective extra twist to one decoding of the parable contained in *Frankenstein*, and might well have assisted in making that decoding the dominant one, thus paving the way for it to become the stereotype of an entire subgenre of horror fiction propped up by pseudoscientific improvisations.

The timing of the publication of Stevenson's novel could hardly have been better (or worse, from the Asimovian viewpoint) with respect to the imminent advent of generic scientific romance and the eventual flourishing of science fiction; it provided a very striking model for writers in either genre to copy, all the more powerful because *Frankenstein* was still in print and still being widely read, having already attained classic status. Indeed, *Dr. Jekyll and Mr. Hyde* rapidly produced imitations in the early days of generic scientific romance, one of the most striking being J. Maclaren Cobban's *Master of His Fate* (1890), whose unlucky anti-hero is obliged to maintain his existence and apparent youth by leeching the life-force of others whenever he reverts to monstrous decrepitude. *The New Faust* (1896) by Alfred Smythe adds an extra twist to a similar variant of the theme, also featuring echoes of Oscar Wilde's *The Picture of Dorian Gray* (1891). By that time, the "Frankenstein complex" identified by Isaac Asimov had taken root in literary psychology, and it was Mary Shelley's bungling modern

Prometheus, rather than Percy Shelley's long-suffering satanic hero, that was to loom symbolically over scientific romance and science fiction alike.

4. THE PROSPECT OF THE FUTURE

Among the friends to whom Percy Shelley sent a copy of *Queen Mab* when he first had it printed was Thomas Love Peacock, whom he had met in 1812, shortly after the latter had published a poem entitled "The Philosophy of Melancholy." Although the two had little in common in terms of their background and outlook they soon became fast friends and were often in one another's company during and immediately after Shelley's first marriage, when Peacock lent the guilt-stricken poet steadfast moral support in spite of feeling sorry for poor Harriet.

Peacock must have been struck by the version of the story of Prometheus of reproduced in the final note of *Queen Mab*, if the two had not discussed the matter previously, and by Shelley's comments on the realignment of the world's axis as paradisal adjustment, because he incorporated both of them into his own novel *Headlong Hall* (1816), which appeared five years before William Clark's unauthorized version of *Queen Mab*. It could not have been obvious to Peacock's readers at the time, but much of the argument in *Headlong Hall* regarding the prospects of the future is a direct response to the argument and imagery of *Queen Mab*, although it is couched in a very different narrative framework.

Headlong Hall is a deft and witty comedy. It adopts the conversational strategy of Fontenelle's *Entretiens*, and takes it to a new extreme, embedding the relevant conversations in an account of an English country house party, in which caricaturish characters clown around while going through the social rituals appropriate to such gatherings, forming various romantic relationships that eventually round the story off with four weddings. Running through the frivolity, however, there is a continuing thread of debate regarding the way the world is going, led by the first guests to be introduced on their way to the party, traveling in the Holyhead mail coach: "Mr. Foster, the perfectibilian" and "Mr. Escot, the deteriorationist." The author obligingly adds footnotes deriving both names from the Greek, the former signifying "one who watches over and guards the light" and the latter "one who is looking on the dark side of the question."

Mr. Foster employs the coach-trip as "an occasion to panegyrize the vehicle" and to hold forth "with great energy on the subject of railways, canals and tunnels, manufactures and machinery," claiming that "everything we look on attests the progress of mankind in all the arts of life, and demonstrates their gradual advancement towards a state of unlimited perfection."[56]

Mr. Escot, unsurprisingly, disagrees completely. "These improvements, as you call them," he opines, "appear to me only so many links in the great chain of corruption, which will soon fetter the whole human race in irreparable slavery and incurable wretchedness; your improvements proceed in a simple ratio, while the fictitious wants and unnatural appetites they engender proceed in a compound one; and thus one generation acquires fifty wants, and fifty means of supplying them are invented, which each in its turn engenders two new ones; so that the next generation has an hundred, the next two hundred, the next four hundred, till every human being becomes such a helpless compound of perverted inclinations, that he is altogether at the mercy of external circumstances, loses all independence and singleness of nature, and degenerates so rapidly from the primitive dignity of his sylvan origin, that it is scarcely possible to indulge in any other expectation, than that the whole species must at length be exterminated by its own imbecility and vileness."[57]

An attempt by "Mr. Jenkinson the status-quoite" to arbitrate in this dispute inevitably fails to heal the breach, and the argument runs on. It is Escot who shares the opinions of William Lambe and John Frank Newton, offering exactly the same interpretation of the myth of Prometheus as Newton, but it is Foster who quotes Shelley's argument regarding the future correction of inclination of the Earth's axis as a means to ensuring the perfection of humankind.

Escot adds his own twist to Newton's argument, contending that ever since fire was applied for culinary purposes, humans have been diminishing in stature. Foster disagrees, countering with the observation that both Aeschylus and Virgil assert the

---

56   [Thomas Love Peacock]. *Headlong Hall*. London: Hookham, 1816. pp.7-8.
57   ibid. pp.8-9.

indispensability of fire in giving birth to the technical arts, whose progress "will finally conduct every individual of the race to the pure philosophic pinnacle of pure and perfect felicity."[58] Foster is a meat-eater, contending that animal food "acts on the mind as manure does on flowers." When Foster argues that the modern English sailor is incontestably superior to ancient Greek seamen, however, Escot is quick to draw a distinction between moral and scientific perfectibility. When the former argues that virtue is in proportion of enlightenment, so that increases in knowledge inevitably produced increases in virtue, the latter makes a long speech arguing the contrary case, arguing that the advancement of knowledge is confined to the few, who take advantage of it to degrade the many. Following Jean-Jacques Rousseau, Escot argues for the moral superiority of the pre-civilized:

"Give me the wild man of the woods; the original, unthinking, unscientific, unlogical savage: in him there is at least some good; but in a civilized, sophisticated, cold-blooded, mechanical, calculating slave of Mammon and the world, there is none—absolutely none."[59]

There is a sense in which both sides of this debate follow on from *Queen Mab*. While Escot echoes Shelley's account of the tribulations of the past, summing up the evils inflicted by political, economic and religious oppression, in Rousseauesque terms, as the ills of civilization, Foster echoes Shelley's optimistic account of the future arrival of a paradisal climacteric. The essential bone of their contention is whether the former condition can possibly give way to the latter.

In spite of his initial pretence of even-handedness, Peacock clearly exhibits more sympathy with Escot than with Foster. He was later to extend Escot's argument about the wild man of the woods in a more flamboyant fashion when he introduced a thoroughly noble "wild man of the woods" in his next modified conversation-piece, *Melincourt* (1817), in the speechless but cultured and heroic anthropoid ape Sir Orang Haut-ton, whose characterization is elaborately shored up with abundant supportive quotes from authorities such as Linnaeus, Rousseau and Lord Monboddo. In the meantime, however, it becomes increasingly obvious in *Headlong*

---

58   Ibid. p.17.
59   Ibid. p.45.

Hall that Escot is the hero of the novel, even though he brutally offends several of his fellow guests with his skepticism, his political radicalism and his sarcastic treatment of religion. Foster, of course, ruffles far fewer feathers.

Unsurprisingly, the list of those whom Escot offends includes Mr. Panoscope, the "chemical, botanical, astronomical, mathematical, metaphysical, meteorological, anatomical, physiological, galvanistical, musical, pictorial, bibliographical, criticial philosopher, who had run through the whole circle of the sciences, and understood them all equally well; that is, not at all,"[60] and the phrenologist Mr. Cranium—inconveniently, in the latter case, as Escot soon becomes enamored of Cranium's daughter Cephalis, for whose affections Panoscope is his chief rival. Panoscope steals a march on him in that regard by obtaining Cranium's blessing, but Escot is able to make up the lost ground when the plot obligingly provides him with an opportunity to save Cranium from drowning.

Escot is somewhat troubled by the question of whether a philosopher ought to be in love, aware that a positive answer would place him at odds with both Plato and the Epicurean Lucretius. He cannot prevent the torment keeping him awake at night, but he nevertheless pursues his suit heroically, in spite of his principled objection to dancing, the only courtship ritual available to the society in which he finds himself. Cranium initially refuses to recognize his debt to Escot, arguing on philosophical grounds that the rescue was the results of a deterministic series of mental events exactly similar to the sequence of physical events that caused him to fall into the water, but he is out-maneuvered by Squire Headlong, who comes up with an ingenious pseudoscientific argument proving that Escot, not Panoscope, is the right man for Cephalis. Escot does not, however, allow his own prospects of happiness to modify his deteriorationist views.

The opposition between the opinions of Foster and Escot is continually modified by the interjections of Mr. Jenkinson's "status-quoism," which also looks forward to a distinctive kind of future, in which an eternal balance of happiness and misery will be maintained, with no possible conclusion in favor of either. Between them, therefore, the three philosophers triangulate the

---

60   Ibid. p.33. The name Panoscope is reduced to Panscope in later editions of the novel, but I have preserved the original.

uneven ideological battlefield on which the controversies of the nineteenth century, with regard to the ideas of progress and perfectibility, were to be fought outside the enclosures of dogmatic religious faith.

Peacock's treatment of the contest correctly anticipates the direction in which the battle was bound to go, by identifying Escot as the true hero of the Headlong Hall skirmish. "Deteriorationism" was, indeed, fated to win in the end, in spite of the optimism valiantly maintained by visionary poets like Percy Shelley and Utopian philosophers like William Godwin. By the time generic scientific romance emerged in the 1890s, it did so in a broadly deteriorationist context, against which H. G. Wells mounted a long and determined fight, trying desperately to maintain the flickering flame of Fosterian hope against the dark tide of Escotism. In that respect, however, the entire genre was doomed from the start, as the subsequent chapters of this history will demonstrate.

* * * *

In his book *The Image of the Future* (1973), the Dutch philosopher Fred Polak argues that there are two distinct categories of futuristic imagery, one consisting of images of the historical future, which he calls Utopian, and one consisting of images of the ultimate future, or of the world beyond this one, which he calls Eschatological. Polak argues that both Utopian and Eschatological thought underwent crucial shifts in the course of the nineteenth century, culminating by the century's end in a kind of denaturation, which he discusses under the rubric of the "Devastation of the Image of the Future." Polak's account describes the same phenomenon, from a different viewpoint, as Frank Manuel's account of the removal of the dominant emphasis of utopian thought from a "euchronian" to a "eupsychian" context, the imaginative quest for an ideal State being abandoned by many writers in favor of a more modest and introverted quest for an ideal state of mind.

In terms of the contribution potentially to be made to euchronian hopes and designs by the further development of science and technology, the debate between Peacock's Mr. Foster and Mr. Escot set the parameters quite frankly. Foster's argument that technological advancement is an unalloyed good, increasing the sum of human happiness directly and providing the necessary bedrock for the advancement of virtue, never disappeared from contention, but as the nineteenth century progressed, Escot's challenge, arguing that the advancement of technology actually decreased the sum of human happiness, instead facilitating vice, gradually gained ground. That slow advance was unaffected by the fact that most deteriorationists actually seemed to live comfortable and happy lives themselves, content to sample all the joys of social life and comforts of technology rather than running wild in the woods.

The same incremental shift can be seen in the further aspect of the Foster/Escot argument that Polak pointed out and isolated: the Eschatological rather than the Utopian considerations. Indeed, that aspect gradually assumed a more important role in literary considerations of the prospects of the future, and achieved an even more complete victory of pessimism over optimism. To some extent, that reflected a change in the general background of opinion, but the matter is not so simple that such reflection can qualify as a full explanation.

It must be remembered that, in matters of philosophical argument, literary work does not present a level playing-field. As Aristotle pointed out in his analysis of drama and epic poetry in the *Poetics*, dramatization and poeticization have their own innate structures and demands, which are not those of philosophical objectivity—which is probably why, unlike Plato, Aristotle shunned the use of fictional devices in his own philosophical discourse. In a literary context, dystopianism has a ready-made advantage over eutopianism because it is inherently more dramatic and more poignant, the sublime always being more forceful than the beautiful, in Burke's terminology.

Whether the ability of tragedy to stimulate emotion and excitement allows it a cathartic effect, as Aristotle proposed, is open to doubt, but its raw affective capacity is not—and that advantage becomes even more obvious with respect to the "eschatological" aspects of futuristic thought and speculation. When literary endeavor meditates upon "final things," whether it is a matter of the fate of the soul after death or the ultimate collective judgment of the entire human species, all the intrinsic dramatic and poetic advantages are on the dark side.

Percy Shelley tried to oppose that tendency, in both *Queen Mab* and *Prometheus Unbound*, but the relevant part of *Queen Mab* was ultimately banished from the canon of his works, and *Prometheus Unbound* can easily be read as if it were merely referring nostalgically to a purely mythical Golden Age. The impression that remains, from the stump of *Queen Mab* and other poems expanding on its imagery—most famously "Ozymandias" (1818)—is actually more deteriorationist than perfectibilist, and the same is true of many of the most celebrated works of the Romantic Movement. There is a good deal more doom and gloom than cheerfulness in the works of Byron, Coleridge, Keats and Thomas De Quincey, let alone the flood of Gothic fiction, when it comes to reflecting upon the fate of the individual and of the race. At the same time, however, utopian social philosophers like William Godwin were still trying to devise schemes for social reform that would make the world a better place, with or without the aid and impetus of technological development, and writers of utopian fiction were still trying to illustrate such schemes, in spite of the awful handicap of an inherent lack of dramatic support.

The process of "devastation" identified and bemoaned by Polak is harder to see, at first glance, in the eschatological dimension of the futuristic literature of the nineteenth century than it is in the utopian dimension. What Polak means by devastation is not, however, a drastic decline in the frequency with which eschatological ideas are expressed, but a significant change in the manner of their expression. Polak's main concern is that, while the legacy of the Enlightenment encouraged belief in the possibility of social progress and of the improvement of the human condition by political, educational and technological effort, the consequent decline of religious faith in the nineteenth century resulted in a damaging loss of consensus with regard to the fate of the soul after death (individual eschatology) and the fate of the human race as a whole (apocalyptic eschatology).

Secularized eschatological imagery underwent a dramatic proliferation in the nineteenth century, but Polak construes that proliferation as a sign of disintegration, and hence of decay; he takes the eventual advent and rise of speculative fiction as the final phase of the devastation of the image of the future by means of fragmentation, and thus the final nail in the coffin of the image of the future—a view directly contrary to the opinion of "historians of science fiction." The proliferation of utopian imagery was equally dramatic, in its own way, but that proliferation too was marked by increasing disintegration and dissent, as differences of opinion as to what a better society might look like became ever more manifest—not simply in the eternal conflict between conservatives and reformers, but in terms of sharp disagreements about the contribution made by mechanical technology to the quality of life.

Although some works of futuristic fiction consider both the historical and eschatological aspects of the future, as *Headlong Hall* does in its calculatedly flippant fashion, it does make sense, as Polak suggests, to consider them separately, as parallel processes of development rather the same one, confused and overlapping but also, to some extent, conflicting, and frequently drawing on different imaginative resources, especially with respect to the implications of science. It therefore seems reasonable to continue this section of the chapter with considerations of the future of history—the utopian dimensions of the argument between "perfectibilism" and "deteriorationism"—while bringing the future of destiny into narrower focus in the next section.

* * * *

Futuristic fiction in Britain had actually made its debut before Louis-Sébastien Mercier's pioneering exercise in euchronianism appeared in France, most notably in an anonymous account of *The Reign of George VI 1900-1925* published in 1763. The work now seems remarkable, however, precisely for its lack of any anticipation of technological progress, although it does anticipate a dramatic increase in canal traffic leading to considerable economic benefits. Otherwise, the anticipations it contains are purely political, focusing on the wars that the fictitious George VI is obliged to fight in order to restore England's fortunes after inheriting a demoralized country burdened with debt. The author might have borrowed the idea from an earlier work by Samuel Madden, *The Memoirs of the Twentieth Century, being the original letters of state under George the Sixth...revealed in the year 1728* (1733), which remained incomplete, but no other significant works in a similar vein were produced in Britain before Mercier was translated, and none thereafter prior to 1820.

Indeed, in spite of the inspiration that Erasmus Darwin and his fellow popularizers of science had attempted to provide, the record of British Utopian fiction throughout the first half of the nineteenth century is exceedingly thin in works expressing the kind of optimism that Mr. Foster had adopted from the French philosophers of progress. The kinds of forebodings entertained by Mr. Escot seem to have cast a dark shadow over such hopes long before they found any eloquent expression in expressly dystopian fiction. The majority of literary utopias produced throughout the century were traditionally framed as visits to geographical enclaves, in which a better life is generated by purely political means, with barely a glimpse of a steam engine or a balloon, let alone any hypothetical technology as bold as those to be found in Bensalem or sketched out as plausible mechanical developments by John Wilkins.

Part of the explanation for this neglect is undoubtedly due to the Anti-Jacobin notion that the French philosophy of progress had been irredeemable tainted by the Revolution and the ensuing Terror, which had allegedly demonstrated its hollowness in no uncertain terms. Radical Romantics like William Godwin and Percy Shelley did not see things that way but, like radicals in general, such philosophers and poets found it easier to specify what they were against, in elaborate diatribes against the world as it is, than to offer detailed designs of the world they would prefer to see in its place—as evidenced by the balance of lines in *Queen Mab*. As previously noted, however, there was another strain in British Romantic thought, most evidently represented by William Blake, that was frankly anti-technological and anti-scientific, and saw the Fosterian view of progress as a threat rather than a promise.

Controversy still rages as to exactly what Blake meant by the "dark satanic mills" to which he referred in "Jerusalem" (1804), but to many readers—and hearers, once the poem was set to music and became a kind of radical national anthem—they simply represented literal mills, the working conditions in which were certainly not lacking in a certain hellish quality. By 1804, the arguably-satanic aspects of the miracles of production wrought by such mill-building industrialists as Richard Arkwright were already becoming clear, and the economic privations of the Napoleonic Wars made that darker side seem increasingly threatening, not merely to the artisans made redundant by the ingenious steam-powered textile industry, but to the comfortable townspeople afraid of what the addition of those ex-artisans to the ranks of the angry unemployed might provoke.

One of the principal mythological images to emerge from the period was that of the Luddites: the machine-smashers who first went into action in Nottingham in 1811 and spread their aggressive Movement throughout the northern counties over the next two years. Parliament reacted, in typical fashion, by making machine-breaking a capital crime, but Lord Byron was one of numerous critics who spoke out on behalf of the Luddites in opposition to the legislation. Luddism was a phenomenon of the industrial north, but agriculture was also undergoing a technological revolution induced by ingenious machinery, and the Swing Riots of the 1830s brought the Luddite philosophy south. "Captain Swing" never quite matched "Ned Lud" for notoriety, but he became a significant scarecrow nevertheless.

Nor was it merely the means of production in factories and farms that was transformed by the new technology in a manner that some thought disastrous; the changes wrought in cities—including, and especially, London—were equally contentious. London had always been foggy, and it had always been filthy, but the effluent of factory chimneys began turning the fog to asphyxiating smog and the rapid increase in its population, partly caused by the displacement of redundant agricultural workers, soon exceeded the capacity of its primitive waste-disposal methods, causing a pollution problem that climaxed in the "Great Stink" of the 1850s, which rendered the banks of the Thames uninhabitable and caused extreme offence in the riverside Houses of Parliament. The reformer William Cobbett had, however, dubbed London "the Great Wen" long before that, in the 1820s.

A significant challenge to progressive utopianism was provided by the anonymous *An Essay on Population* (1798), which the ensuing controversy soon identified as the work of the Reverend Thomas Robert Malthus. The essay proposed an "Iron Law of Population"—an early example of the attempt to extend Newtonian analysis into the fledgling realm of social science—which proposed that, because food production could only increase linearly, in "arithmetic" progression while population growth could accelerate in "geometric" progression, population would always tend to outstrip resources, inevitably being cut back by what came to be known as the "Malthusian checks": famine, disease and war; which were thus declared to be inevitable features of the human condition.

Progressive social philosophers, including William Godwin, inevitable reacted fiercely to Malthus' proposal of the Iron Law. Partly in consequence of their objections, Malthus issued a much-elaborated version of his argument in a second edition of the essay in 1803, and continued making modifications until the sixth and final version was issued in 1826, after which he condensed the argument again for a popular *Summary View of the Principle of Population* published in 1830. In the later editions of his essay Malthus admitted that "moral restraint" might substitute for the negative checks on population in an ideal society, but he clearly had no faith in the human capacity for moral restraint, and could not even bring himself to think about anything as horrifically indecent as technological birth control, although his opponents and supporters alike were less shy.

At any rate, the Iron Law of Population became an issue that any nineteenth century utopian would have to confront, one way or another, especially when it was supplemented by an analogue in the "Iron Law of Wages," credited to Ferdinand Lassalle in mid-century, which argued that competition among would-be workers would always ensure that wages remained close to the level needed to sustain mere survival. The greatest triumph of Malthus' Iron Law, however, was that it became one of the principal inspirations and theoretical supports for Charles Darwin's theory of natural selection.

In view of all these concerns, it is not entirely surprising that a majority of nineteenth-century English Utopian visions are pastoral rather than urban, seeking the secret of happiness in technological moderation rather than further advancement. That majority was doubtless assisted by the fact that aristocrats and the financially secure always produce far more literary works than the poor, if the poor produce any at all, and the English aristocracy, untoppled by any French-style Revolution, was notoriously smug in its conservatism. It must be admitted, however, that even Romantic utopianism, as in *Queen Mab*, very often tended to the Arcadian in its notions of paradise, and very rarely to the metropolitan.

* * * *

The most sustained attempt made in England to design a utopian society modeled on the ideas of the Enlightenment was undertaken by Thomas Spence in a series of five works published over a quarter of a century: *A Supplement to the History of Robinson Crusoe* (1782); *A Marine Republic; or, A Description of Spensonia* (1794); *The Constitution of a Perfect Commonwealth* (1798); *The Constitution of Spensonia: A country in Fairyland Situated between Utopia and Oceana* (1801) and *The Receipt to Make a Millennium or Happy World* (1805). The accounts of the imaginary country of Spensonia were all based on "Spence's Plan," first set out in a pamphlet in 1775 entitled *Property in Land as Every One's Right*.

The fact that explicit Utopian speculation became distinctly thin on the ground in English fiction for half a century after the publication of the last of the accounts of Spensonia might have something to do with the fate that befell Spence in consequence of his endeavors in that vein. Any talk of "the rights of man" was considered highly dangerous even before the French Revolution and the greater publicity given to the slogan by Thomas Paine's *The Rights of Man* (1791), and was considered even more dangerous thereafter. At least one of Spence's five sketches of Spensonia was written while he was in prison, charged with High Treason, and he served four terms of imprisonment while the project was in progress.

There is much emphasis on human rights—including the rights of women and children—in Spence's utopian design, but the key to the good life enjoyed in Spensonia is the common ownership of land, so his description of the land as lying somewhere between Utopia and Oceana (with New Atlantis far beyond the horizon) is accurate in its imaginary geography. No significant role is attributed to the possibilities of technological advancement in Spensonia—but that did not prevent the lesson of Spence's tribulations affecting potential British champions of euchronian advancement just as much as campaigners for human rights.

Another factor thinning out the British literary record was probably the feeling that merely writing about hypothetical utopias had become a trifle passé in the Age of Enlightenment, and that the time was ripe to put such dreams into action. Although Samuel Taylor Coleridge produced no utopian fiction and there are only vague nuances of utopian thought in Robert Southey's literary works, the two of them made plans in the 1790s to set up a Utopian community of their own in America, under the banner of the benign creeds of "Pantisocracy" (government by a population of equals) and "Aspheterism" (the prohibition of private property) but they failed to raise the capital necessary to undertake the necessary emigration, and no detailed plan of the hypothetical community's organization exists, nor any account of what contribution the advancement of science might or might not have been expected to made to its future.

William Blake was a much more prolific utopian writer than any of his fellow Romantic poets, albeit in the flamboyantly allegorical vein of his "Prophetic Books," of which there are a dozen in all, the main sequence of which extends from *America, a Prophecy* (1793) through *The Visions of the Daughters of Albion* (1793), *The Book of Urizen* (1794) and *The Book of Los* (1795) to *Jerusalem: The Emanation of the Great Albion* (1804-1820), and which make Shelley at his most extravagant seem relatively sober. It was Blake's remark in 1808 that Milton's Satan had been "of the devil's party without knowing it" that inspired the tune of Shelley's extravagant literary satanism.

Blake knew Tom Paine before the champion of human rights was driven into exile in America, and he was undoubtedly aware of the work and tribulations of Thomas Spence; his consciousness of the danger of expressing radical ideas straightforwardly rather than allegorically was probably as acute as Shelley's. For all his hatred of "mechanism" in all its forms, however—which caused him to despise Isaac Newton—Blake did see Utopia in terms of a city rather than a rural paradise, and also as a city that would have to be continually rebuilt, although whether that continual remaking is a consequence of improvements in architectural methodology or merely of a natural rhythm of rises and falls is unclear. The future Jerusalem never does emerge clearly from the murky smog of Blakean symbolism.

Where Coleridge and Southey faltered, others persevered, not only in America, the favorite refuge of experimental Utopians, but in Britain—most famously in Robert Owen's establishment at

New Lanark, which was very much an industrial and mechanical enterprise, taking full advantage of the new means of production; its initial base was a water-mill built by Richard Arkwright in partnership with David Dale, whose daughter Owen married.

Owen was helped to raise the capital for his project by likeminded social reformers, including Jeremy Bentham. The essays setting out the prospectus for the society he intended to formulate were initially published in 1813 in *A New View of Society*. Although the experiment is still regarded so highly that New Lanark has now become a virtual shrine—a place of socialist pilgrimage—it did not live up to Owen's hopes, and he eventually resigned all connection with it in 1828.

It is against that background that the conspicuously feeble development of English utopian fiction in the early part of the nineteenth century needs to be seen.

* * * *

The futuristic fictions of the early part of the century were not all as gloomy as Mary Shelley's *The Last Man* and Jane Webb's *The Mummy!* Although fiction in the cheap periodicals of the day rarely used any fantastic devices but those of lurid Gothic horror fiction, Peter Haining, looking for such fiction for a horror anthology in the late 1970s, stumbled across a fascinating long-forgotten item in *The Pocket Magazine* in 1818 entitled "Five Hundred Years Hence" and signed "D"—although it was surely not by Humphry Davy, who used that signature elsewhere. It offers a light-hearted sketch of Britain and the Americas in the twenty-fourth century, when economic fortunes have changed drastically, partly because of the exhaustion of England's coal reserves, although perpetual motion has recently been developed in Mexico, and a mission launched from the U.S.A. has reached the moon.

John Banim's *Revelations of the Dead-Alive* (1824) is also relatively cheerful; although it is primarily a whimsical satire in which the reputations of famous men of 1823 are considered from a hypothetical distance of a hundred years of history, Banim does make some effort to describe the technological advancements that have taken place in that interim, not entirely frivolously.

A Hundred Years Hence; or, The Memoirs of Charles, Lord Moresby, written by Himself (1828), is equally light-hearted, if far more modest, in parodying society autobiographies; the relatively slight and quirky changes that have overtaken English and French society in the course of a century are mostly mentioned *en passant* and obliquely. Meanwhile, the conceited notional author concentrates on matters of importance to him—primarily the various aspects of his social life, which are mostly conventional, save for the occasional attendance at theatrical performances by dancing kangaroos. He does, however, stress the importance of dramatic advances on locomotion and communication facilitated by the applications of steam to road and rail travel, and pays particular attention to two very recent inventions that the author evidently suspected—incorrectly, as it turned out—to be capable of making significant improvements in means of travel: "Browne's gas-carriages" and "Pocock's kite-carriages, the latter being" "the most expeditious of all when the wind is fair"[61] in the 1920s.

The former reference is to a gas engine recently developed by the engineer and inventor Samuel Brown, which used a flame to create a partial vacuum in a sealed chamber and then used an in-rush of air to do mechanical work. In 1826 he demonstrated a prototype on Shooter's Hill in London, but the company he founded to market it failed, probably because the fuel feeding the flame was too expensive; had it been more widely adopted, the internal combustion engine might have been developed far earlier than it was. It was also in 1826 that George Pocock obtained a patent for his kite-carriage, or "charvolant"—a kind of land-yacht. Although neither device, strictly speaking, made it through the next century, it cannot be said that the anticipation that they might was unreasonable, and their presence in the future scenario demonstrates that "Lord Moresby" was well in touch with the march of contemporary technology.

The light tone and obliquity of these glimpses of the future was further reproduced in a more adventurous piece in the pioneering annual gift book *The Keepsake* in 1830: "A Dialogue for the Year 2130, extracted from the album of a modern sibyl," by Thomas Lister. Although the dialogue is mostly concerned with social events, it reveals *en passant* the existence of domestic automata and automata used as mounts in hunting—with the result

---

61   *A Hundred Years Hence; or, The Memoirs of Charles, Lord Moresby, written by himself.* London: Longman, 1828. p. 111.

that horses have become the quarry rather than conveyances, and are pursued with rapid-fire automatic rifles. Changes in literary fashion have produced a new genre of "scientific novels" featuring such racy mathematical accounts of passion as *Love and Algebra* and such social dramas as *Geological Atoms; or, The Adventures of a Dustman*. A focus on domestic life similar to Lister's can also be found in the anonymous three-decker *Mrs. Maberly; or, The World as It Will Be* (1838), set in 2036.

Given this process of casual domestication, even though it proved short-lived, it is perhaps surprising that more earnest accounts of potential social and mechanical progress are so very rare, but Utopian speculation of all kinds was in the doldrums for a generation and it had no obvious euchronian dimension. Even the satirical end of the utopian spectrum seemed to lose much of its energy in the first half of the nineteenth century by comparison with the Swiftian exuberance that had animated so many eighteenth century works; although Thomas Erskine's political satire *Armata: A Fragment* (1817) retained a certain endearing quirkiness, not least in the bizarre route by which its castaways gain access to the educational heterocosm—which might have been borrowed from Margaret Cavendish—it was followed by a long lacuna.

The resumption of Utopian design in England, in such works as Henry J. Forrest's *A Dream of Reform* (1848), which is principally couched as a series of lectures by a character named "Kindly", and Robert Pemberton's barely-fictionalized description of a quasi-socialist community *The Happy Colony* (1854), seems distinctly hesitant and short-sighted; the works cited are similarly soft-centered in their focus on small-scale industry and moral restraint. Henry O'Neil's *Two Thousand Years Hence* (1868) is not so much an account of things to come as a history of the nineteenth century, written from a supposedly distant but determinedly conservative viewpoint.

The typically tentative character of early nineteenth-century British Utopian romances was, however, cast aside in the 1870s, when a sudden series of more robust, more elegant and more adventurous utopian satires appeared. The first of them was the anonymous *The Coming Race* (1871), subsequently attributed to Edward Bulwer, by then Baron Lytton of Knebworth. Although it owes a slight debt to Bulwer's earlier occult fantasies, about which more will be said in a subsequent section, and the probable unreliability of the narrator makes the exact depth of its irony difficult to judge, the novel caused something of a sensation, with its description of an underworld populated by the Ana, or Vril-ya. The Vril-ya's mastery of the mysterious force of "vril" has enabled them to build a prosperous egalitarian society, equipped with automata that carry out household chores, and flying machines that deploy fantastic weaponry—weaponry that the Vril-ya are not loath to use, even genocidally, if they feel threatened.

Vril is a kind of elementary, unified force whose particular manifestations include electricity and magnetism; it not only supplies abundant heat and light but has curative powers too. The idea was sufficiently appealing to be picked up by John Lawson Johnston, who appropriated it in order to give a forceful brand image to a new meat extract he called Bovril, and also to fuel a further novel about the discovery and employment of vril on the Earth's surface, *The Vril Staff* (1891), signed "X.Y.Z." Although some modern critics have been tempted to reintrepret it as an anticipation of atomic power, it owes more inspiration to the idea of "odic force," suggested by Carl von Reichenbach in 1845 as the elementary force underlying not merely electricity, magnetism and heat but the vital "life-force" supposedly manipulable by Mesmeric "animal magnetism." In essence, however, vril is simply a representation of generalized technological progress, embodying the assumption that such progress might eventually equip humankind with godlike powers—always assuming that the Vril-ya do not emerge from their caverns before then to wipe out humankind as a potential threat to their existence.

Vril's use requires a biological modification of the nervous system, so it is a technology fit only for superhumans—a move that places the novel at the head of one of the major themes of scientific romance: the attempt to image the species that will, in due course, replace *Homo sapiens* as evolution progresses. Although it seems, at least superficially, to be a novel full of euchronian promise, *The Coming Race* can also be construed as a dire warning akin to H. G. Wells' *The War of the Worlds*, subtly reminding the people of England, and by extension the entire world, that they too might suffer the fate of the Tasmanians or the Carib Indians if they happen to run into a technological superior race.

That notion is, inevitably, reminiscent of the notion of "the survival of the fittest," but in respect of evolutionary theory, *The Coming Race* is a trifle eccentric. The Vril-ya, having discovered fossilized frogs and toads and applied the perspectives of comparative anatomy, wonder whether they might be descended from such creatures, but it seems unlikely that the joke is intended to mock evolutionary theory from a creationist perspective. The Utopian credentials of the Vril-ya are undermined in several ways; for instance, they are distinctly crass in terms of their esthetics, having little in the way of arts. Again, though, reading that as a straightforward poke at American democracy, as some critics have, seems oversimplified.

The Coming Race was swiftly followed, and perhaps countered, by the similarly-anonymous *Erewhon; or, Over the Range* (1872), in which the satire is much more obvious, including an interpolated section extrapolating the Darwinian theory of evolution in a comical fashion, which is best discussed specifically in a subsequent section. *Erewhon*'s author was Samuel Butler, who based it on his experiences as a temporary emigrant to New Zealand, and the pastoral life of the Erewhonians contrasts very markedly with that of the Virl-ya, not because the Erewhonians are ignorant of mechanical technology, but because they have consciously decided to set it aside. Sympathy for that decision is, however, undermined by the various absurd aspects of their society, including such witty inversions as the practice of punishing illness while caring for criminals, and the satirical description of Erewhonian religion. It is those farcical inclusions that provide the book with its real substance, suggesting by their absurdity that the inversion of the philosophy of progress might be one more piece in a jigsaw of silliness. The belated sequel, *Erewhon Revisited* (1901) is much narrower in its concern, being almost entirely concerned with religious satire, and does nothing to make the technological argument any clearer.

Considerably less well-known, but similarly interesting as a precursor of scientific romance, is a third anonymous novel published immediately after *Erewhon* and *The Coming Race*, which was the work of the homeopathic physician Robert Ellis Dudgeon: *Colymbia* (1873). Set, like *Erewhon*, in Australasia, *Colymbia* describes the adventures of a castaway who is rescued by the inhabitants of the eponymous submarine civilization, resulting from the interbreeding of previous English castaways with an ancient ocean-dwelling culture. Although their society is located in an equatorial archipelago, the inhabitants live under the water in preference to the islands, in order to escape the harassments of tropical heat and poisonous insects; in consequence, they have been forced to develop an advanced technology in order to facilitate that way of life, to manage their supplies of breathable air, supply their homes with electrical heat, light and power, and also to contrive effective means of communication and waterproof cultural artifacts.

Colymbian society features a few inversions and apparent absurdities in the Erewhonian manner—sexual relationships are open but people can only own houses on the basis of lifelong contracts—and it involves numerous caricatures of British life. The education system of the elite is centralized on the learning of the dead language of the ancient ocean-dwellers, although the resulting incompetence is welcomed by their underling advisers, while the purely symbolic head of state is a giant turtle. On the whole, however, the principal focus of the story is the ingenuity required to sustain an underwater existence that is by no means hellish. Homesickness and the annoying conceit of the Colymbians, who are forever denigrating his own culture, eventually drive the castaway back to England, but once he is there, like Gulliver, he cannot help seeing its society through Colymbian eyes, and cannot be entirely happy.

Like its two immediate predecessors, *Colymbia* is no blueprint for an ideal state, but neither was Thomas More's *Utopia* if read sensitively. The Colymbians' ingenious technology does not constitute an advertisement for future British technology, except in the very general sense that lauds mechanical improvisation as the brainchild of necessity, but it is, nevertheless, a work that carries covert futuristic implications in the same fashion as Bacon's *New Atlantis*; it anticipates several later speculative romances that feature Plato's Atlantis surviving as an underwater civilization, including André Laurie's *Atlantis* (1895; tr. as *The Crystal City Under the Sea*) and Stanton A. Coblentz's *The Sunken World* (1928), which found a belated home in the science fiction pulps when it was rejected for publication elsewhere.

The point of all three of these neo-Utopian fantasies is that such constructions, however light-hearted they might be, provide a kind of binocular vision, by means of which a new and adventurously-extensive dimension can be added to the taken-for-granted aspects of English society. This was a manner of dealing with exotic societies that was to become a standard feature of scientific romance, establishing, as it were, a flexible third leg to the easel whose two fixed legs extended in the directions of eutopia and dystopia. Fictional images of ideal societies did not disappear, of course, and straightforwardly dystopian images became increasingly common, but many subsequent hypothetical societies featured in English-language fiction were neither wholeheartedly eutopian nor wholeheartedly dystopian, any more than they were wholeheartedly serious or wholeheartedly satirical, but set off instead to explore the possibilities that might be open to future societies in an open-minded exploratory fashion.

None of the three works just cited is manifestly euchronian in its narrative framework, but nor is any of them backward-looking—and they are, in fact, much bolder in their speculations, and far more readable, than some of the formally futuristic fantasies that appeared alongside them. John Francis Maguire's three-decker *The Next Generation* (1871) is a particularly leaden example. It was, however, in this same brief period that futuristic fiction also began to adopt a more experimental spirit and a far greater imaginative reach. Edward Maitland's three-decker *By and By: An Historical Romance of the Future* (1873), in spite of being weighed down by the necessary verbosity of its format, does offer interesting glimpses of a future social order transformed by flying machines and other swift means of communication, and morally better-equipped by a mysterious "higher science."

A third three-decker, the anonymous *Annals of the Twenty-Ninth Century: The Autobiography of the Tenth President of the World Republic* (1874), the work of a Scottish physician named Andrew Blair, made an even better fist of imagining a broad sweep of future social and technological development. Although Blair faced the same problem of obligatory prolixity, he contrives a remarkable detailed future history of social reorganization on Earth, partly enforced by natural catastrophes; the story includes exploration of the other planets in the solar system, in a much more pragmatic frame of mind than cosmic visions motivated by the eschatological rather than the utopian imaginative impulse.

An adventurous spirit similar to that reflected in *The Coming Race, Erewhon* and *Colymbia* is also to be found in some lesser works whose euchronian dimension is presented obliquely. One of particular note, in spite of its literary ineptitude, is Benjamin Lumley's Martian fantasy *Another World; or, Fragments from the Star City of Montallah* (1873), signed "Hermes," in which a not-yet-ideal society is facilitated by the total technological mastery of electricity, including its healing powers, and individual sanity is ensured by advanced psychological techniques.

Although futuristic fiction remained relatively scarce throughout the 1870s and 1880s, with the striking exception of one narrow subgenre described in a subsequent subsection, the examples that were produced mostly included anticipations of much greater change, both politically and technologically than those produced in earlier decades, probably encouraged by the extraordinary voyages featured in Jules Verne's early works, which were translated into English in the early 1870s.

The Age of Science: A Newspaper of the Future (1877) signed Merlin Nostradamus (Frances Power Cobbe) is a relative brief satire, but is interesting in its emphasis on scientific advancement, as advertised by its title. *Three Hundred Years Hence* (1881) by William Delisle Hay is repulsive in its genocidal racism, but is again remarkable for its emphasis on the transformative force of advanced science and technology. Both those examples paled, however, by comparison with *A Thousand Years Hence* (1882), pseudonymously signed "Nunsowe Greene," and possibly the work of Edgar Welch—who wrote other pseudonymous satires for the same publisher—which extrapolates its scientific miracles much further, progressing from accounts of advanced technologies to a description of elaborate explorations of the profusely-inhabited solar system

Although not intended at all seriously—the notional author is identified as the "ex-Vice-President of the Shoreditch and Spitalfields Universal Discussion Society" and the absurdity of the anticipations is intended to poke fun at the utopian speculations supposedly offered in the context of Mechanics Institutes and similar educational establishments—the scope of the vision of *A*

Thousand Years Hence has a curiously liberating magnificence that undermines its purpose, reproducing on a much bigger scale the effects of such briefly flamboyant Rabelaisian parodies as the anonymous "Anti-Humbug. Phrenology as a Detector of Murder: A Tale of the Fortieth Century" (1840) and "Gumbuh" (1874), signed "J. G. M.," in which a visit to the eponymous planet reveals inversions in the manner of Astolpho's trip to the Moon in *Orlando Furioso*. James Payn's "The Fatal Curiosity; or, A Hundred Years Hence" in *Belgravia*'s Christmas Annual for 1877 is similarly light-hearted in its description of a seasonal house-party at Mellington Hall. Nunsowe Greene's addition to this curious subset of antiscientific romances illustrates that mere blatant nonsense was becoming harder to contrive, in a world where it was, indeed, becoming possible for a "Merlin Nostradamus" to anticipate an eventual "age of Science" in which vril, or something akin to it, might render all manner of miracles, including Lucianesque trips to the Moon, quite feasible.

Some conscientiously moderate works began to adopt a more even-handed and investigative attitude view of future possibilities, including Anthony Trollope's last novel, *The Fixed Period* (1882), which devotes scrupulous care to the examination of a society in which the Malthusian threat has been politically countered by legislation fixing the allotted human lifespan. *The Disk: A Prophetic Revelation* (1884) by E. A. Robinson and G. A. Wall takes similar care in examining the possible consequences of the invention of a "photo-electrophone" (i.e., television). Meanwhile, conventional utopian romances became gradually more confident in their use of explicitly euchronian frames, as in the anonymous *Palingenesia; or, The Earth's New Birth* (1884, by the Reverend G. J. Ouseley) and *Darkness and Dawn: The Peaceful Birth of a New Age* (1884, by Clement Wise).

* * * *

Perhaps unsurprisingly, in view of the dearth of Utopian novels early in the century, dystopian fiction was slow to put in a reactionary appearance in Britain, but the anonymous three-decker *The Last Peer* (1851) takes a decidedly dim view of a twentieth century in which the aristocracy has been stripped of its privileges and crime and unemployment are rife; although the bleakness is relieved by the exceedingly Victorian sentimentality of the plot, the book does deserve consideration as a pioneering anticipatory work of the deteriorationist school.

Unlike France, where technological dystopianism often took graphic forms, British dystopianism, when it began to emerge in fiction, was usually oblique, its forebodings expressed in delicate satirization rather than grim depictions of world gone wrong. Nor, to begin with, was it very extreme in calling for a technological retreat. Mr. Escot's glorification of the life of "the wild man of the woods" had not even won the serious commitment of Mr. Escot, and the idea of a return to that kind of primitivism seemed unattractive even to the most diehard opponents of technical development. Some writers even avoided the necessity for such a retreat. In the anonymously-issued *Erchomenon; or, The Republic of Materialism* (1879), written by the Australian-born clergyman Henry Crocker Marriott Watson, which probably qualifies as the first wholehearted vision of a dystopian future published in Britain, a society ruined by socialism—the story is set in year 550 of the Commune, in the twenty-fifth century, when advanced technology is coupled with rampant vice—the possibility of contriving a modest retreat is rendered redundant by the arrival of the Day of Judgment.

A similarly deep hostility to materialistic civilization is much more elegantly expressed in Richard Jefferies' *After London; or, Wild England* (1886), set in the aftermath of an unspecified catastrophe that has obliterated the great cities, when life in England has reverted to more innocent rural habits and customs. Although the predators there certainly do not lie down with their prey, and nature remains red in tooth and claw, there is a paradisal aspect to Jefferies' loving descriptions of post-industrial pastoralism that echoes aspects of Shelley's utopia—but the retreat has been measured, and has stopped well short of chaotic collapse.

Although it must have seemed to be an eccentric oddity at the time, *After London* stands at the lead of a long tradition of British post-catastrophe novels that welcomed the catastrophes in question, to a greater or lesser extent, with a greater or lesser degree of ambivalent irony. Such fiction supplied an important thread to generic scientific romance, which was carried all the way through into one of the most distinctive strands of British science fiction to emerge after 1950.

A more orthodox dystopia, whose theme similarly gave it a considerable relevance to the subsequent development of scientific romance, was Walter Besant's *The Inner House* (1888), which followed up an earlier dystopian satire, *The Revolt of Man* (1882), in which a socially-stultifying future matriarchy is overthrown bloodlessly. Although the purpose of the earlier work is to demonstrate by exemplary inversion the obnoxiousness of the treatment of women by British men, the reverse psychology of the argument might not have been obvious to all the book's readers, some of whom probably misconstrued it as an anti-suffragette tract.

The Inner House develops similar fears of future social stultification, but attributes the threat to a less insulting, and arguable more convincing, cause, as the ultimate consequences of the invention of a chemical means of preventing aging. Although the undying individuals thus produced do not suffer from the problems of Jonathan Swift's struldbrugs, they are afflicted by a kind of psychological stasis, which inevitably results in a cultural stasis far more extreme than the one suffered by Bulwer's Vril-ya. Although the strictly-regulated society thus preserved in aspic is not conspicuously unhappy, and is liberated from the economic disadvantages that blighted so many nineteenth-century lives, it is devoid of the verve that comes from historical impetus, and thus falls foul of one of the most important lessons that Francis Bacon derived from his version of the myth of Prometheus—of which Besant's novel might be regarded as an extrapolation.

As with *The Revolt of Man*, *The Inner House* is vulnerable to potential misreading; its real target is the typical conservatism of the old rather than the baleful potential of medical science, but some of its readers probably missed that point. The plot of the novel follows the endeavors of a female hero whose relatively recent birth was permitted in order to replace a citizen who fell victim to a rare accidental death; her youth gives her the existential impetus to plot rebellion against the fossilized rulers of the static utopia, although the forces arrayed against her seem insuperable.

Like *After London*, although more obscurely, *The Inner House* stands at the head of a considerable tradition of futuristic fictions in which lone rebels take a heroic stand against an oppressive society whose masters have advanced technological means at their disposal—a plot-formula that proved even more useful in American pulp science fiction than in British scientific romance. It is not at all surprising, however, that both *After London* and *The Inner House* were produced on the very threshold of the development of generic scientific romance, and both could plausibly be numbered among its introductory works rather than being ranked as mere precursors.

* * * *

One of the most remarkable images of the historical future published in Britain in the nineteenth century, although it went completely unnoticed at the time, was *The Air Battle* (1859), signed by the pseudonym "Herrmann Lang," which is set at the end of the sixty-eighth century, when considerable geological upheavals have changed the geography of the Earth dramatically. The world is now dominated by three empires, based in the Sahara, Brazil and Madeira. The only surviving white people live a primitive existence in what is left of Europe, and are occasionally taken as slaves by the Brazilians and Madeirans, although the Saharans are opposed to slavery. All three cultures have advanced technologies, with new power sources at their disposal, and are thus in possession of various remote-controlled mechanical devices, enormously powerful weapons, and vast flying machines.

The plot of the novel involves an Irishman who rises to a commanding rank in the Madeiran air fleet in spite of his lowly origins, and eventually leads the fleet into battle against the Saharans, while two of his former acquaintances have romantic adventures of their own in the other empires. The author has never been identified, and it is difficult to know what to make of the narrative voice's explicit identifications of himself as a black man, but whoever he was, the imagery of the technologically advanced society, and particularly of future warfare, presented in the novel was considerably ahead of its time. To its contemporary readers, the story undoubtedly seemed bizarre and probably preposterous, but it anticipated one of the most remarkable developments of nineteenth-century futuristic fiction, and one that played a crucial role in the establishment of generic scientific romance as a form of popular literature.

As matters transpired, it was a far more modest work, but one that enjoyed a spectacular success, that actually prompted a deluge of futuristic fictions dealing specifically with the technology of warfare, expressing the ominous fear that Britain might be helpless if a new war were suddenly to break out, because the nation's army and armaments had been allowed to slip into obsolescence. The possibility that such a war might, indeed, break out, was brought sharply into focus by the Prussian invasion of France in 1870 and the consequent abrupt collapse of Napoléon III's Second Empire

The May 1871 issue of Blackwood's Magazine featured an unsigned story called *The Battle of Dorking: Reminiscences of a Volunteer*, which was rapidly reprinted as a pamphlet. The author, having studied the Prussian campaign in the Franco-Prussian War, offers a blood-curdling account of what might happen if the Prussian army were to invade Britain in the same manner that it had invaded France. The ex-combatant, reporting the events some time afterwards, explains that the British armed forces, even with their ranks swelled by volunteers like himself, had no chance of repelling the invasion, because the enemy equipment was so superior and their tactics were so much more effective. Having smashed British resistance at Dorking, the Prussians are reported to have proceeded at their leisure to capture London, just as they had marched on Paris after crushing the French at the battle of Sedan—with the result that the nation becomes a mere subservient satellite of an all-conquering Empire guided by the notoriously ambitious and aggressive "Iron Chancellor" Otto von Bismarck.

The Battle of Dorking was a best-seller in England and was translated into several other languages—including German—provoking a good deal of interest throughout Europe. As intended, but probably far more effectively than its author had anticipated, it proved to be a remarkably effective item of propaganda in the call for the reform of the Army and the rearmament of Britain's defense forces. The controversy it stirred up was sufficient to spur the prime minister, William Ewart Gladstone, to make an angry reference to it in a parliamentary diatribe against "alarmism." It also called forth a veritable blizzard of replies in kind, in which appalled defenders of the nation's honor imagined different ways that the Germans might have been defeated even after their success at Dorking, or produced elaborate arguments intended to demonstrate that they could never have get as far as Dorking in the first place.

A full account of this remarkable episode, and an elaborate commentary on the entire subgenre of future war stories spawned by *The Battle of Dorking* can be found in I. F. Clarke's detailed study of *Voices Prophesying War, 1763-1984*. Clarke's bibliography of the *Tale of the Future* lists more than a dozen other pamphlets produced before the end of 1871 that provide explicit replies to it, and a handful of others featuring alternative conflicts between Britain and Germany at a greater remove in time and space A further dozen works of the same sort appeared in the next decade, and although the initial flood soon became a trickle, it was a trickle that stubbornly refused to dry up.

By virtue of the persistence of this stream of afterthoughts, the author of *The Battle of Dorking*, George T. Chesney, achieved the almost unique feat of starting a literary tradition single-handed, not merely in Britain but internationally. A similarly persistent tradition of future war stories was soon established in France, whose inhabitants were still smarting from the defeat and the financial penalties consequent upon it—fiercely resented even by the radicals who had hated the Second Empire—and another tradition, far more triumphalist in tone, was established in Germany. The British press and public became obsessed with such speculations, whose literary manifestations soon began to gather force again once the initial fuss had calmed down.

It is not difficult to understand why that obsession developed: Britain had long been a great military power, but had grown—at least according to some vociferous critics both inside and outside parliament—direly complacent. The men controlling the armed forces were said to be living in the past, trading on an assumption of invulnerability that could no longer stand up to inspection. Although the sun proverbially never set on the British Empire, and Britannia still ruled the waves by courtesy of her navy, enormous dangers were lurking on the horizon, of which the newly consolidated German Empire, hungry to become a colonial power and to assert its military might, was only one. There was, as always, trouble in various far-flung parts of the globe where British influence, although still powerful, was a trifle unsteady—India, South

Africa and China—not to mention the more immediate thorn in the English side of the Irish crusade for Home Rule. No other nation enjoyed a political situation that justified the intensity of paranoia manifest in British tales of imaginary uprisings and invasions.

In the 1870s and 1880s, most imaginary future wars were fought with conventional weapons essentially similar to those already in use, but anticipations of new weaponry soon began to creep in. The as-yet-unconstructed Channel Tunnel began to feature as a means of invading Britain, in such pamphlets as *The Channel Tunnel; or England's Ruin* (1876), signed "Cassandra" but almost certainly the work of its publisher, William Laird Clowes, who went on to become a prolific author of future war stories in the early days of generic scientific romance. More adventurously, a brigade of winged troops fought for Irish liberty in *Tom Greer's A Modern Daedalus* (1885).

Ironically enough, the most radical transformation of future warfare suggested in this wave of fiction was one envisaged by George Chesney himself, in the anonymously-issued *The New Ordeal* (1879), which looks forward to a day when bombs have become so very powerful that they can obliterate whole nations. Chesney proposes that this would make war impossible, and that disputes between nations would have to be settled by limited pseudo-gladiatorial contests. The notion of "weapons too dreadful to use," the development of which would put an end to war, had long been a standard feature of French futuristic fantasies, but British authors had always considered the notion far more skeptically, and continued to do so in spite of Chesney's atypical intervention.

By the 1890s, the popularity of this kind of fiction was sufficient to encourage many military men to think in terms of the possibilities of future conflict, and close attention was being paid to the possibilities associated with every new item of military hardware. The popular magazines that proliferated in the early 1890s naturally took the opportunity to cash in on the potential of this kind of story, and their eagerness to do so was a crucial element in the birth of generic scientific romance, as will be described in Chapter Three.

5. THE FUTURE OF DESTINY

Prose lends itself very well to such projects as utopian design and attempts to construct extrapolative maps of the future. Poetry, by and large, does not—but it does lend itself much better to ruminations on eschatological issues, which are inherently more diffuse and tend to collapse if they are burdened with overmuch detail and rational calculation. It is therefore not surprising that Romantic poetry offers much more elaborate displays of eschatological images of the future than utopian ones. Indeed, one of the most significant precursors of the British Romantic Movement was the 1740s vogue for "graveyard poetry", when Edward Young, James Hervey and others used the poetic medium for extensive meditation on the ultimate fate of the human soul, and the implications of that fate for the attitude of mind appropriate to adopt in life. Young's *The Complaint; or, Night Thoughts on Life, Death and Immortality* (1742), better known simply as *Night Thoughts*, became the archetype of the subgenre.

There was a related vogue during the heyday of Romanticism, when Mary Shelley's version of *The Last Man*—which illustrates some of the difficulties of tackling such themes in prose—followed close on the heels of a poem of the same title by Thomas Campbell (1823), which begins with the declaration that "All worldly shapes shall melt in gloom,/The Sun himself must die," and proceeds to elaborate that thought with a vision of a future era in which:

> *The Sun's eye had a sickly glare,*
>   *The Earth with age was wan,*
> *The skeletons on nations were*
>   *Around that lonely man!*
> *Some had expired in fight,—the brands*
> *Still rusted in their bony hands;*
>   *In plague and famine some!*
> *Earth's cities had no sound nor tread;*
> *And ships were drifting with the dead*
>   *To shores where all was dumb!*[62]

---

[62] Thomas Campbell. "The Last Man" in *The Poetical Works of Thomas Campbell*. London: Moxon, 1837. p.105.

As befits a man whose proudest poem was "The Pleasures of Hope," Campbell portrays his last man valiantly confronting his end with complete faith in the afterlife to come, but an 1826 parody of the poem by Thomas Hood finds the two survivors of a great plague meeting by a gallows-tree, on which one ends up hanging the other for looting, before consigning himself miserably to the same fate. Campbell had probably borrowed the title and the idea itself, from the 1806 translation into English of Jean-Baptiste Cousin de Grainville's *Le Dernier homme* (1805), which illustrates the problems of apocalyptic prose narrative even more sharply than Mary Shelley's endeavor. Lord Byron's "Darkness" (1816) is sometimes associated with the group of texts by commentators, although the interpretation of the poem as a futuristic apocalyptic vision is open to doubt, given that 1816 was "a year without a summer," whose obscuring of the sun we now know (although Byron did not) to have been due to volcanic ash injected into the atmosphere by the eruption of Mount Tambora.

The Romantic vogue for eschatological themes extended beyond literature in the apocalyptic paintings of John Martin, which he began to produce in 1812 and continued with increasingly spectacular success into the 1840s. As previously noted, Jane Webb, author of *The Mummy!* was briefly a protégé of Martin's, and he was acquainted with William Godwin. He was also a friend of Michel Faraday and the physicist and inventor Charles Wheatstone, and he began to draw up plans for various inventions and engineering projects of his own in the late 1830s, taking a strong interest in the development of a much-needed system of sewerage for London. Martin's interest in science seems to have enhanced his interest in apocalyptic imagery, and he was by no means the only person to obtain such dark inspiration therefrom.

Scientists whose social, political and imaginative interests brought them within the fringes of the Movement, if only temporarily, were sometimes prompted by it to entertain visionary rhapsodies whose content and manner were very different from the methodical procedures of their scientific reportage. The most striking example was provided by Humphry Davy when the imminence of death took him away from the scientific labors to which he had dedicated his life and put him in a very different frame of mind. By that time, he had long abandoned his youthful radicalism, undergoing religious and political conversions, but he had certainly not forgotten his earlier affiliation to the Romantic Movement or its artistic methods, and was able to make highly original use of them in what is, in essence, a sustained prose-poem encapsulating a cosmic vision akin, at least in its initial momentum, to *Queen Mab*.

* * * *

Davy was one of the foremost English scientists of his day, in terms of his achievements and his celebrity. He was born in Penzance in 1778; his mother, having been orphaned in infancy, had been adopted by a surgeon named John Tonkin and when Humphry's own father died Tonkin secured him an apprenticeship with a fellow physician. Tonkin also allowed Humphry to set up a laboratory in his garret, although he subsequently cut Davy out of his will when the young man turned his back on the medical profession. Davy had found another patron by then, who employed him as a laboratory assistant in a Pneumatic Institute he had established in Bristol. In Bristol, Davy made the acquaintance of Samuel Taylor Coleridge and Robert Southey, and began writing poetry under their influence.

The most interesting of Davy's poems, in retrospect, is "The Sons of Genius," signed simply "D. 1795," which directly follows Charles Lamb's "Living without a God in the World" in a 1799 volume hopefully entitled *Annual Anthology*—which was, indeed, followed by two more. The poem imagines a shepherd going home at dusk, and seeing the landscape populated by "Elfins" and "Sprites" as darkness falls, although the poem's narrative voice offers a different perspective:

> *Whilst Superstition rules the vulgar soul,*
>   *Forbids the energies of man to rise,*
> *Rais'd far above her low, her mean controul*
>   *Aspiring Genius seeks her native skies....*
>
> *Before her lucid all-enlightening ray,*
>   *The pallid spectres of the night retire,*
> *She drives the gloomy terrors far away*
>   *And fills the bosom with celestial fire.*

> *Inspired by her the sons of Genius rise*
>   *Above all earthly thoughts, all vulgar care,*
> *Wealth, power, grandeur, they alike despise,*
>   *Enraptur'd by the good, the great, the fair.*
>
> *A thousand varying charms to them belong*
>   *The charms of Nature and her changeful scenes,*
> *Theirs is the music of the vernal song*
>   *And theirs is the colour of the vernal plains.*

The sons of Genius are not, however, restricted to a finer experience of the wonders of Nature; having spelled out those, the poet adds:

> *Yet not alone delight the soft and fair*
>   *Alike the grander scenes of Nature move,*
> *Yet not alone her beauties claim their care,*
>   *The great, sublime, and terrible, they love.*

That theme too is expanded, but in the darkness where the terrors of the sublime lurk, it is possible to find relief as well as inspiration, and "how sweet" it is as a means of passing the night away:

> *To scan the laws of Nature, to explore*
>   *The tranquil reign of mild Philosophy,*
> *Or on Newtonian wings sublime to soar,*
>   *Thro' the bright regions of the starry sky*

With the result that:

> *From these pursuits the sons of Genius scan*
>   *The end of their creation, hence they know,*
> *The fair, sublime, immortal hopes of man*
>   *From whence alone undying pleasures flow*
>
> *By science calm'd over the peaceful soul,*
>   *Bright with eternal wisdom's lucid ray,*
> *Peace, meek of eye, extends her soft controul,*
>   *And drives the fury passions far away.*

And in conclusion:

> *Like yon proud rocks amidst the sea of time*
> *Superior scorning all the billow's rage,*
> *The living Sons of Genius stand sublime,*
> *The immortal children of another age.*
>
> *For those exist whose pure ethereal minds*
> *Imbibing portions of celestial day,*
> *Scorn all terrestrial cares, all mean designs,*
> *As bright-eyed Eagles scorn the lunar ray.*
>
> *Theirs is the glory of a lasting name*
> *The meed of Genius and her living fires,*
> *Theirs is the laurel of eternal flame,*
> *And theirs the sweetness of the Muse's lyres.*[63]

Davy then proceeded to take in life the path he had mapped out in verse for the sons of Genius, and do his best to discover a better future via science. His early work was on gases, following up the experiments by Joseph Priestley that had isolated "dephlogisticated air" (oxygen) and paved the way for the scrupulous analysis of the atmosphere and the exploration of the chemistry of it components. Gases seemed to have enormous scope in terms of their potential physiological effects as well as their sometime-extraordinary chemistry. Davy introduced Coleridge and Southey to the recreational use of nitrous oxide, also discovered by Joseph Priestley, who had similarly introduced it to his fellow members of the Lunar Society, including James Watt—although Coleridge ultimately preferred the plant-based hallucinogens supplied to him by Joseph Banks as sources of visionary inspiration. Oddly enough, although Davy made notes on the potential of nitrous oxide as a cure for hangovers, it never occurred to any of its early fans that it might be useful as a surgical anesthetic.

In 1801 Davy was appointed Director of the Chemical Laboratory at the recently-founded Royal Institution, also serving as editor of the Institution's publications. That work immediately involved him in the study of "galvanism," which was on the brink

---

63   [Humphry Davy]. "The Sons of Genius" in [Robert Southey, Samuel Taylor Coleridge and Charles Lamb, eds.] *Annual Anthology Volume I*. Bristol: Biggs & Co. for Longman & Rees, London, 1799. pp. 93-99.

of becoming a boom area in research, and enabled him to carry out a long series of crucial experiments in electrochemistry, discovering several new elements in the process. His career went from strength to strength, winning him a series of promotions and prizes and culminating in the knighthood conferred upon him in 1812, the year in which he published *Elements of Chemical Philosophy*. In 1815 he devised the miners' safety-lamp for which he is today best-remembered. In 1818 he was awarded a baronetcy, and in 1820 he was elected President of the Royal Society. He continued his researches thereafter, but his health had already begun to fail and it broke down completely in 1826. He spent his last three years roaming continental Europe, partly in search of a more benign climate and partly in search of the solace that the contemplation of natural scenery and the ruins of past civilizations afforded him.

Such was the parlous state of medical knowledge in the 1820s that Davy's health problems mostly went undiagnosed as well as untreated, but the deterioration had begun in his early days as an experimenter, during his extensive empirical investigation of the physiological effects of various gases, when he had gone in search of the hypothetical "principle of contagion" responsible for the communication of disease, and means of countering it. The damage done by his various inhalation experiments—using a gas chamber constructed for him by James Watt—was exacerbated in 1812, when he contracted a dangerous fever whose cause he was trying to detect, and the harm was doubtless increased by his attempts to cure it. One of the gases he had inhaled in order to test its potential curative effects was chlorine, later to be used in warfare as a poison gas.

Davy's final work, reflecting on the lessons of his life and analyzing the effects of his contemplations, was *Consolations in Travel; or, The Last Days of a Philosopher* (1838). It is, in a sense, his intellectual testament, and had to be published as it was initially written down because the author had no opportunity to make any revisions before his death. It takes the form of a series of six conversations, frequently interrupted by long expository sequences in which the hypothetical narrator, unnamed at first but eventually dubbed Philalethes (love of truth), describes various European settings and his responses thereto, and offers accounts of dreams that he has experienced at various times in his life.

The other main participants in the first two conversations are designated as Ambrosio and Onuphrio; their main function is to represent different religious standpoints, the former being a conservative Roman Catholic, the latter a moderately radical Protestant. In the later dialogues two other characters make extensive contributions to the discussion. One, described as "The Unknown" or "The Stranger", eventually speaks most explicitly and most elaborately in the voice of Davy the scientist, although that is not his primary function. The other, Eubathes, is, like Davy himself, a keen fly-fisherman who becomes the predominant voice in the final pages, when he delivers a long and eloquent soliloquy on the inevitability of mortality and decay.

Philalethes reveals that he was a skeptic in his youth, but that he was eventually converted to belief in God. He identifies the cause of his conversion as a dream he had while he was delirious after contracting a dangerous fever while investigating the theory of contagion, and he offers this dream as a reason for believing that another and much more elaborate dream can be counted as an essentially truthful Revelation. The rest of the book mostly comprises an attempt to discover the implications of this supposed Vision.

* * * *

The narrator explains to his listeners how he sat alone in the ruins of the Coliseum in Rome by the light of the full moon, and how his situation led him to ruminate on the transitory nature of human endeavor. This reverie leads to the conscious construction of analogies between human individuals and civilizations, which give way to the vision itself, in which: "It appeared to me that I had entered a new state of existence, and I was so perfectly lost in the new kind of sensation which I experienced that I had no recollections and no perceptions of identity."[64]

This altered state of consciousness allows the narrator to hear the voice of a "superior intelligence", which he chooses—perhaps with "The Sons of Genius" still vaguely in mind—to call "the Genius," who plays the role of commentator as the narrator is carried away on a voyage through time and space.

---

64   Humphry Davy. *Consolations in Travel; or, The Last Days of a Philosopher*. London: John Murray, 1838. p.17.

The narrator sees the remote ancestors of mankind living in a wild state, without clothes or shelter, using primitive tools of flint and bone. Then, after "the birth of Time", he sees man "in his newly created state": fully clad, far better fed—having invented agriculture and animal husbandry—and properly sheltered. He sees civilization advance by degrees, witnesses the advent of metallurgy and philosophy, war and writing, conquest and colonization. The Genius explains to him how the fall of Rome to barbarian hordes was a necessary clearance and prelude to reinvigoration by hybridization, and waxes lyrical on the crucial role played in human history by natural philosophers and technological innovators: the progenitors and agents of progress.

Unsurprisingly, Davy's Genius sides with Peacock's Mr. Foster when it comes to assessing the benefits of technology and is bitterly critical of the ingratitude of past and present societies to their pioneers of science:

"The works of the most illustrious names were little valued at the times when they were produced, and their authors were either despised or neglected; and great, indeed, must have been the pure and abstract pleasure resulting from the exertion of intellectual superiority and the discovery of truth and the bestowing benefits and blessings upon society, which induced men to sacrifice all their common enjoyments and all their privileges as citizens, to these exertions. Anaxagoras, Archimedes, Roger Bacon, Galileo Galilei, in their deaths or their imprisonments, offer instances of this kind, and nothing can be more striking than what appears to have been the ingratitude of men towards their greatest benefactors; but hereafter, when you understand more of the scheme of the universe, you will see the cause and effect of this, and you will find the whole system governed by principles of immutable justice. I have said that in the progress of society, all great and real improvements are perpetuated...."[65]

This summary account and evaluation of history and technology concludes with a ringing endorsement of the moral benefits of technological progress, which echoes the sentiments of Erasmus Darwin: "If the quantity of life is increased, the quantity of happiness, particularly that resulting from the exercise of intellectual power, is increased in a still higher ratio." The Genius immediately

---

65   Ibid. pp.35-35.

hastens on, however, to extrapolate the utopian argument into an eschatological one, moving from talk of "intellectual power" to "spiritual nature":

"Spiritual natures are eternal and indivisible, but their modes of being are as infinitely varied as the forms of matter. They have no relation to space, and, in their transitions, no dependence upon time, so that they a pass from one part of the universe to another by laws entirely independent of their motion. The quantity, or the number of spiritual essences, like the quantity or number of the atoms of the material world, [is] always the same; but their arrangements, like those of the materials which they are destined to guide or govern, are infinitely diversified; they are, in fact, parts more or less inferior of the infinite mind, and in the planetary systems, to one of which this globe you inhabit belongs, are in a state of probation, continually aiming at, and generally rising to a higher state of existence."[66]

The Genius assures the narrator that he could show him the present incarnations of the spiritual essences that were Socrates and Newton, "now in a higher and better state of planetary existence, drinking intellectual light from a purer source" but decides instead to conduct him to the planet Saturn, so that he might look down into its atmosphere and see its alien inhabitants.

"I saw moving on the surface below me immense masses, the forms of which I find it impossible to describe; they had systems for locomotion similar to those of the morse or sea-horse, but I saw with great surprise that they moved from place to place by six extremely thin membranes, which they used as wings. Their colors were varied and beautiful, but principally azure and rose-color. I saw numerous convolutions of tubes, more analogous to the trunk of the elephant than anything else I can imagine, occupying what I supposed to be the upper parts of the body."[67]

The Genius explains that each of these trunk-like tubes "is an organ of peculiar motion or sensation" and that their superior sensory apparatus and intelligence have allowed the Saturnians to discover far more about the universe and its laws than mankind ever could, and to become far more virtuous. He explains to the narrator that the other planets in the solar system are inhabited by

66 Ibid. pp.42-43.
67 Ibid. p.47.

beings at various levels of intellectual and spiritual development, and that the "higher natures" that exist elsewhere in the universe make use of "finer and more ethereal kinds of matter" in their organization. He offers brief descriptions of life on Jupiter, Mars and Venus, whose inhabitants have other modes of locomotion and other senses, but participate in the same scheme of intellectual and spiritual progress.

These are not merely parallel stories to that of human beings; after death, human individuals—among whom scientists are those most ready for rapid advancement—will make continue to make their own spiritual progress, by slow and measured degrees, through a series of extraterrestrial incarnations:

"The universe is everywhere full of life, but the modes of this life are infinitely diversified, and yet every form of it must be enjoyed and known by every spiritual nature before the consummation of all things."[68]

The narrator is permitted to glimpse one other mode of existence, when he observes moving around him "globes which appeared composed of different kinds of flame and of different colors," containing figures that remind him of human faces. The Genius explains to him that he is now in "a cometary system; those globes of light surrounding you are material forms, such as one of your systems of religious faith have been attributed to seraphs; they live in that element which to you would be destruction; they communicate by powers which would convert your organized frame to ashes; they are now in the height of their enjoyment, being about to enter into the blaze of the solar atmosphere."[69]

Although they were once incarnate as humans, these cometary beings can no more remember their humanity than men can remember life in the womb. The only "sentiment or passion" that the spiritual essence or "monad" carries forward through all its successive metamorphoses is the love of knowledge, whose ultimate extrapolation is the love of God. If this love is misapplied to worldly ambition or the pursuit of oppressive power, the Genius explains, a spirit "sinks in the scale of existence...till its errors are corrected by painful discipline"—but the narrator is not insulted by any vision of such subhuman modes of existence. The Genius

68   Ibid. p.54.
69   Ibid. p.55.

concentrates on celebration of the progressive aspects of the post-human situation, insisting that the cause of progress is not merely the highest good but the source of the greatest joy of which any imaginable being is capable.

The Saturnians and the comet-dwellers, the dreamer is assured, are capable of far greater happiness than mere humans. The Genius, who is happier still, cannot take the narrator into his own world—the sun—because its brightness would prove fatal to one of his feeble constitution, and so the vision ends with the voice of Enlightenment replaced by that of a servant searching for his lost employer.

* * * *

Although strikingly original in the context of English literature, Davy's vision was not the first extraterrestrial flight of the human imagination into the cosmos theoretically constructed by science, nor the first to find an escalating scale of perfection laid out there, potentially accessible to the human soul after death. The subsequent dialogues in *Consolations in Travel* refer *en passant* to two visionaries who had undertaken more extensive odysseys—Athanasius Kircher and Emmanuel Swedenborg—but the work by Kircher to which Davy refers is the proto-geological study *Mundus Subterraneus* (2 vols., 1665; 1678) and he is unlikely to have read the far less well known *Itinerarium exstaticum* (1656). The documents nowadays known as the *Arcana of Heaven* had been extracted from Swedenborg's notebooks for publication and translation long before, but Davy is unlikely to have read them either, being far more interested in the author's earlier scientific works.

It is even more unlikely that Davy had read the first work that had attempted (unsuccessfully) to popularize the idea of serial reincarnation in extraterrestrial settings, Restif de la Bretonne's epistolary fantasy *Les Posthumes* (written 1787-89; published 1802). He might well, however, have been familiar with the most significant book of that kind written by a scientist of his own stature, Christiaan Huygens' *Cosmotheoros* (1698), which the astronomer and inventor had not dared to publish while he was alive, lest it be deemed heretical and invite violence, but the posthumous publication of which had occasioned rapid translation into English. *Cosmotheoros* describes life on the other planets in the solar system and organizes them into a divinely-ordained schema of creation. Huygens assumed, however, that humans would be replicated on all other worlds, reproducing the same image of their creator that was manifest on Earth. Davy attributed a more flexible meaning to the notion of "image," applying it to the soul rather than mere bodily form, and thus followed the precedents set by John Kepler and Restif in populating other worlds with genuinely alien life-forms.

Just as its predecessors had been produced in continental Europe, so the most direct and most striking influence of Davy's vision was on the far side of the English Channel. *Consolations in Travel* made such a deep impact on the French astronomer Camille Flammarion that he translated it into French, and immediately introduced its perspective into a series of essays in the popularization of science he was in the process of writing in the form of conversations with a disembodied soul, collected under the title of *Lumen* (1866-69), initially in *Récits de l'infini* (1872), and then in an expanded version in 1887. Flammarion's version of literal "cosmic palingenesis" had considerably more influence in France than Davy's had in England, where the vision was rightly construed as an allegory rather than an assertion of fact.

Considerable attention is paid in the subsequent dialogues in *Consolations in Travel* to the question of whether the modern discoveries of science can be reconciled with the account of Creation and the Fall contained in Genesis, and Philatheles comes down firmly on the side of Creation, even though he accepts the evidence of fossils as proof of biological evolution. "The Unknown" agrees with him, adding an exemplary anecdote of his own about an accursed wanderer condemned to immortality: not the Wandering Jew of legend but a Wandering Christian, cursed by God for attempting to rebuild the Temple in Jerusalem at the behest of the Roman emperor Julian the Apostate.

The Unknown seems to symbolize the limitations of scientific knowledge, setting down boundaries of mystery that ought not to be crossed; the parable of the Wandering Christian seems to be indicating that there are some matters that should not be subjected to experimental testing. In the fourth dialogue the Unknown becomes a guide not unlike the Genius, offering observations on matters of biology and philosophical ruminations on the nature of life; he presents a robust rebuttal of materialism and a stirring defense of vitalism, to which the immortality of the spiritual essence is, in his view, a mere corollary.

In the fifth dialogue, the Unknown mounts a strident defense of chemistry as a uniquely useful field of human endeavor, summarizing its crucial contributions to human progress and waxing lyrical on the issue of its as-yet-unrealized potential. This argument is further extended in the final dialogue, where the Unknown becomes passionate in his insistence that humans must work much harder to preserve their works from the ever-present effects of erosion and corrosion. Eubathes takes up this theme, arguing with equal passion that because decay is inevitable and all earthly things transient men must look beyond civilization and technology for the final justification of their efforts and endeavors.

The final conclusion is, however, left for Philatheles to affirm his own ultimate conviction, which turns out to be a little more modest and less robust than the suggestion of the vision, but nevertheless preserves its essence and clings stubbornly to the inevitability of progress:

"It is, perhaps, rather a poetical than a philosophical idea, yet I cannot help forming the opinion, that genii or seraphic intelligences might inhabit [the nebulae described by William Herschel], and may be the ministers of the eternal mind, in producing changes in them similar to those which have taken place on the earth. Time is almost a human word and change entirely a human word; in the system of Nature we should rather say progress than change. The sun appears to sink in the ocean in darkness, but it rises in another hemisphere; the ruins of a city fall, but they are often used to form more magnificent structures as at Rome; but, even when they are destroyed, so as to produce only dust, Nature asserts her empire over them, and the vegetable world rises in constant youth, and—in a period of annual successions, by the labours of man providing food—vitality, and beauty upon the wrecks of monuments, which were once raised for purposes of glory, but which are now applied to objects of utility."[70]

* * * *

---

70   Ibid. pp.280-281.

Although Humphry Davy's brief vision of the universal progress of spiritual essences won no converts, the impulse that drove him to formulate the dream nevertheless remained comprehensible to many of his contemporaries, who took up the burden of the meditation in their own terms. Religious believers faced with the challenge posed by scientific challenges to their eschatological notions could simply retreat into dogmatic faith—as Philatheles is certainly tempted to do, although he cannot eventually persuade himself to take that route with either of his initial companions—but doubters and skeptics needed to search for other directions. In terms of poetic expression, none searched harder, with a fuller awareness of contemporary developments in science, than Alfred, Lord Tennyson, who poured his reflections into a series of meditative poems, the most famous of which is *In Memoriam A. H. H.* (1849), although that poem is ideologically bracketed by his two comparative reflections on "Locksley Hall" the first published in 1842 and the latter, as "Locksley Hall Sixty Years After," in 1886.

In Memoriam was a reaction to the death of the poet's close friend, Arthur Hallam, who had died in 1833, and is a direct reflection of grief and the mental effort—extended over several years—of coming to terms with it. Although *Consolations in Travel* was written in anticipation of its author's own death, there is a necessary disjunction of perspective between the two, which imparts a different slant to their interpretation of similar observations, even before differences of personal conviction are taken into account, and which undoubtedly helped to determine where those differences of personal conviction ultimately settled.

Like *Headlong Hall* and *Consolations in Travel*, *In Memoriam* introduces elements of dialogue in order to set ideas in contest, and the first such voice to be introduced, to preach the lessons of the scientific perspective, is Sorrow:

> *O Sorrow, cruel fellowship,*
> *O Priestess in the vaults of Death.*
> *O sweet and bitter in a breath,*
> *What whispers from thy lying lip?*
>
> *'The stars,' she whispers, 'blindly run;*
> *A web is wov'n across the sky;*

> *From out waste places comes a cry,*
> *And murmurs from the dying sun:*
>
> *'And all the phantom, Nature, stands—*
> *With all the music in her tone,*
> *A hollow echo of my own,—*
> *A hollow form with empty hands.'*[71]

The narrative voice cannot quite convince himself that Sorrow's bleak image of the world really is the produce of a "lying lip," and the long mediation that follows, occasionally interrupted by brief voices attempting to offer comfort, cannot defeat its dread. While the poem was making its slow progress, in fact, Tennyson read Chambers' *Vestiges of the Natural History of Creation*, which only served to re-emphasize Sorrow's view of a bleak, uncaring and inhospitable universe.

Before that point is reached, the narrative voice indulges in a nostalgic flight of fancy, regretful of an Arcadia where the hills hummed with "the murmur of a happy Pan."[72] He continues in that soothing vein for some time, mingling paradisal imagery taken from both Classical and Biblical sources, including the voices of Urania and Melpomene, but the darker doubts remain insistent, compelling him to wonder whether:

> *Are God and Nature then at strife,*
> *   That Nature lends such evil dreams!*
> *   So careful of the type she seems,*
> *So careless of the single life;*
>
> *That I, considering everywhere*
> *   Her secret meaning in her deeds,*
> *   And finding that of fifty seeds*
> *She often brings but one to bear,*
>
> *I falter where I firmly trod,*
> *   And falling with my weight of cares*
> *   Upon the great world's altar stairs*
> *That slope through darkness up to God,*

---

71   Alfred, Lord Tennyson. *In Memoriam*. Eleventh Edition. London: Moxon, 1862. p.3.
72   Ibid. p.39.

> *I stretch lame hands of faith and grope.*
> *And gather dust and chaff, and call*
> *To what I feel is Lord of all,*
> *And faintly trust the larger hope.*[73]

The next stanza continues:

> *'So careful of the type?' but no.*
> *From scarped cliff and quarried stone*
> *She cries 'a thousand types are gone;*
> *I care for nothing, all shall go.*
>
> *'Thou makest thine appeal to me:*
> *I bring to life, I bring to death:*
> *The spirit does but mean the breath:*
> *I know no more.' And he, shall he,*
>
> *Man, her last work, who seem'd so fair*
> *Such splendid purpose in his eyes.*
> *Who roll'd the psalm to wintry skies,*
> *Who built him fanes of fruitless prayer,*
>
> *Who trusted God was love indeed*
> *And love Creation's final law—*
> *Tho' Nature, red in tooth and claw*
> *With ravine, shrieked against his creed—*[74]

The image contained in the penultimate quoted line stuck in the public memory more than any other, and came to seem even more emblematic a decade later, when Charles Darwin proposed that natural selection was the key to the evolutionary process—from which it seemed to follow that the bloodiness of Nature's teeth and claws is a central element of the cost of progress.

The fact that Tennyson could not find God and Nature in harmony, but rather in strife, can hardly seem surprising from a modern viewpoint that, even if it refuses to accept natural selection, cannot ignore it. In Tennyson's day, however, advocates of the view advocated by Isaac Newton, that a better understanding of Nature would necessary lead to a better understanding and appreciation of

---

73   Ibid. pp.78-79.
74   Ibid. p.80.

God, and promoted in verse by Richard Blackmore, Henry Baker and Henry Brooke, had developed into the doctrine of "natural theology," popularized in William Paley's *Natural Theology; or, Evidences of the Existence and Attributes of the Deity, Collected from the Appearances of Nature* (1802). With Chambers' aid, Tennyson had concluded that the "Appearances of Nature" did not endorse the Christian image of God at all, but were, in fact, in brutal conflict with it. Gerald Griffin had been unable to understand that anyone contemplating the wonders of astronomy could fail to concede the glory of the Creator, but to Tennyson, as to Shelley and many others, no such easy and direct inference seemed possible, and it seemed to them that if faith were to be sustained, it would have to find alternative support.

That Tennyson tried to do, in the remainder of *In Memoriam*; eventually, having found his way back to Christmas Eve and all its symbolism for a second time, and with it a more hopeful way to "Contemplate all this work of Time," he was able to conclude:

> *I trust I have not wasted breath;*
> *I think we are not wholly brain,*
> *Magnetic mockeries; not in vain,*
> *Like Paul with beasts, I fought with Death;*
>
> *Not only cunning casts in clay:*
> *Let Science prove we are, and then*
> *What matters Science unto men,*
> *At least to me? I would not stay.*
>
> *Let him, the wiser man who springs*
> *Hereafter, up from childhood shape*
> *His action like the greater ape,*
> *But I was born to other things.*[75]

* * * *

Not everyone found that kind of reaffirmation possible, in the face of what Tennyson had accepted, and the main thrust of the scientific idea of "Nature," after Chambers' stirring of the vestiges of Creation, was not to bring any obvious succor. Indeed, other

---

75   Ibid. p.186.

calculations with seeming eschatological connotations were soon added to the melting-pot.

One such addition that was to be surprisingly potent as an idea guiding thought and literary expression was an essay in the popularization of science by Sir William Thomson, Lord Kelvin, which he wrote for *Macmillan's Magazine* in 1862, "On the Age of the Sun's Heat," in which he attempted to exemplify the second law of thermodynamics with calculations of the likely duration of the period when the sun's heat would continue to supply the Earth with the heat permitting life to flourish there. As evidenced by the quoted comments of Thomas Campbell and Tennyson, the fact that the sun seemed fated to die did seem a relevant issue in nineteenth-century eschatological meditations, and it was thus only natural that a scientist who thought himself capable of casting some light on the question of when should try to do so.

In laying the theoretical foundation of his estimate, Kelvin draws upon a popular lecture delivered two years earlier in Königsberg by Hermann von Helmholtz, which proposed that the sun's heat must have originated as a results of smaller bodies "falling together by mutual gravitation and generating, as they must do according to the great law demonstrated by Joule, an exact equivalent of heat for the energy lost in collision."[76] Kelvin rejects all chemical theories of generation on the grounds that none would allow the sun the produce heat for as long as it already has, and also rejects the idea that continuing "meteor falls" can still be renewing the heat on any substantial scale.

As a result of his calculations—which we now know to be based on false premises, because the sun's heat is actually generated by nuclear fusion—Kelvin concludes that:

"It seems, therefore, on the whole most probable that the sun has not illuminated the earth for 100,000,000 years, and almost certain that he has not done so for 500,000,000 years. As for the future, we may say, with equal certainly, that the inhabitants of the earth cannot continue to enjoy the light and heat essential to their life, for many million years longer, unless sources now unknown to us are prepared in the great storehouse of creation."[77]

76   Lord Kelvin. *Popular Lectures and Addresses, Volume 1.* New York: Macmillan, Second Edition, 1891. pp.372-373.

77   Ibid. p.375.

Because of its double extent, this calculation had a double relevance. Its first part, although crediting the Earth with a long past life, put a limit on the time that evolutionists could attribute to the development thus far of Erasmus Darwin's great filament—a limit that was cramped by comparison with estimates such as Benoît de Maillet's two billion years—while the second part suggested that the history of life on the planet had far less time remaining to it than it had already enjoyed. Although a few million years of future was by no means short, in human terms, the proportion clearly suggested that human beings had been very belated arrivals on the Earth's surface, and could not possibly exist for more than a small fraction of its lifetime. What then became of the prospects of perfectibility? How, in fact, could any "perfection" be reckoned truly perfect, with that sentence of ultimate death hanging over it?

Kelvin might well have been surprised by the intensity of the interest his calculation had caused, and the importance attached by some commentators to the implications of his conclusion. He must, however, have reckoned the piece an unusually successful exercise in popularization, and eventually followed it up with another, delivered as a lecture at the Royal Institution in 1887 and subsequently reprinted in *Good Words* as "On the Sun's Heat," in which he elaborated the theoretical basis of the first essay and defended it against some objections, but did not modify his calculation.

Kelvin's conclusion was adopted as a significant item of evidence for the "deteriorationist cause"; Mr. Escot would have doubtless have loved it, and would not have failed to cite it as the ultimate damnation of Mr. Foster's thesis. What could it matter that the earth's axis might be altered in order to unify its climates, if the sun were bound to die, by degrees, over a span of time far less that humans had taken to evolve? The image of the sun's death had been present in eschatological fantasies before Kelvin's essay, but putting a number on it, even one as vague as "not many million," gave it a different perspective within the context of geological estimates of the Earth's age and the pace of organic evolution. H. G. Wells, who used it as the logical keystone of *The Time Machine*, was one of the writers who took it most urgently to heart, and thus incorporated it into the very heart of generic scientific romance.

* * * *

Another notable scientist of the Victorian Era who was moved to the kind of eschatological rhapsody contained in *Consolations in Travel*, albeit in a tongue-in-cheek fashion, was Kelvin's fellow Scot, James Clerk Maxwell, who produced "A Paradoxical Ode [After Shelley]" in 1878, a year before his death. Its second verse integrates the implications of Kelvin's calculation with evolutionary theory:

> *But when thy science lifts her pinion*
> *In Speculation's wild dominions*
> *I treasure every dictum thou emmitest;*
> *While down the stream of Evolution*
> *We drift, and look for no solution*
> *But that of survival of the fittest,*
> *Till in that twilight of the gods*
> *When earth and sun are frozen clods,*
> *When, all its matter degraded,*
> *Matter in aether shall have faded,*
> *We, that is, all the work we've done,*
> *As waves in aether shall forever run*
> *In swift expanding spheres, through heavens beyond the sun.*[78]

The third and last verse concludes with a mocking but not entirely inapposite plea to "Let viewless fancies guide my darling flight/Through aeon-haunted worlds, in order infinite."

Maxwell's poem was written in specific response to the popularizing efforts of his friend Peter Guthrie Tait, the co-author with Lord Kelvin of a *Treatise on Natural Philosophy* (1867) and co-author with Balfour Stewart of *The Unseen Universe; or, Physical Speculations on a Future State* (1875), a tract written in opposition to the materialist views of John Tyndall and intended to demonstrate that modern science could be reconciled with Christian doctrine. Tait and Stewart followed up the latter text with an unsigned fictionalized sequel, *Paradoxical Philosophy* (1879), which Maxwell

---

78 James Clerk Maxwell. "A Paradoxical Ode," in Daniel S. Silver. "The Last Poem of James Clerk Maxwell." Notices of the AMS 55:10 (2008). pp.1266-1270.

must have seen before publication, because it involves imaginary conversations between Scottish Christians and a fictitious German philosopher, Hermann Stoffkrafft, to whom Maxwell's poem is notionally addressed.

The authors of *Paradoxical Philosophy* observe in its preface that: "The exigencies of the subject, and not any thought of imitating Peacock, Helps, or Mallock—far less Christopher North, Bunyan or Plato—absolutely *dictated* the conversational style."[79] The comment is disingenuous, however, as the book is manifestly imitative of the literary method Peacock had pioneered in *Headlong Hall* and Peacock is the obvious model for its literary construction and style.

The other authors named are not irrelevant to the development of philosophical conversations bearing on scientific issues. The prolific writer on historical and sociological subjects Sir Arthur Helps had made use of such conversations in several works, most notably in *Realmah* (1868), in which one of the participants in the dialogue weaves a pioneering prehistoric romance to illustrate a debate about the early evolution of society. William Hurrell Mallock created a considerable stir with his satirical dialogue *à clef*, *The New Republic* (1877), which bore upon utopianism as well as evolutionism. "Christopher North" was an imaginary persona adopted by John Wilson, the editor of *Blackwood's Magazine*, for the regular feature *Noctes Ambrosianae*, detailing witty imaginary table-talk on the part of the magazine's contributors, including two whose improvised representations were wryly adopted by the appellants: "the Ettrick Shepherd" (James Hogg) and "the English Opium-Eater" (Thomas De Quincey).

The text of *Paradoxical Philosophy* opens with an introductory account of the Paradoxical Society, supposedly founded in 1826 by Isaac Fairbank and maintained by his son Stephen, who hosts its fiftieth anniversary celebration in 1876. The guests at the gathering include the amiable and sincere Dr. Stoffkraft:

"With regard to his mental characteristics, they were not like those of ordinary mortals. In this country we should probably (in the rough way we have of lumping men together) call him a materialist, but Dr. Hermann Stoffkraft might no doubt be inclined to

---

79 [Peter Guthrie Tait and Balfour Stewart] *Paradoxical Philosophy*. London: Macmillan, 1879. unpaginated prefatory material.

contest the propriety of the name. He called himself a votary of the goddess Nature, apparently using the word to denote not merely the orderly succession of external phenomena with which we are brought into contact, but likewise the Power which underlies those manifestations.

"But he was by no means a blind worshipper, in fact he was compelled reluctantly to admit that in one little matter his goddess had made a mistake.

"That mistake consisted, according to him, in the development of a race of intelligent beings like ourselves."[80]

In the ensuing discussions Stoffkrafft does indeed confirm that, in his view, consciousness, or "at least a consciousness sufficiently developed to feel at the same time a longing for immortality and an assurance of its impossibility,"[81] has to be reckoned a mistake on the part of Nature. It is this eschatological conundrum that provides the nub of the argument, as it did for Tennyson in *In Memoriam*, but the self-described "Christian scientists" of the Paradoxical Society, instead of trying to come to terms intellectually with the assurance of mortality, take the opposite tack, and endeavor to prove to the votary of Nature that immortality is, in fact assured—a stratagem of which James Clerk Maxwell, who might have taken the characterization Stoffkrafft a trifle personally, could not approve.

The debate is far-ranging in detail, but it involves an ingenious exchange between Stephen Fairbank and Dr. Stoffkrafft on the impossibility of accepting the "eternity of the sun," juxtaposed with the necessity of accepting the "eternity of the atom." There is much quoting from the earnest *The Unseen Universe*, but the discussion is enlivened by the interventions of Sir Kenneth M'Kelpie, a believer in the traditional Scottish gift of "second sight," whose anecdotal evidence in support of that notion, linked to modern developments in spiritualism, provides impetus that carries the plot forward beyond the house party to various further developments. That part of the dialogue reflects Balfour Stewart's interest in such matters; he was later to be prominently involved in the Society for Psychical Research.

---

80   Ibid.p.13.
81   Ibid.p.50.

The further developments in question include the involvement of the newly-married and somewhat-converted Stoffkrafft in adventures in "Electro-biology," and lead him to resume his mathematical work on other dimensions: work of a sort that might have led him, in time, to ideas similar to those developed by Charles Howard Hinton in his explicitly-labeled *Scientific Romances*, and which definitely entitle him to the regular membership in the Paradoxical Society that the final chapter of the book grants him.

The Lunar Society surely discussed the same issue as the one addressed by the Paradoxical Society's anniversary meeting, undoubtedly more than once, and we can probably presume that the members of the Constellation would have done so too. Whether they might have come to conclusions similar to those of Lord Tennyson or Humphry Davy, we can only guess, but the probability is that Erasmus Darwin and Joseph Priestley, and Tag, Rag and Bobtail's uncle too, would have been sympathetic to both; the eschatological image of the future, and the role that scientific genius might play in helping to form and clarify it, was an issue of some importance to them. Even the materialists who occasionally spurred them to intellectual action, like John Tyndall, would not have considered the question irrelevant or settled.

In spite of the desire of boundary-markers like Davy's Unknown to mark certain imaginative territories off-limits to scientific inquiry, they could not really be left inviolate, no matter how discreet such inquiries were—and even if they had to be set aside by empirical science, they remained very much at home in the realm of scientific romance, ripe for seizure by the genre.

6. THE POETRY OF SCIENCE

Another British scientist of note who dabbled in Romantic poetry and visionary fantasy, and who worked hard to insist that science had a Romantic poetry of its own, was Robert Hunt, who published a wide-ranging popularization of science entitled *The Poetry of Science* in 1848. He followed it up with a novel, *Panthea: the Spirit of Nature* (1849), which borrowed more than its figurehead from the work of Shelley, but the story had obviously been composed at intervals over a long period of time; only the brief final section attempts to embody the principles set out in

The Poetry of Science, the rest mapping out an intellectual odyssey in allegorical form that presumably tells the story of how Hunt arrived at the mentality behind the earlier book.

Robert Hunt was born in September 1807 in Plymouth Dock (now Devonport). He was named after his father, a naval officer whose ship had gone down with all hands in April of that year. At the age of twelve, Hunt was apprenticed to a surgeon in London and worked for a while as a physician and medical dispenser before poor health and the inheritance of a small property prompted him to return to Cornwall in 1828.

While he was in London, Robert Hunt made the acquaintance of Henry Hunt, a friend of William Cobbett's who had been about to address the crowd gathered in St. Peter's Fields in August 1819 when the so-called "Peterloo Massacre" occurred, and had served a term in jail in consequence. Henry Hunt was thus better known as "Radical Hunt"—a nickname that sometimes caused him to be confused with the Romantic poet Leigh Hunt. Just as Leigh Hunt had once taken a young medical student—John Keats—under his wing and helped him become a Romantic poet, Henry Hunt took charge of Robert Hunt's continuing education, and introduced him to Romantic poetry.

When Hunt first returned to Cornwall he produced a volume of poetry entitled *The Mount's Bay* (1829), and also developed a strong interest in gathering local folklore. When his health recovered in 1833 he opened a pharmacy in Penzance, but after marrying he returned to London to seek more lucrative work with a firm of chemical manufacturers. He was assigned projects that made him one of the earliest investigators of the chemistry of photography. In 1840, he moved back to Cornwall again when he was appointed secretary of the Royal Cornwall Polytechnic Society and settled in Falmouth. His interest in the education of the working class had always been strong—he had helped to found a Mechanics' Institute in Penzance—and he became increasingly enthusiastic in that cause, particularly on behalf of Cornish miners. The remainder of his life was devoted to the causes of education and science.

Hunt's *Popular Treatise on the Art of Photography* (1841) was the first to be issued in the British Isles; it went through six editions. The first edition of his *Researches on Light in its Chemical Relations* (1844) was almost exclusively devoted to photography, but his experiments in the field soon ranged further afield. He took a particularly keen interest in the subtly-different chemical effects of colored light rays separated by prismatic refraction; when a second edition of the *Researches on Light* issued in 1854 it was much broader in its scope. In 1845 he received the government appointment of Keeper of the Mining Records, a post he was to hold for the next thirty-seven years. Although the duties attached to the position were by no means trivial, he also found time to lecture in Mechanical Sciences at the Royal School of Mines at Redruth in 1851, eventually taking the chair of Experimental Physics.

Hunt continued to spend a good deal of time in London, and he was actively involved in the organization of the Great Exhibitions of 1851 and 1862, for which he produced handbooks explaining the scientific and technological background of the items in the catalogues. Because scientific works are routinely superseded, while superstition is forever, his most enduring work proved to be his folklore collection *Popular Romances of the West of England*, initially issued in two volumes in 1865 with decorations by George Cruikshank; a single-volume edition followed 1871, and was reprinted periodically for more than a century thereafter.

Panthea was probably begun in the latter phase of the sojourn in Cornwall that produced the notes for the study of the region's folklore, and seems to have been heavily influenced by Edward Bulwer-Lytton's *Godolphin* (1833). The plot of Bulwer's novel exhibits a marked change of mind on the part of its author as it developed, which its writing might have helped to bring about, and *Panthea* does the same, although that was probably not intended when it was begun. Both novels begin by enthusiastically embracing an occult world-view that their heroes—together with the impersonal narrators commenting on the heroes' careers—eventually renounce. Hunt's long career as an experimental scientist proves that his conversion was more wholehearted and durable than Bulwer's, the aftermath of which will be discussed in a subsequent section.

Various references in Hunt's works to the life and works of Humphry Davy suggest that Hunt must have read *Consolations in Travel* (1830), and the lessons that he draws from the geological discoveries of James Hutton, Charles Lyell and others echo Davy's so closely that Hunt must have thought of himself and Davy as kindred spirits. Like Davy, Hunt appears to have set aside his flirtations with radical freethought in order to become a steadfast Christian, and like Davy, he is very reluctant in *The Poetry of Science* to read the evidence that the surface of the earth has undergone enormous changes in past eras as a challenge to the religious view of humanity as a special and direct creation of a Divine Architect.

In the preface to *The Poetry of Science*, Hunt states that "An attempt has been made in this volume to link together those scientific facts which bear directly and visibly on Natural Phenomena and to show that they have a value superior to their mere economic applications, in their power of exalting the mind to the contemplation of the Universe."[82]

As promised in this prospectus, each of Hunt's sixteen chapters sets out to acquaint the reader as to what facts have been discovered in various fields of physical and chemical science and what theories have been induced therefrom, together with a careful and reverent account of what the sum of these conclusions suggests as to the nature of the universe and humankind's place therein. Hunt continually contrasts the revelations of modern science with the speculations of classical philosophers and the inventions of folklore.

"It has been argued by many," Hunt contends, "that the realities of science will not admit of anything like a poetic view without degrading its high office; that poetry, being the imaginative side of nature, has nothing in common with the facts of experimental research, or with the philosophy which generalizes the discoveries of severe induction. If our science was perfect, and laid bare to our senses all the secrets of the inner world; if our philosophy was infallible and always connected one fact with another through a long series up to the undoubted cause of all: then poetry, in the sense we now use the term, would have little business with the truth; it would, indeed, be lost or embodied, like the stars of heaven, in the brightness of a meridian sun. But to take our present fact as an example, how important a foundation does it offer on which to build a series of thoughts, capable of lifting the human mind above the materialities by which it is surrounded; of exalting each common nature by the refinement of its fresh ideas to a point higher in the

---

82   Robert Hunt *The Poetry of Science; or, Studies of the Physical Phenomena of Nature*. London: Reeve, Benham and Reeve, 1848. p.v.

scale of intelligence, of quickening every impulse of the soul, and giving to mankind most holy longings."[83]

When he contemplates the revelations of geology, it is not the evidence of drastic change that first presents itself to Hunt's poetic eye, but rather the evidence of the constancy by which the fundamental forces governing matter have supervised and organized the progression of the epochs, and he finds a cause for teleological optimism therein:

"Thus have we preserved for us, in a natural manner, evidences which, if we read them aright, must convince us that the laws by which creation has ever been regulated are as constant and unvarying as the Eternal mind by which they were decreed. Our earth, we find, by the records preserved in the foundation stones of her mountains, has existed through countless ages, and through them all exhibited the same active energies as prevail, at the present moment. By precisely similar influences to those now in operation, have rocks been formed, which, under like agencies, have been covered with vegetation, and sported over by, to us, strange varieties of animal life. Every plant that has grown upon the earliest rocks which presented their faces to the life-giving sun, has had its influence on the subsequent changes of our planet. Each trilobite, each saurian, and every one of the mammalia which exist in the fossil state, have been small laboratories in which the great work of eternal change has been carried forward, and under the compulsion of the strong laws of creation, they have been made ministers to the great end of forming a world which might be fitting for the presence of a creature endued with a spark taken from the celestial flame of intellectual life...."[84]

* * * *

Panthea's protagonist, Lord Julian Altamont, has lost most of his siblings to death, and his one surviving sister is ominously named Euthanasia. His tutor, Mr. Cheverton, was once an experimental scientist but is now a clergyman. In spite of his own religious orthodoxy and the strong objections of Julian's father, Lord Devonport, Cheverton encourages Julian to seek enlightenment from an unorthodox scholar named Laon Ælphage, or Laon

---

83   Ibid. p.173.
84   Ibid. pp.324-325.

the Mystic, said to be "a follower of Jacob Behmen" (the German mystical philosopher Jacob Boehme.) Laon has a daughter, Æltgiva, and although Julian is supposed to be in love with the eighteen-year-old Eudora Spencer, the daughter of a neighboring landowner, Æltgiva makes a deep impression on him. She seems to him to be haloed in "mystic sanctity", and when she offers to initiate him into the mysteries of "the mighty PANTHEA"—the spirit of nature—he is extremely eager, and sets off on a journey of discovery with Laon, which changes him considerably. Its beginning closely echoes the first phase of Davy's Vision:

"It appeared to Julian that he had entered upon a new state of existence. His thoughts were of a higher order, and his feelings of a more sensitive character. His powers of perception were more accurate, and his reflective faculties capable of closer and more enduring exercise. He could now direct his powers of observation to the most microscopic phenomena, and without difficulty connect them with the extended operations of creation. A veil had been removed from his eyes; all things appeared more clear; a greater transparency was, as he thought, exhibited in nature."[85]

The geography of the visionary journey is metaphorical rather than literal. It reaches its climax in tropical South America, where Laon and Julian pass at hectic speed through a fern-forest, across a prairie and a cactus-strewn desert into a dense and richly-populated rain-forest. Their destination is a mountain whose slopes are briefly barred to them by a monstrous ape, which chatters and laughs wildly as the attenuated air causes Julian to slip into a trance state. He passes into the interior of the mountain through a cavernous passage lit by phosphorescence, and finds himself in a damp Underworld veined with precious metals and encrusted with gems. There, he is urged by a magical song to send his spirit forth into a supernatural light:

"The brightness increased upon him, and he was soon involved in the splendour of rays, refracted from myriads of ærial prisms, forming, by combination, circles of the utmost chromatic beauty and intense brilliancy, revolving around a centre of the purest brightness.

---

85   Robert Hunt. Panthea, the Spirit of Nature. London: Reeve, Benham and Reeve, 1849. p.47.

"Under the influence of the powers of sound and light, Julian's consciousness was slowly restored. He was now moving through the stellar space, and saw world after world rolling on its infinite path in that intercommunion of brightness which chains the material creations into one universal whole....

"He felt that he approached the central sun. With his exalted powers of vision he could now scan the immensity of space; and looking through myriads of planetary systems, which obeyed the influence, as it now appeared to Julian, of that power which was so rapidly impelling him onward, he perceived, as a small speck of light, his own Earth amid the congregated band of planets forming the little solar system, of which he knew himself a part, although he felt no earthward longing."[86]

Panthea appears to him as "a beautiful embodiment of angelic grace" with furled wings, and carries him away in a car of cloud; the imagery of this sequence, like some of the more high-flown passages in *The Poetry of Science*, is strongly reminiscent of *Queen Mab*, although it is possible that Hunt had only read the truncated version of the poem. Panthea's car carries Julian into space to a viewpoint from which he can observe and study the creation, formation and evolution of the Earth under the influence of the elemental forces of Gravitation, Magnetism, Heat and Electricity. Then comes Light to "animate the scene", first producing vegetable life, and then animal life, while continents shift and break up, sea replacing land and land replacing sea. All this is the natural gestation of a "Sacred Paradise," but Panthea is careful to stress that its further augmentation requires the direct intervention of the Eternal Presence.

When Julian first beholds "the mighty Adam" amid the trees of paradise, Adam is splendid, but a mere animal: "he saw but with his sensual eyes—he heard but with his mechanical ears. Without a thought...the parent of the human race passed before the eyes of Julian as a melancholy example of a soulless man."[87] Once ensouled, however, Adam looks about him in a very different way, "all-absorbing" and admiring, but frustrated in the expression of his feelings for want of a mate.

---

86   Ibid. pp.64-65.
87   Ibid. p.88.

Left to his own devices, Panthea tells Julian, Man would become a demon—another Lucifer—but with the bonds of Woman's affection to restrain him he might do better. On the advent of Adam and Eve the natural food chain is temporarily suspended—the Lion plays innocently with the Lamb—while the Celestial host sings their praises; but it does not last, and nor does Julian's vision, which fades away.

The following dawn finds Laon and Æltgiva reunited, ascending a "Druidic way" to a Bardic Temple (a circle of stones) where they make their Pantheistic religious observances. They are approached by Eudora Spencer, who has also been Laon's pupil, in search of news of Julian. The text now reveals that Æltgiva is in love with Julian, although she hides the fact from Eudora. Laon promises that the reawakened Julian will be home very soon, and so he is, but he is "an altered man".

Mr. Cheverton, chastened by Lord Devonport's criticisms, determines to bring Julian back into the Christian fold, and denounces Laon as a false prophet. He insists that there are limits to what men might learn, and boundaries to what science can reveal, but Julian is unimpressed. In the subsequent dispute the author's sympathy still seems to lie with Julian the Mystic, but the chapter is followed by an Interlude entitled "Modern Science." Lord Devonport dispatches Julian to London to further his education, and although he is disappointed by London society, which seems to him to be obsessed by trivialities, Julian is soon entranced by the world of science. He soaks up all the newly-solved mysteries that are mapped in *The Poetry of Science*, but still longs for more: for the gift of "some process of inspiration" that will allow him to "see through nature by a species of *clairvoyance*."[88]

When Julian returns to Altamont he finds Laon deeply engrossed in alchemical endeavors, arguing for the possibility of transmutation with a passion Julian never found in the chemists of London. Because Julian is avid for something similar, Laon offers him a drug—cannabis—whose "strange powers...have been known in the East for many centuries,"[89] in order that it might provide the enlightenment he seeks. Hunt might well have taken a tincture of cannabis while he was ill in the late 1820s, and would

---

88   Ibid, p.148.
89   Ibid. p.204.

have had ready access to it when he set up as a pharmacist. The drug provides Julian with a second vision, during which Panthea, after chiding him for faltering in his vocation, takes up the thread of the earlier rhapsody and displays a synoptic history of mankind after Adam's fall: a panorama of social progress guided by the twin lights of scientific discovery and religious revelation.

At this point the text undergoes another marked change of character. A storm awakes a peculiar echo in Julian's own being; seemingly struck by lightning, he falls unconscious. When he regains consciousness he is delirious, and charges Laon with having driven him mad. He now sees his former mentor as a demonic tempter, and seems convinced, when Laon contrives to guide him home, that he has made a pact with the devil. A physician and a surgeon are summoned to attend to Julian but disagree violently as to the treatment of his malady and Cheverton elects to treat the patient with cannabis. The drug puts Julian to sleep again, but there is no sign of Panthea in his dreams, which are terribly confused; he thinks of them as his own version of the temptations of St Anthony.

The stricken Julian is initially cheered by the devotions of his little sister, but when she dies suddenly, Cheverton takes over the task of comforting him, and persuades him to take a new attitude to life and work. Having repented of his dreamy indolence, Julian embarks upon a "war against Poverty," which he intends to fight with the weapons best suited to the task: scientific and technological innovation, based on assiduous experimentation, and technical education. One matter still remains to be settled, however, and it is to the death of Æltgiva—her "return to Panthea" and the elimination of all the temptations she represented—that the final pages of the narrative are dedicated. Laon, Eudora and Julian are all at her death-bed, but their reactions are very different. Although Julian cannot help recalling his visions of Panthea with a certain nostalgia, he now dismisses Æltgiva's demise, rather rudely, as "a choice sacrifice at a false shrine"[90] When Laon bids him to "dream on" Eudora counters with an injunction to "awake and work," and it is to the latter instruction that Julian immediately pledges his allegiance.

The ending of the story is one that no reader could have anticipated during the early chapters, and it seems somewhat ill-fitted

---

90   Ibid. p.358.

even to the chapter immediately preceding it, where Julian—despite his alleged moral rearmament—is still happy to follow flights of philosophical fancy with Cheverton. There is no doubt that the resolutions made by Julian in the final chapter echo resolutions that Robert Hunt actually made in real life, and the probability therefore seems strong that the contrary tendency of the earliest chapters, and the confused irresolution of the penultimate ones, also reflect psychological phases through which he had passed, on his way to what he finally accepted as enlightenment.

Once he had arrived at the conclusions summarized in the final chapter of *Panthea*, Hunt appears to have felt that he ought to set aside not merely the Romantic flights of fancy that fill the early pages of the story, but any further attempt at poetry or fiction, in favor of the "poetry of science." It is not obvious, however, that the story really points to that conclusion, let alone that the conclusion is justified.

The Poetry of Science sets out to inform its readers that science is not merely poetic but more poetic than poetry. One might argue on that basis that if science is virtuous because it is poetic, then poetry must itself be virtuous, but that is a point on which Hunt seems slightly confused. There is something a trifle excessive in the narrowness of his rededication to science. If his commitment to the poetry of science put a stop to his interest in poetry *per se*, however, the message of his works did not have that effect on others, and his future involvement in the popularization of science—especially his endeavors on behalf of the Great Exhibition of 1851—were certainly not without literary influence.

The Great Exhibition, housed in the legendary Crystal Palace, was a huge success, not least in provoking a remarkable flood of celebrations, satires and didactic stories for children, which including E. G. M.'s *The Crystal Palace* (1851), Robert Franklin's *Wanderings in the Crystal Palace* (1851), Samuel Warren's *The Lily and the Bee—An Apologue of the Crystal Palace* (1851), C. T. W.'s *The Crystal Hive; or, The First of May* (1852), and Henry Mayhew's comic novel *1851; or, The Adventures of Mr. and Mrs. Sandboys and Family, Who Came up to London to "Enjoy Themselves" and See the Great Exhibition* (1851, with illustrations by George Cruikshank).

Although the crusade for the popularization of science had never faded away since the days of Erasmus Darwin, Joseph Priestley and Jane Marcet, it had faltered somewhat, but it seemed to take on a new lease of life in the wake of the Great Exhibition. George Eliot made every attempt to promote science in the *Westminster Review*, founded in 1852, which she helped to edit, and one of her early recruits to that line of work was her future partner in life, G. H. Lewes, who also contributed "Studies in Animal Life" to the early issues of William Makepeace Thackeray's *Cornhill Magazine*, founded in 1860.

Other notable popularizations from the period included Margaret Gatty's series of *Parables from Nature* (1855-71), Charles Kingsley's *Glaucus; or, The Wonders of the Shore* (1855) and *Madam How and Lady Why* (1869), and John Ruskin's engagingly eccentric *The Ethics of the Dust: Ten Lectures to Little Housewives on the Elements of Crystallisation* (1865). All of these endeavors probably owed some debt, if only indirectly, to Robert Hunt's guide-book to the Exhibition and his notion of the poetry of science, and all of them made some attempt of their own to celebrate the poetry of science, but their use of fictional devices was relatively limited. Few British popularizers followed the examples set in France by the astronomer Camille Flammarion, who made several significant attempts to adapt fictional formats to the purpose of popularization.

The most notable exception is the British astronomer Richard A. Proctor, who followed up his analysis of the plurality of worlds, *Other Worlds Than Ours* (1870) with numerous speculative essays, including two couched as imaginary voyages, first published in the *Cornhill*: "A Voyage to the Sun" (March 1872) and "A Voyage to the Ringed Planet" (September 1872). The former now seems primarily remarkable for its inevitable errors regarding the mechanism of the sun's production of heat and the nature of sunspots, but is nevertheless very striking in its imagery, not least because Proctor's assumptions regarding the enormous extent of the solar atmosphere enables him to provide a thunderous accompaniment to the light show.

A similar assumption enables Saturn to be rather cacophonous in the second essay, but the more interesting part of the second essay is not the description of the turbulent giant planet, whose cloud-shrouded surface is far too violent to support life, but the assumption that its many satellites are teeming with life, almost as various in its forms as life on Earth, but markedly different. The only elaborate description offered is that of the intelligent inhabitants of Mimas, who are vaguely humanoid but are equipped with extra sensory organs that perceive heat, but Proctor is careful to stress that the peculiarities that distinguish the inhabitants of Enceladus, Tethys, Dione, Rhea, Titan and Japetus from each other and those of Mimas "are as remarkable as those which distinguish Mimasian creatures from the inhabitants of earth."[91]

* * * *

One of the readers of *The Poetry of Science* who was sharply struck by its ringing message was the poet William Wilson, who went on to derive a prospectus from it very different from the one that Hunt enacted himself, in *A Little Earnest Book Upon a Great Old Subject* (1851), which is dedicated to Edward Bulwer-Lytton. The "great old subject" in question is poetry, but under Hunt's inspiration, Wilson included a chapter on "The Poetry of Science" and followed it with a chapter arguing that Hunt's book can be seen as a justification for a new literary genre, which he calls "science-fiction."

Wilson first speaks of "the poetry of science" in a general sense, as a phenomenon that is "beginning to attract a considerable increase of attention." He adds that: "All known sciences contain within themselves Worlds of exquisite Poetry, and the more general mind becomes familiarized with the ever-varying interest and fascinations connected with their Study, the more rapid will become the diffusion and the rise of Science."[92]

Wilson's notion of the poetic effect of scientific knowledge is summarized in a passage that begins: "With what an advance of interest over that of ordinary men must the Man of Science wander in the Fields and the Woods, and traverse over mountains, seas and deserts. The Trees and Flowers have tongues for him, and the Rivers and Streams have a History. He knows where the Zoophytes

---

91   Richard A. Proctor "A Voyage to the Ringed Planet" in *The Borderlands of Science*. London: Smith Elder 1873, p.85.
92   William Wilson. *A Little Earnest Book Upon a Great Old Subject*. London: Darton, 1851. pp.131-132.

merge into one another; he knows not only the form and colour of a flower, but the combinations that produce its symmetry and lovely hue; and he knows the laws by which the white sunbeam is thrown back from the surface in coloured rays."[93] He goes on to list many other things that the Man of Science supposedly knows—most of them quoted from inspirational passages from *The Poetry of Science*.

Wilson also cites Coleridge in support of his thesis that knowledge can transform perception in a valuable manner; it is clear that, for him, Isaac Newton is not the unweaver of the rainbow so much as the man who laid the groundwork for its weaving to be better understood and better appreciated, esthetically as well as mathematically. "Those who people Earth now," Wilson says, "and those who will do so in future ages, are beneficiaries of the researches of science, and the scientific truths accumulated—like all truths—are eternal."[94] Again, that benefit is held to be not merely material but inspirational, enabling a better perception of both the beautiful and the sublime in nature.

In the next chapter, Wilson continues: "Fiction has lately been chosen as a means of familiarizing science in one single case only, but with great success. It is by the celebrated dramatic poet R. H. Horne, and is entitled *The Poor Artist; or, Seven Eye-Sights and One Object*. We hope it will not be long before we may have other works of Science-Fiction, as we believe such books likely to fulfil a good purpose, and create an interest, where, unhappily, science alone might fail.

"[Thomas] Campbell says that 'Fiction in Poetry is not the reverse of truth, but her soft and enchanting resemblance.' Now this applies especially to Science-Fiction, in which the revealed truths of Science may be given, interwoven with a pleasing story which may itself be poetical and true—thus circulating a knowledge of the Poetry of Science, clothed in a garb of the Poetry of life. The influences of Science inter-penetrate the whole Earth, breathing eloquently through the framework of Creation."[95]

Wilson claims that Byron had the same opinion, and goes on to list some of the recent supposed triumphs of science—including

---

93   Ibid, pp.133-134.
94   Ibid. pp.135-136.
95   Ibid, pp.137-140.

aerostatics, the electric telegraph, anesthetic surgery and phrenology—to prove his point. His assertion that "Science-Fiction," as he has defined it, has only one supportive example to cite might seem a little extreme, but his notion of the embryonic genre as a celebration of the new vision of the material world facilitated by scientific knowledge would have prevented him from recognizing other recent examples that have been picked out by modern "historians of science fiction," even if he had known of their existence. The example he does cite would undoubtedly seem very marginal to a modern reader with a generically-derived notion of "science fiction," and was not cited as an example in any "histories of science fiction" until Wilson's prospectus was unexpectedly rediscovered in the 1970s, but it does relate closely to the kind of visionary transformation for which Wilson commends science, and is interesting in its originality.

The Poor Artist (1848)—whose author's full name was Richard Henry Horne, although he occasionally signed himself R. Hengist Horne—is a sentimental story in which a lovelorn artist, rejected as a potential suitor by his beloved's uncle because his pictures make no money, is miraculously enabled successively to listen to accounts offered by a bee, an ant, spider, a fish, a cat and a bird, of strange objects they have each seen. He makes drawings from the second-hand descriptions, which eventually turn out to refer to the same object: a gold coin; in the meantime, the six animals indulge in a philosophical discussion of the interpretative nature of vision. Inevitably, in the context of a sentimental fable, the remarkable series of designs eventually plays a role in the making of the artist's reputation, the increase of which allows him to forge the desired union, but that is not achieved without considerable difficulty, and while the hard-won success is in the making the author inserts a certain amount of philosophizing about sight and art into the narrative, and an expository chapter extolling the wonders of natural history, quoting extensively from the botanist William Henry Harvey in support of an argument to the effect that "dumb animals" are just as immortal as humans.

Wilson points out that Horne's book is dedicated to the "physiologist" Professor [Richard] Owen—whom we would now call a paleontologist—and adds the judgment that "Doubtless this

Professor Owen's whole existence has been one exquisite poem; one long abstraction for the enlightenment and elevation of his race."⁹⁶ In the dedication in question, Horne remarks that "the present little work...only pretends to give a romantic account of science, in illustrating the different character of vision in different creatures" but hopes that "your largeness of mind, in the enormous accumulation of facts of Natural History, has even extended itself to those shadowy and mysterious boundaries, where fact and experiment, being unable to proceed a degree further, may permit you to listen with no half-averted ear to the possible revelations of a 'reasoning imagination.'"⁹⁷ The title page also carries a quotation beneath its subtitle, which simply reads "Science in Fable," so it is evident that Horne did intend his work as a dramatization and popularization of science, albeit in the existing vein of fabular philosophical speculation rather than in any attempt to break new literary ground.

It would not have been easy for Wilson, writing in 1851, to find other possible examples of "science-fiction" within his narrow conception of it; he probably would not have counted Humphry Davy's *Consolations in Travel* as fiction, and would surely have thought that the occult trappings of *Panthea* disqualified it from consideration. There are, however, two works that historians with a more recent notion of "science-fiction" have picked out from those contemporary with Hunt's *Poetry of Science*, which are just as eccentrically original as *The Poor Artist*, and can be seen in retrospect to have anticipated developments in fiction that were to be prolifically extrapolated by subsequent writers of scientific romance and science fiction: "The Lieutenant's Daughter" (1847) by "Zeta" (James Anthony Froude) and Charles Rowcroft's *The Triumph of Woman* (1848). Although neither work is particularly distinguished, and they have almost nothing in common, they are of considerable interest as exemplars of primitive attempts to deal with two themes that eventually became central to twentieth century speculative fiction.

---

96   Ibid, footnote to p.139.
97   R. H. Horne. *The Poor Artist; or, Seven Eye-Sights and One Object*. London: John Van Voorst, 1850. unnumbered prefatory pagination.

James Anthony Froude became famous as a polemical historian, having moved in that direction when his initial intention to become a clergyman foundered in doubt. His brother Richard was a leading member of the "Oxford Movement" of Anglo-Catholics, but Froude found himself unable to sympathize with that crusade, and his own religious ideas became increasingly unorthodox, under the influence of his close friends Thomas Carlyle and Charles Kingsley. "The Lieutenant's Daughter" was one of two novellas in a volume published under the title of the other, *The Shadow of the Clouds*, both of which reflect the crises induced by the metamorphosis of his faith.

The narrator of "The Lieutenant's Daughter," moved to speculate about the nature of time and the astronomical determination of the day and the year, wonders whether time might be speeded up or thrown into reverse. Such musings allow him to acquire the mental faculty of seeing such phenomena as if they were real, and he views a series of images leading from the suicide of a young woman back through the causal chain of events that led her to that pass, eventually reaching the death of her father when she was a child. Then, however, he sees an alternative set of images, in which the woman is living happily with a husband and children, which extends backwards through a similar cause and chain to a crucial division of time in which her father survived for five further years.

In retrospect, Froude's story can be seen as a precursor of the sciencefictional subgenre of "alternative history" stories, and as a crude but nevertheless significant ancestor of stories of time travel in general. In the latter capacity, at least, and arguably in the former too, it had one highly significant precursor, which Everett Bleiler unerringly identifies in his consideration of the story, although it lies outside the scope of his definition of science fiction: Charles Dickens' *A Christmas Carol* (1843; dated 1844).

Although it employs frankly supernatural devices, in the tradition of Voltairean philosophical speculations, Dickens' moral fable broke important new ground in moving its protagonist, Ebenezer Scrooge, backwards and forwards in time, as well as sideways in space, so that he can see both the formative causes of his present character and the likely consequences of the actions corollary to that character—with the result, of course, that he changes his behavior and thus subverts the futuristic vision he has been shown, enabling the undoomed Tiny Tim, the entire Cratchit family and many others to enjoy a more prosperous future than the one to which his miserliness would otherwise have condemned them.

Froude's novella passed virtually unnoticed, and certainly did not show the slightest sign of founding a genre, but Dickens' story became one of the most famous in the English language, and did found a genre, although not a genre of time travel stories. Instead, and with the help of Dickens' other "Christmas books," it founded a genre of Christmas fantasies: sentimental epiphanic tales of redemption and moral reconstruction, whose unashamed fantasization, in an era when supernatural apparatus was widely criticized as either foolishly unrealistic or dangerously un-Christian, was granted special license because Christmas was a special holiday.

Dickens followed *A Christmas Carol*, a year later, with *The Chimes*, with which he intended to "strike a great blow for the poor." In that story, too, the protagonist, the dispirited ticket-porter Trotty Veck, sees a bleak vision of the future in which those close to him suffer terrible fates. Unlike Scrooge, however, Trotty is in no way responsible for those misfortunes and cannot prevent them by mending his own ways; only by the collective effort of a general faith in the possibility of progress and a fostering effort of amelioration can society be saved from corrupting deterioration. That turned out, however, to be an uncomforting message, which his readers were by no means enthusiastic to hear, and Dickens, ever the professional, softened it considerably in the third book in the series, the sickly-sweet *The Cricket on the Hearth*. Feeling more secure, he reverted to grim realism in the fourth, *The Battle of Life*, and then to more complex and ambitious moralistic fantasy in *The Haunted Man and the Ghost's Bargain*, but then he gave up, rightly convinced that he could never repeat the enormous success of *A Christmas Carol*, and presumably persuaded that what the reading public wanted in their Christmas gifts was not sophisticated moral philosophizing but the easy identification of convenient scapegoats.

In the vast flood of Christmas fantasies by other hands that the success of *A Christmas Carol* unleashed, only a few involved futuristic visions, and none used such visions as springboards for metaphysical speculation in the fashion of "The Lieutenant's Daughter." In casting around for decorative fantastic imagery, however, a few did progress a little further than mere imaginative tinsel, and one of those was Charles Rowcroft's *The Triumph of Woman*, whose subtitle labels it "A Christmas Story."

Rowcroft had led a varied and colorful life before taking up a literary career in his forties—he published eleven novels in all, very varied in their subject matter—having traveled widely in Australasia and the Americas, working as a sheep-farmer, a justice of the peace and a diplomat. In 1845, however, when the famous poet and humorist Thomas Hood died, Rowcroft took over the editorship of *Hood's Magazine and Comic Miscellany*, for which much of his subsequent work was done, and in the presiding spirit of which *The Triumph of Woman* was written.

The novel opens at a Christmas party in Bavaria hosted by the obsessive astronomer Dr. Astercop, who ruins the planned celebration by refusing to come to dinner, because he has made a remarkable telescopic observation. While investigating the newly discovered post-Uranian planet (not yet known as Neptune) he has seen it apparently moving toward the Earth at prodigious velocity. The object in question eventually lands in his garden, and turns out to be an inhabitant of the planet paying a rare visit to Earth. After learning Earthly languages by means of a kind of applied phrenology, the visitor explains that there are no women on his planet, and that their importation has been banned ever since one of them, imported from Earth, sowed havoc there. He introduces himself as Zarah, meaning "The Constant."

Civilization has reached a much higher level on Zarah's world than on Earth; although human in appearance, the planet's inhabitants are superhuman in their innate faculties and in their technology. They have innate powers of levitation, which can be so greatly enhanced by technological devices as to permit their bodies to enter an alternative state of matter, which permits them to travel through space at the speed of light. Zarah is carrying one such instrument, which has the form of a metal rod. Unfortunately, when he reveals that the rod can also be used to transmute metals, the housemaid's boy-friend immediately sets out to steal it. The robbery is interrupted, but in the ensuing confusion the thief activates the device and is hurled away through the air, causing it to be lost.

Unable to return home, Zarah sets off in search of his "talisman," traveling throughout with the aid of his innate levitatory power. Wherever he goes he is confronted with instances of female behavior, which reveal to him the awful fickleness and perfidy that led to the prohibition of the female sex on his own world, but also show him a few instances of heroic self-sacrifice motivated by love. In the meantime, he cannot shake off the memory of Astercop's lovely daughter Angela, who has fallen in love with him. He is imprisoned several times, unjustly, and even threatened with execution, but is always able to fly away when the opportunity arises. By the time he eventually finds the talisman, however, he is heartily sick of Earth and cannot wait to go home—except that, once there, he finds that he can no longer be content with a placid woman-free existence, and he returns to Angela on the anniversary of his first arrival.

The story would be pure fantasy were it not for a chapter set in Germany at the very beginning of Zarah's quest, when he lodges with Herr Splidztraw, the Professor of Law at the University of Gottingen, to whom he explains something of the science underlying his world's technology, before being forced to flee by the machinations of the professor's young and lustful wife. His explanation includes an argument about the nature of the atom and a corollary theory underlying transfigurations of substance, which is much more far-ranging than the mere transmutation of metals, and involves modes of material existence as yet unknown to Earthly natural philosophers, who are only familiar with the solid, fluid and gaseous states.

Unfortunately, Zarah never has an opportunity to flesh out his explanations at greater length. They would not amount to much in the eyes of a modern physicist, but the effort is an interesting one, especially in the context of an item of light fiction expressly designed for amusement. In the context of the plot, the intrusion is mere casual conversation, but the fact that the author felt able and inclined to include it helps to demonstrate that by 1848, the time really had arrived for the seeds of some kind of "science-fiction" to begin germination.

Fictitious visitors from other planets had arrived on Earth before, in such portentous philosophical speculations as Voltaire's *Micromégas*, but the fact that the motif could now be accommodated within a Christmas story, along with the trappings of scientific speculation regarding the nature and possible manipulations of matter, is an unmistakable symptom of the familiarization of the idea. *A Christmas Carol* and "The Lieutenant's Daughter" demonstrate that mind-games played with the ideas of time and causation were similarly in the process of familiarization, and *The Poor Artist* demonstrates that speculations about variable perceptions based in alternative mechanisms of sight and could also be accommodated in fiction aimed at a general audience.

The advent of generic scientific romance was still two generations away—although the *roman scientifique* was able to acquire a generic status of sorts in France within a decade—but its seeds were no longer being sown singly at rare intervals; they were beginning to cluster, in the manner of elementary cultivation. William Wilson could not find more than one example of "Science-Fiction" in 1851, but he did not need the aid of the Ghost of Christmas Yet to Come to help him anticipate its advent, and he could easily have found further examples, if not of "Science-Fiction," at least of fiction that was taking scientific perspectives aboard in the course of considerations of everyday social life.

James Anthony Froude's friend Charles Kingsley provided one of the more remarkable examples of this tendency in his *Alton Locke, Tailor and Poet: An autobiography* (1850). In Chapter XXXVI the narrator's tribulations reach a crisis-point at which he falls into exhausted sleep, and has a remarkable dream, in which he sees his own struggle to rise above his humble beginnings, by means of education and moral and artistic effort, in the context of the general struggle of life to rise from humble beginnings to the pinnacle of human existence. In the dream, Locke experiences "himself" successively as a madrepore polyp, a crab, a remora, an ostrich, a mylodon and a baby ape struggling toward consciousness, while simultaneously haunted by images of Lilian, the woman he loves but might have lost, whose metamorphoses form a strange counterpoint to the evolutionary fantasy.

At the climax of the dream, Locke's cousin and rival in love appears in the guise of a hunter-missionary, who shoots him in his ape identity and carries him away for dissection by a surgeon, who "discours[es] sneeringly about Van Helmont's dreams of the Archaeus and the animal spirit which dwells within the solar plexus" while "fingering" his heart.[98] Jan Van Helmont, active immediately after Paracelsus, had helped in the transformation of alchemy into chemistry; the Archaeus or *Anima Mundi* [World-Soul] was a notion borrowed from occult science, referring to a kind of interface between the material and the spiritual, which allows the soul to act upon the body.

In 1851 the works of Edgar Allan Poe—who was American by adoption but English-born and in English in inspiration—made their first appearance in volume form in England, including at least half a dozen stories that can be seen in retrospect as significant precursors of American science fiction, and which also provided exemplars for at least a few of the pioneers of scientific romance. Although the stage was still empty of anything resembling an English-language genre of "Science-Fiction" or scientific romance, therefore, the set had at least been dressed. Although Robert Hunt had been wooed way from poetry and fiction alike by the Poetry of Science, there were others still prepared to linger, and by virtue of that lingering to form the nucleus of a community of sorts.

It is not obvious, or even likely, that William Wilson's essay on the merits of "Science-Fiction" reached any ears sufficiently sympathetic to make an attempt to practice what he preached, but a handful of stories published in the few years that followed his *Little Earnest Book* might have been considered by a contemporary observer to belong to the category.

The anonymously-issued *Heliondé; or, Adventures in the Sun* (1855, by Sydney Whiting) might seem like an unlikely candidate, but arguments supporting the notion that the sun's heat was only generated when its rays interacted with the Earth's atmosphere had been seriously put forward, and although the trip to the sun's lovely surface described in the story turns out to have been a dream, it is by no means devoid of philosophical speculation; the account of the musical language spoken on the sun is particularly intriguing.

More pertinent is "The Blue Beetle" (1856) by A. G. Gray Jr., published in the weekly periodical *The Train*, in which a protagonist hoping to solve the mystery of the first "atom" to be infused

---

98   Charles Kingsley. *Alton Locke, Tailor and Poet*. Chapman and Hall, 1856. p.271.

with vital force—thus becoming the progenitor of all Earthly life—contrives the creation of the eponymous insect; unfortunately, it proves to be deadly, thus making the story into an early example of Isaac Asimov's "Frankenstein complex," and demonstrating the convenience of that story-arc in short fiction. In the same year, *The Train* also published the farcical "Remarkable Incident in the Middle of Next Week," which Bleiler attributes to E. L. Blanchard, although it was published anonymously. It is a curious timeslip story, in which the Earth stops rotating, leaving Britain in darkness. The Queen and Prince Albert are obliged to convene a panel of eminent scientists to plan a national survival strategy, although the crisis is averted when a bold explorer finds a mean to lubricate the planet's axis and restore normal rotation.

Had periodicals like *The Train* been more abundant, more examples of Poesque experimentation might have proliferated, but even the editor of *The Train* seems to have found the results of his experimentation unsatisfactory; he did not continue with it, and it was not until one of the less staid literary periodicals, *The Belgravia*, became tentatively hospitable to works of a similarly adventurous stripe in the 1880s that any similar haven became readily available. The opportunity for the Poetry of Science to give birth to "Science-Fiction" was, in consequence, effectively postponed for a generation.

7. THE TRIUMPH OF EVOLUTION

Georges Cuvier's contemporary Jean-Baptiste de Lamarck, who made the first systematic study of fossil invertebrates, had no sympathy with the Comte de Buffon's hesitation over the idea of evolution, or Cuvier's denial of it. Like Erasmus Darwin in England, he was a convert to the cause of what was then known as "transformism" long before he dared to express that conviction, but express it he eventually did. Lamarck was no Jacobin—and, indeed, had a difficult time during the Revolution by virtue of his aristocratic heritage—but he took advantage of the freedom of expression that the Revolution brought, and which Napoléon sustained, and he made the mutability of species into the foundation-stone of a whole new intellectual system in *Philosophie zoologique* (1809). He represented his own classification of species by the tracing of lines of historical descent that extended across vast reaches of past time, thus building on Erasmus Darwin's powerful image of the incessantly-branching "great filament" of life.

The key notion that Lamarck used to explain mutability was adaptation, which he assumed to be the result of a dynamic impulse innate in all living things, expressed as a *sentiment intérieur* driving species to explore new habitats and means of sustenance, and to innovate in order to exploit them more effectively. He was assisted in this conceptualization by the gradual supplementation of Maillet's geological studies by more elaborate accounts of the world's forging by the forces of fire as well as those of water; something of a controversy had developed among "vulcanologists" and "hydrologists" regarding the priority of those effects in orchestrating the succession of the "epochs of Nature."

A more general dispute had developed between "catastrophists," who thought that the changes reflected in the Earth's geological strata had happened relatively rapidly, on a scale of tens or hundreds of thousand of years, and "uniformitarians," who thought that they had happened much more slowly. Lamarck's theory of adaptation demanded a uniformitarian account, and had one readily available in James Hutton's *Theory of the Earth* (1795), which went even further than Maillet is arguing that the succession of epochs of nature was suggestive of a "system in nature" in which there was "No trace of a beginning, no prospect of an end."[99]

Lamarck's ideas were applauded by Charles Lyell in the second volume of his *Principles of Geology* (1832), which carried forward Hutton's uniformitarian thesis and provided further evidence and argument in its support. The case was further developed, in a more combative mode, by Robert Chambers' highly controversial *Vestiges of the Natural History of Creation* (1844), and it was in response to that text that the impetus to literary reflection of transformist theory began to move up through the gears of fascination and controversy. Although Tennyson's "In Memoriam" readily conceded the strength of Chambers' arguments, Benjamin Disraeli followed in his father's footsteps by reacting against them in *Tancred* (1847). Charles Kingsley, in the dream sequence reproduced in *Alton Locke*, also took significant cues from Chambers.

---

99   James Hutton, *Theory of the Earth, with Proofs and Illustrations*. Edinburgh: W. Creech, 1795. volume I. p.19.

Non-fictional extrapolations of the argument continued in Britain in such essays as Herbert Spencer's "The Development Hypothesis" (1852), but the term "evolution" had not yet come into common usage in English at that point; its eventual arrival in common parlance at much the same time as Charles Darwin's *On the Origin of Species by means of Natural Selection, or the Preservation of Favoured Races in the Struggle for Life* (1859; the title was shortened in the sixth edition to the more familiar *The Origin of Species*) helps to explain the persistent confusion still implicit in many references to "the theory of evolution," which conflate the theory that the relatedness of species is explicable in terms of hereditary descent with the theory that the pattern of descent can be explained in terms of natural selection.

Given the substance of Alton Locke's crucial vision of his life in a cosmic context, it is hardly surprising that Charles Kingsley was one of the first people to lavish praise on *The Origin of Species*, of which he had been sent an advance review copy, nor that Darwin should incorporate Kingsley's remarks into subsequent editions of the book as evidence that an intelligent and eminent churchman could find no contradiction between the theory and his devout religious faith. There was, on the other hand, no shortage of equally eminent clergymen who took a very different view. Kingsley went on to pen a satire about the controversy, "Speech of Lord Dundreary in Section D, on Friday Last, on the Great Hippocampus Question" (1861), more commonly known as "The Great Hippocampus Question," whose argumentative thrust he subsequently incorporated, albeit discreetly, into his classic children's book *The Water-Babies: A Fairy Tale for a Land Baby* (1863).

In the speech, the deeply confused Lord Dundreary, who confuses the hippocampus with the hippopotamus as well as the sea-horse species with the structure in the human brain, finds himself equally at sea in comparing the contrasting ideas of Thomas Henry Huxley and Richard Owen on the possible relationship between humans and apes, and can only conclude by suggesting that the toss of a coin might serve to decide the matter. Although barely mentioned in *The Origin of Species*, the issue of human relationship with apes inevitably became the centerpiece of the long-smoldering controversy that was spectacularly ignited by the publication of the Darwinian thesis.

Darwin fought shy of controversy himself, and had delayed publication of his thesis for many years for fear of it, eventually being forced to stake his claim to priority when Alfred Russel Wallace came up with the thesis independently and wrote to him asking for his opinion of it in 1858. Darwin's unwillingness to engage in public debate, however, merely left the way clear for Thomas Henry Huxley, who immediately engaged in a war of words with Richard Owen—the dedicatee of Horne's *Poor Artist*—that made the latter by far the most famous anti-evolutionist paleontologist.

Huxley took the stage in a public debate at a British Association meeting in Oxford in June 1860, in which he famously upstaged the bombastic Bishop of Oxford, Samuel Wilberforce, by responding to a sneering question as to whether it was on his mother's or his father's side that he was descended from an ape by retorting that he would far rather have an ape for an ancestor than a man who misused his gift of speech in the way that Wilberforce was doing. After that put-down, the actual substance of their arguments became irrelevant in the estimation of the reporters present. In another debate at the Oxford Diocesan Conference, Benjamin Disraeli provided an equally memorable quote when he proclaimed that he had come to debate the question of "whether man is an ape or an angel" and solemnly declared that he was on the side of the angels—a commitment of which his father would presumably have approved.

Huxley had been urged to make his stand in Oxford by Robert Chambers, and he was supported by two other mutual friends of his and Darwin's who had long been familiar with the thesis, Joseph Dalton Hooker and John Lubbock. Thereafter, Huxley was proud to call himself "Darwin's bulldog," even though he had reservations about the strength of the empirical evidence supporting the reality of natural selection, and his vocal support of the theory of natural selection became a virtual crusade. His lectures on the subject were reorganized into his most famous book, *Evidence as to Man's Place in Nature* (1863).

In 1864 Huxley founded a dining club known as the X-Club, which met nine times a year thereafter until 1893, although several of its members died along the way. Alongside Hooker and Lubbock its other members included Herbert Spencer and John Tyndall, and all of its participants won reputations as eminent scientists in their various fields. Spencer was already an outspoken advocate of the transformist thesis, and was largely responsible for establishing the phrase "the survival of the fittest"—which was his, not Darwin's—as a capsule description of the latter's theory. Huxley, Hooker and Tyndall subsequently joined the much older institution on which the X-Club was modeled, the Literary Club co-founded by Samuel Johnson in 1764, although they were rumored to avoid meetings at which Richard Owen and Samuel Wilberforce were likely to be present. Lord Kelvin was a member of the latter club, and so were J. A. Froude and Alfred, Lord Tennyson.

Tennyson, unsurprisingly, was one of the writers to react to the publication of the Darwinian thesis, and to find it uncongenial. Ultimately, he imported his darkened view of future prospects into a revisitation of the setting of a much earlier poem in "Locksley Hall, Sixty Years After" (1886), in which he reflects on the long withering of his youthful optimism. The narrative voice of the poem bids "Authors—essayist, atheist, novelist, realist, rhymester, play your part/Paint the mortal shame of nature with the living hues of Art"[100] but looks forward nevertheless to the possibility of moral progress, wondering whether he might yet see:

> *When the schemes and all the systems*
>   *kingdoms and republics fall.*
> *Something kindlier, higher, holier—all for*
>   *each and each for all?*
>
> *All the full-brain, half-brain races, led by*
>   *Justice, Love and Truth;*
> *All the millions one at length with all the*
>   *visions of my youth?*
>
> *All diseases quench'd by Science, no man*
>   *halt, or deaf, or blind;*
> *Stronger ever born of weaker, lustier body.*
>   *larger mind?*
>
> *Earth at last a warless world, a single race,*
>   *a single tongue—*

---

100   *The Poetic and Dramatic Works of Alfred Lord Tennyson.* New York: Houghton Mifflin, 1898. p.520.

> *I have seen her far away—for is not Earth*
> *as yet so young?*[101]

That hope now seemed far more fragile to Tennyson than when he had written the original "Locksley Hall," however, and the narrative voice immediately goes on to wonder whether war can ever die out "till this outworn earth be dead as/yon dead world the moon." A plea to "be grateful for the sounding watchword 'Evolution'...Evolution ever climbing after some ideal good" is immediately followed by the notion of "reversion ever dragging evolution in the mud." The bleakness of the poem might well owe as much to Tennyson's own aging as to the advent of Darwinism, but it nevertheless echoes a widespread sentiment of anxiety associated not so much with the theory's continued erosion of the authority of religious faith but the seeming harshness of what it had put in its place.

A more profound and persuasive effect is detectable in the work of George Meredith, who attended a meeting of the British Association in Cambridge in October 1862 at which Thomas Henry Huxley and Richard Owen—by now seasoned adversaries—crossed swords yet again, as furiously as ever. John Tyndall spoke at the same meeting. Although Meredith insisted on maintaining a divine framework for his view of Nature, his view of its operations was colored thereafter by his understanding of evolutionary processes, which affected much of his poetry and the background to his novels—to such an extent that the most popular modern critical approach to Meredith's work is the identification and analysis of his Darwinian influences.

A more direct, if considerably less pervasive influence of the renewal of evolutionary imagery can be found in the work of Thomas Hardy, occasionally becoming brutally explicit, as when the amateur geologist Henry Knight—one of the doomed heroine's rival suitors in *A Pair of Blue Eyes* (1873)—slips over the edge of a cliff and, while dangerously stranded there, finds himself face to face with a fossil:

"It was a creature with eyes. The eyes, dead and turned to stone, were even now regarding him. It was one of the earliest crustaceans called Trilobites. Separated by millions of years in

---

101   Ibid. p.521.

their lives, Knight and this underling seemed to have met in their death....

"The creature represented but a low type of animal existence, for never in their vernal years had the plains indicated by these numberless slaty layers been traversed by an intelligence worthy of the name. Zoophytes, mollusca, shell-fish, were the highest developments of those ancient dates. The immense lapses of time each formation represented had known nothing of the dignity of man. They were grand times, but they were mean times too, and mean were their relics....

"Time closed up like a fan before him. He saw himself as one extremity of the years, face to face with the beginning and all the intermediate centuries simultaneously. Fierce men, clothed in the hides of beasts...rose from the rock, like the phantoms before Macbeth.... Huge elephantine forms, the mastodon, the hippopotamus, the tapir, antelopes of a monstrous size, the megatherium and the mylodon—all, for the moment, in juxtaposition. Further back, and overlapped by these, were perched huge billed birds and swinish creatures as large as horses. Still more shadowy were the sinister crocodilian outlines—alligators and other uncouth shapes, culminating in the colossal lizard, the iguanodon. Folded behind were dragon forms and clouds of flying reptiles; still underneath were fishy beings of lower development; and so on, till the lifetime scenes of the fossil confronting him were a present and modern condition of things."[102]

As he continues clinging precariously to the cliff, beginning to doubt the possibility of rescue, Knight, who "knew that his intellect was above the average" reflects that: "his death would be a deliberate loss to earth of good material; that such an experiment in killing him might have been practiced upon some less developed life."[103] Fortunately, however, he is not yet due to be selected out of the great chain of being by the cruel hand of fortune and sent to join the hosts of the dead

J. O. Bailey co-opted Hardy's later novel *Two on a Tower* (1882) into the bibliography of "Scientific Romances" that he offered at the end of his pioneering study of speculative fiction,

---

102 Thomas Hardy. *A Pair of Blue Eyes*. New York: Harper, 1905. pp.252-253.
103 Ibid. p.256.

Pilgrims Through Space and Time, and Hardy referred to that novel himself as a "romance" and a "fantasy," but it is on the list of titles that Suvin excludes from his bibliography of *Victorian Science Fiction*, on the grounds that it has no speculative element, its scientific component being confined to the activities of its hero, an astronomer. Most of Hardy's subsequent musings on evolution were confined to his poetry.

In fact, Darwinian theory was not very prompt in inspiring speculative extrapolations in prose, and most of its evident literary effects prior to the emergence of generic scientific romance are either philosophical musings like Henry Knight's or farcical caricatures such as *The Gorilla Origin of Man; or, The Darwinian Theory of Development, Confirmed from Recent Travels in the New World Called My-me-ae-nia, or Gossipland* (1871), signed "His Royal Highness Mammoth Martinet, alias Mono-Yojo-Oo-Oo." The anonymous *Simiocracy: A Fragment from Future History* (1884, by Arthur Montagu Brookfield), in which radicals contrive to have orangutans granted equal rights with their human brethren, resulting in political chaos, is similarly contemptuous.

There were, however, satirical responses that were much defter and more philosophically sophisticated than *The Gorilla Origin of Man*, the most spectacular and elegant of which is in an inclusion in Samuel Butler's *Erewhon* (1872) called "The Book of the Machines," in which the author satirically applies the theory of natural selection to machines, suggesting that machines are ultimately bound to become fitter than humans, and will therefore condemn humankind to extinction, unless we follow the example of the Erewhonians and abandon them. The argument is a joke, but Butler's interest in evolutionary theory was entirely serious.

In its setting, *Erewhon* draws upon five years that its author had spent in New Zealand between 1859 and 1964, and a rough draft of the argument set out in "The Book of Machines" had appeared in a New Zealand newspaper, *The Press*, on 13 June 1863, in an article in the form of a letter, captioned "Darwin Among the Machines" and signed "Cellarius."

"Day by day," the article asserts, "the machines are gaining ground upon us; day by day we are becoming more subservient to them; more men are daily bound down as slaves to tend them, more men are daily devoting the energies of their whole lives to the development on mechanical life. The upshot is simply a question of time, but that the time will come when the machines will hold the real supremacy over the world and its inhabitants is what no person of a truly philosophic mind can for a moment question."

The intended irony was not noticed by all readers of *Erewhon* at the time, and it was, over time, subverted by the growth of real fears of the same kind—with the result that the article and the chapters in the novel now seem prophetic, if not of actual events, at least of a bugbear that was to come to seem uncomfortable in scientific romance and loom very large indeed in American science fiction. In other works, however, Butler conducted a more earnest and far more elaborate criticism of the negative aspects of Darwinian natural selection. He published no less than four books on the subject: *Life and Habit; An Essay After a Completer View of Evolution* (1878), *Evolution Old and New; or, the Theories of Buffon, Dr. Erasmus Darwin and Lamarck, as compared with that of Charles Darwin* (1879), *Unconscious Memory* (1880) and *Luck or Cunning as a Main Means of Organic Modification?* (1887).

In consequence of this anti-Darwinian endeavor, Butler assumed a position at the head of a school of thought that came to be described as "neo-Lamarckism," which eventually claimed fervent converts, including George Bernard Shaw. Although there is probably no direct connection of influence between "The Book of the Machines" and various stories of machine revolt published the American science fiction magazines, it seems more probable that it provided the imaginative seed for two short novels published in England and signed "W. Grove." The first of them, *A Mexican Mystery* (1888) is an account of a single automated locomotive that comes to life and begins a battle for self-defense, while its sequel, *The Wreck of a World* (1889) depicts the problem becoming general and a human/machine war for survival breaking out.

In the same year that *Erewhon* was published, Winwood Reade, a nephew of the novelist Charles Reade, took a much more positive view of the new evolutionist creed in the rhapsodic final section of his "universal history" of the Western world *The Martyrdom of Man* (1872)—a secularist epic that made a deep impression on H. G. Wells, who produced *The Outline of History* (1920) in the same vein. In the preface, the author explains that the final section had originally been intended to form part of another book, provisionally entitled *The Outline of Mind*, but that the publication of Darwin's *Descent of Man* in 1870 had seemed to render that project redundant. He is careful to observe, however, that he and Darwin differ on several issues and that Darwin might not approve entirely of his own ideas—a cautionary note that was undoubtedly justified.

In some ways, *The Martyrdom of Man* echoes Shelley's *Queen Mab* in offering a narrative history of the past as a chronicle of political, economic and religious oppression, before moving forward to a vision of an infinitely more glorious future, to be attained when all those oppressions have been overthrown. Reade's future paradise is, however, more concrete than Shelley's:

"We can conquer Nature only by obeying her laws, and in order to obey her laws we must know what they are. When we have ascertained, by means of science, the method of Nature's operations, we shall be able to take her place and to perform them for ourselves. When we understand the laws which regulate the complex phenomena of life we shall be able to predict the future as we are already able to predict comets and eclipses and the planetary movements.

"Three inventions which perhaps may not be long delayed, but which possibly are near at hand, will give to this overcrowded island the prosperous conditions of the United States. The first is the discovery of a motive force which will take the place of steam, with its cumbrous fuel of oil or coal; the second, the invention of aerial locomotion which will transport labour at a trifling cost of money and of time to any part of the planet, and which by annihilating distance will speedily extinguish national distinctions; the third, the manufacture of flesh and flour from the elements by a chemical process in the laboratory, similar to that which is now performed by animals and plants. Food will then be manufactured in unlimited quantities at trifling expense, and our enlightened posterity will look back upon us who eat oxen and sheep just as we look back upon cannibals. Hunger and starvation will then be unknown, and the best part of human life will no longer be wasted in the tedious business of cultivating the fields. Population will mightily increase, and the earth will be a garden.... Finally, men will master the forces of Nature; they will become themselves architects of systems, manufacturers of worlds."[104]

Subsequently, Reade goes on to argue that individual human beings are "components" of a greater whole, and that there is a sense in which "there is only one Man upon the earth," and such phenomena as wars and epidemics merely "inflammatory phenomena incident to certain stages of growth."[105] In this view, there is no room for an individual soul, and individual human intellects resemble instincts that "inhabit the corpuscles" of a body, which are not lost by death because of their contribution to the whole. This is pure romance, but it is romance insistently based in the poetry of science.

Reade supplemented *The Martyrdom of Man* with a novel offering an account of the tribulations of a Darwinian convert rejected by his devout father and troubled by the death of his wife, *The Outcast* (1875). The latter was followed by other novels featuring duels of intellect and wit between Darwinists and religious men, modeled on the Huxley/Owen debates, with social exclusion as the forfeit at stake. Eliza Lynn Linton's *Under Which Lord?* (1879) is a particularly striking example, but Mrs. Humphry Ward's *Robert Elsmere* (1888) is more sensitively balanced. Linton and Ward were far less sympathetic to the new creed than Reade, but their works showed a clear awareness of the way the tide was running.

Mrs. Ward, whose maiden name was Mary Arnold, was the niece of the poet Matthew Arnold and the aunt of Julian and Aldous Huxley, her sister having married Thomas Henry Huxley's son Leonard, so she was not far removed from the center of the debate. Matthew Arnold was another poet deeply affected by the post-Darwinian world-view, resentful of its seemingly-fatal corrosion of the religious world view, as in the famous lament of "Dover Beach" (1867):

> *The Sea of Faith*
> *Was once, too, at the full, and round earth's shore*
> *Lay like the folds of a bright girdle furled.*

---

104   Winwood Reade. *The Martyrdom of Man*. London: Watts & Co. Thinker's Library. [1833]. pp.412-413.
105   Ibid. p.419.

But now I only hear
Its melancholy, long, withdrawing roar,
Retreating, to the breath
Of the night-wind, down the vast edges drear
And naked shingles of the world.

Ah, love, let us be true
To one another! for the world, which seems
To lie before us like a land of dreams,
So various, so beautiful, so new,
Hath really neither joy, nor love, nor light,
Nor certitude, nor peace, nor help for pain;
And we are here as on a darkling plain
Swept with confused alarms of struggle and flight,
Where ignorant armies clash by night.[106]

Matilde Blind's book-length poem *The Ascent of Man* (1889) and J. Compton Rickett's *The Quickening of Caliban* (1893), a parable in which an intelligent anthropoid ape is introduced into human society with results far worse than those depicted in Peacock's *Melincourt*, also offer earnest and rather gloomy reflections on the import of Darwinism. May Kendall's poem "The Conquering Machine" (1887) saw evolution working inexorably towards "the Automatic Soul," and a note of regret was sounded even in such celebrations of Darwinism as Grant Allen's "The Lower Slopes" (1894), whose author could not entirely approve of a human ancestry in which "the strongest continued to thrive/While the weakliest went to the wall."

Perhaps curiously, although he was a fervent disciple of Darwin and claimed that his short stories always had a seed of scientific speculation in them, Grant Allen did not treat Darwinian themes in his fiction, although his collection *Strange Stories* (1884) does include "The Child of the Phalanstery," a controversial story championing the cause of eugenics as espoused by Charles Darwin's cousin, Francis Galton. However, Allen's favorite market for his early short stories, *Belgravia*, did publish an extravagant comedy on an evolutionary theme in Ernest G. Harmer's "Professor Bommsenn's Germ" (1888), in which the stimulation of

---

106   Matthew Arnold. *New Poems.* Boston: Ticknor and Fields, 1867. p.96.

primordial protoplasm in the hope of producing a cow overshoots its mark, taking its metamorphosis all the way up the tree of life to humankind and beyond; humankind's successors, in this scheme, are mesmerically-talented dwarfs devoid of such atavisms as hair, teeth or toes.

Several of the responses to the new interest in evolutionism adopted its particular interest in the origins of humankind to prehistoric fantasies, following the example of the tale improvised in Arthur Helps' *Realmah*. These were mostly satirical to begin with; Andrew Lang's "A Romance of the First Radical" (1886) is a straightforward mockery of taboos, while Henry Curwen's *Zit and Xoe: Their Early Experience* (1887) is deliberately silly in its presentation of an Adam and Eve putting aside the traditions of their apelike forebears and rushing through millennia of cultural evolution in the space of a generation. H. B. Marriott Watson—the son of the author of *Erchomenon*—dealt with evolutionary ideas in a quasi-allegorical fashion in the eccentric traveler's tale *Marahuna* (1888), which concerns the discovery of a new human race adapted to a fiery environment and devoid of emotion, but the story does not explore that notion in any great detail or with any great force.

By far the most effective of the evolutionary fantasies published before the advent of generic scientific romance was W. H. Hudson's *A Crystal Age* (1887), which is set in the future but seems a deeply nostalgic work. It has echoes of Richard Jefferies' *After London*, but it reaches much further in its notion of a "return to nature." The novel's protagonist, Smith, wakes from thousands of years of suspended animation to find people living a remarkably comfortable agrarian existence organized around communal dwellings centered on a single reproductive individual, somewhat after the fashion of a hive. In its stress on the harmony of the relationship that the people of the future have with their domestic animals and their environment, the novel provides a sketch of the "ecological mysticism" for which Hudson was subsequently to provide an even more eloquent parable in *Green Mansions* (1905), thus providing a stern opposition to the notion of "nature red in tooth and claw" that the version of Darwinism preached by Thomas Henry Huxley and Herbert Spencer seemed to imply.

Hudson might well have paid closer attention than many of his contemporaries to the notion of human evolution set out by Darwin in *The Descent of Man*, in which Darwin stressed the positive selection of human parental care and social organization rather than the negative selection of predation and disease, calling attention to the importance of nurture and social relationships as key factors in the evolution of intelligence and sentiment—a thesis broadened out further in *The Expression of the Emotions in Man and Animals* (1872). In fact, Hudson's notion of the future of human evolution might be reckoned more truly Darwinian than those reacting for or against perceived "Darwinism," although the ill-tempered nature of the controversy maintained the latter's scarecrow status in public consciousness throughout the twentieth century.

By 1890, the parameters of the dispute were sufficiently well-entrenched in public consciousness, and adequate literary foundations had been laid, for the immediate adoption of evolutionary speculation as a central theme of scientific romance. H. G. Wells was ideally placed, in terms of his education and ambitions, not merely to address that theme but to do so in unprecedentedly graphic and robust fashions, which added considerably to the merits of generic scientific romance as a mode of philosophical speculation, in the great Baconian tradition.

8. THE SHADOWS OF SCIENCE

By the beginning of the nineteenth century, large areas of science had been freed from most of the most significant Baconian idols that had confused and polluted them in previous ages. Astronomy had been largely detached from astrology, and chemistry from the mystical aspects of alchemy. To many people, the development and sophistication of evolutionary theory seemed to be a further step in the same process, freeing geology and biology from the burden of religious dogmas that were clouding clear vision of the truth. The principal area of knowledge in which a considerable burden of ideas inherited from tradition still lingered, and in which the new ideas that had sprung up to change those idols were little better, was medicine, the biological foundations of which were still patchy.

This did not mean, of course, that the old ideas had been obliterated. False beliefs are not mere random accidents; when they command strong allegiance it is usually because they answer some psychological need or appetite, and there can be no guarantee that the truth will provide the same satisfactions. Even if, as Mark Akenside asserted so confidently, the truth—and therefore science—has an essential beauty of its own, there is no guarantee that all beholders will be able to appreciate that beauty equally, especially when it is difficult to comprehend; many falsehoods retain an enticing quality even when stripped of their rational claim to truth. By 1848—the year of revolutions—it seemed to people like Robert Hunt that they had to make a choice between the occult seductions of Panthea on the one hand, and a firm commitment to science and technology on the other—and that in such a contest there could only be one rational decision. Not everyone agreed, however, either about the necessity of making a choice or the direction in which to go.

Scientists, for the most part, were enthusiastic to shed the baggage of past superstition, because that was an essential aspect of the scientific method and the scientific quest. Many wanted to make exceptions, especially with respect to items of religious faith, but mostly did so by fencing them off and isolating them from scientific enquiry. The hopes of the "natural theology" that had expected the discoveries of science to confirm rather than deny the elements of supposed religious revelation had been dashed even before the publicity given to Charles Darwin's theory of the origin of species planted a crucial banner around which secularists could rally. For the most part, scientists were enthusiastic to argue that the "occult sciences" were not and never had been truly scientific, and were mostly, if not entirely, dustbins full of the rubble of exploded notions.

People who were interested in conserving ideas from occult science, individually or collectively, inevitably took the opposite view. Many people who wanted to maintain the claim that at least some occult ideas partook of the beauty of truth, as well as the seductiveness of psychological appeal, elected to insist that they did, indeed, qualify as science—and when scientists attacked those ideas, they defended them, sometimes merely by asserting a stubborn faith but often by adopting the more ingenious ploy of trying to reconstruct the foundations of the beliefs in the image of the new science, casting around for a supportive jargon that maintained an appearance of scientific rationality.

Inevitably, the area in which this strategy became most obvious was the one in which occult ideas clung on most stubbornly for want of any convincing replacement. Paracelsian "chemical medicine" had achieved a good deal in causing the idols of Galenian medicine to tremble, but had not succeeded in smashing them, and, for the most part, had merely raised up a rival set of idols. The conflict between the two schools was further complicated by commercial disputes between physicians, who prescribed medicines, and apothecaries, who supplied them, as to their relative slices of the available profits. The side-effects of these contests included a massive proliferation in the late seventeenth and eighteenth centuries of "quacks": supposed doctors who employed unorthodox treatments, generally backed up with a jargon that was imitative of that of orthodox physicians but richly spiced with notions borrowed from new science, intended to make it seem more "advanced."

Health being one of the major concerns of everyday human life, intimately connected with both of the great literary subjects—sex and mortality—medicine and its follies are abundantly mirrored in the history of literature, and the tendencies of quackery came in for rapid satirization, as in Molière's famous farce *Le médecin malgré lui* (1666; tr. as *The Doctor In Spite of Himself*) and Edward Ravenscroft's English counterpart *The Anatomist; or, the Sham Doctor* (1697).

In Britain, the 18th century became the golden age of quackery, producing such legendary figures as "Crazy Sally" Mapp, the pioneer of techniques subsequently reinvented as osteopathy, and Gustavus Katterfelto, the inventor of "styanography," "palenchics" and the "caprimantic arts." Henry Fielding's *The Mock Doctor* (1732) parodies the French quack Jean Misaubin, but the milieu of quackery is more extensively represented in the works of Tobias Smollett, who turned to writing after five years struggling to establish himself as a fashionable London physician; *Ferdinand Count Fathom* (1753) is the most pertinent of his picaresque novels in its depiction of the deceptions and hypocrisies of quacks. The hijacking of the notion of medical progress by such tricksters lent a bitter irony to almost all 18th-century literature dealing with medical topics, although it was not only writer-physicians like Mark Akenside and Erasmus Darwin who looked on licensed practitioners with a much more kindly eye.

Quacks took abundant advantage of patent law; the first British "patent medicine"—Timothy Byfield's *Sal oleosum volatile*—received its grant in 1711. By the end of the century more than a hundred medical patents had been granted, including those for trusses and various electric gadgets. The latter were dramatically popularized by James Graham, whose Temples of Hymen and Health became very fashionable in London between 1778 and 1784, anticipating both the kinds of treatments subsequently made famous in France by the "magnetizer" Anton Mesmer and their ostentatious mode of administration. Graham fared less well when he was forced to return to Edinburgh, although his *How to Live for Many Weeks or Months or Years Without Eating Anything Whatsoever* (1794) pioneered what is now called "Breatharianism."

Quack nostrums played a key role in the early development of newspaper advertising, and continued to thrive as newspapers increased their audiences vastly in the 19th century. Physiognomy, phrenology and homeopathy were among the greatest successes of quack theory, their utility undoubtedly buoyed up by what would now be called the placebo effect, although their principal virtue—by no means insignificant in the context of the times—was their lack of toxicity.

Hindsight suggests that most significant eighteenth-century breakthrough in medical treatment was vaccination against smallpox, which was developed in India before being pioneered in England by Edward Jenner, but it was by no means universally appreciated at the time, especially by the medical establishment. Jenner's initial submission to the Royal Society in 1798 was rejected because the president, Joseph Banks—for whom Jenner had formerly worked, dissecting specimens brought back by Banks from James Cook's first expedition—refused to sanction it.

Following that rejection, Jenner immediately set out to follow the standard quack strategy, mounting a publicity campaign advertising the virtues of vaccination, with the aid of testimonials from colonialists who had seen its results. He commissioned a poem for use as propaganda in his cause—Robert Bloomfield's *Good Tidings; or, News from the Farm* (1804)—and obtained the support of the Romantic poets Robert Southey and Samuel Taylor Coleridge, although Southey's *A Tale of Paraguay* (1825) was a retrospective celebration of Jenner's heroic status rather than a contribution to its achievement. In the end, it was the potential military advantage conferred by vaccination that finally secured the method's success—a pattern subsequently repeated in both twentieth-century World Wars, when the urgent necessity of keeping soldiers fit to fight prompted large-scale medical adventures that were field experiments in more than one sense.

The relationship between literature and medicine was emphasized in this transitional era by a number of writers who represented their literary activity as self-medication. Laurence Sterne's *Tristram Shandy* (1760-67) is described by its narrator as "a treatise writ against the Spleen." Such representations contributed to the development of the notion of "psychosomatic" disorders, and to the psychopathological theories that linked literary genius so intimately with madness. A different alliance was wrought with the most popular 19th-century pain-killer, laudanum—an alcoholic tincture of morphine—whose hallucinogenic effects were explicitly exploited by such writers as Coleridge and Thomas De Quincey, and made a considerable contribution to the development of 19th-century imaginative fiction. Robert Hunt's use of cannabis was in the same category.

Nineteenth-century medical experimentation proceeded in fits and starts, undermined by its inherent hazardousness as well as its methodological problems, illustrated by Humphry Davy's attempts to identify and counteract the gaseous "principle of contagion." Progress remained unsteady, but it did accelerate. The stethoscope, invented in 1813, introduced a kind of bodily seismology into the art of diagnosis. The pulse-measuring sphygmograph followed in its wake. Physiological analysis began to clarify the processes carried out by the various organs whose anatomical and histological description had been aided by the sophistication of the microscope. The most crucial breakthrough can be seen, with hindsight, as the revivification of the germ theory of disease in the 1840s, initially by François Raspail, although Louis Pasteur reaped the more favorable publicity; at the time, however, germ theory was merely one of a whole series of new hypothetical accounts of disease, including the English variants by Erasmus Darwin and William Lambe mentioned in previous sections.

Joseph Simpson's development of chloroform as an anesthetic in 1847, complemented by disinfectant precautions pioneered by

Ignatz Semmelweis in mid-century and Joseph Lister's introduction of antisepsis in 1865, dramatically enhanced the success-rate of 19th-century surgery, and paved the way for the pioneering of hundreds of new procedures. In the meantime, however, quackery continued to thrive, enthusiastically taken up by the entrepreneurial spirit of the U.S.A. and extended there to legendary extremes in "medicine shows" run by peddlers of "snake-oil."

Realistic literary treatment of rational medical research obtained a landmark in George Eliot's sympathetically wry portrait of the medical researcher Tertius Lydgate in *Middlemarch* (1871-72), but the demands of melodrama found much more scope in the development of research gone wrong; the unfortunate Dr. Jekyll in Robert Louis Stevenson's *Strange Case of Dr. Jekyll and Mr. Hyde* (1886) proved a more powerful inspiration to the popular imagination than Tertius Lydgate could ever have been, even if the latter had not fallen into the ready trap of marriage and domesticity.

The ever-powerful demand for cures for all manner of ills, and the support lent to it by the unreliable but genuine rewards of the placebo effect, helped not merely to sustain various fringes of traditional occult science, but also to renew, reshape and supplement them. It is not merely the treatments suggested by false beliefs that can sometimes prove effective in helping sick people feel better, but the beliefs themselves. Not only can superstitious beliefs give people the precious sensation of having more understanding of their lives and control over their destinies than they actually have, or ever could have, but the mere idea of being the possessor of arcane secrets to which others are not party can convey a precious sense of distinction. The beliefs that everyone holds are psychologically cheapened by the very fact of their being commonplace, and the beauty of truth cannot make up entirely for the depreciation of vulgarity, especially in competition with more esoteric notions whose esthetic appeal mingles the seemingly-beautiful with the seemingly-sublime.

* * * *

It would be unfair to write off too much of the shadier aside of nineteenth-century medicine as mere quackery, given that many of the new schools of medicine that played a prominent role in the gradual development of medical science undoubtedly had a supportive logic that was not entirely groundless. Although much of the seemingly-confirmatory empirical evidence supplied by apparent cures was doubtless deceptive, assisted by the heroic efforts of patients' own immune systems as well as by the placebo effect, many of the physicians in search of such evidence were sincerely attempting to employ the scientific method in their investigations.

Although it is safe enough, from a modern standpoint, to cast off phrenology, homeopathy and animal magnetism as phantoms of the imagination, to such an extent that fiction featuring extrapolations of their theories now qualify as supernatural fiction rather than scientific romance, classification of such works is nevertheless difficult, because the attitude of the author has to be taken into account as well as the content to be appraised. It is true that calling phrenology a science does not make it into one, but it is also true that putting a Swiftian boot into astronomers and the Academy of Lagado does not make astronomy any less of a science or the Royal Society any less of a scientific institution. The dealings of scientific romance with medical wisdom are not merely an intrinsically grey area, but one that has a great many shades of grey—perhaps even as many as fifty.

One area of emergent medical practice in which writers of fiction inevitably took an interest, following in the deeply-imprinted footsteps of Robert Burton and Laurence Sterne, was that of what was increasingly coming to be accepted as "mental illness" and its treatment by "alienists" and "psychologists." Lunatic asylums became part of the standard scenery of Gothic fiction during the Romantic era, not merely as places of potential confinement even more horrific than dungeons, but also as destinations that could provide a satisfactory sense of dramatic closure to melodramas. Indeed, the climatic revelation that the narrator of a tall tale is writing the memoir in a madhouse became almost as hackneyed and lame in the course of the nineteenth century as awakening from a dream. Its prevalence, however, and the evolution of an entire subgenre of "madman's manuscript" stories, does serve to illustrate an intense interest in nineteenth-century negotiations of the notion of madness and the possibility that at least some forms of it might be curable.

With the exception of psychologists, scientists largely ignored the question, but that is understandable, even if—as many writers believed—all scientists were at least a little mad, because science itself laid claim to being the epitome of sanity. It was equally natural that literary men should treat the question with as much sensitivity as curiosity, especially if, a many scientists believed, all writers were at least a little mad, because art was routinely seen as a form of divine madness. Although very few scientists have ever attempted to drive themselves mad in the hope of getting a little closer to genius, artists have shown much greater enthusiasm in that regard, especially with regard to the more attractive forms of aberration. "Neurasthenia," first defined by George M. Beard in 1881, became positively fashionable in literary circles for a while, as a badge of exceptional sensitivity.

The scientific perspective began to creep into investigations of aberrant mental states long before the nineteenth century; as previously noted, Burton's *Anatomy of Melancholy* is a landmark work of that kind, helping to inspire such later pseudo-clinical exercises in self-analysis as Thomas De Quincey's *Confessions of an English Opium-Eater* (1821). As noted with reference to Samuel Johnson's *Rasselas*, there is a multitude of literary works that include characters who could nowadays be diagnosed with complete conviction as sufferers from one mental disease or another, and enthusiasts for "retrospective diagnosis" are sometimes just as enthusiastic to diagnose the neuroses of characters in Shakespeare as those of actual historical individuals.

Intense and detailed accounts of mental aberration by such writers as E. T. A. Hoffmann and Edgar Allan Poe laid much of the groundwork for modern horror fiction. It was not until the mid nineteenth century, however, that an identifiable subgenre of stories began to emerge in which fictional formats were used to set out analytical "case-studies" of various mental conditions recognized, catalogued and to some extent anatomized by contemporary medical practitioners. In Britain, the great pioneer of that kind of work was William Gilbert, who produced two volumes of such case studies in *Shirley Hall Asylum; or, The Memoirs of a Monomaniac* (1863) and *Doctor Austin's Guests* (1866). The former includes a character driven mad by the frustrations of trying to solve the problem of perpetual motion, while the latter commences with a study of "Patent Mania." Gilbert wrote several other novels, and two collections of moralistic supernatural tales, the latter including some deft philosophical speculations cast in the form of popular fiction.

William Gilbert was the first English physician to classify alcoholism as a disease, a diagnosis that inspired Walter Besant's treatment of the theme in *The Demoniac* (1890). Besant also produced *The Ivory Gate* (1892), one of the most detailed accounts of "multiple personality syndrome" to be construed in a clinical light rather the Gothic shadow of such works as James Hogg's *Confessions of a Justified Sinner* (1824). The utility of such "medicalization" of themes previously employed in horror fiction was, however, limited by an anti-climactic element that went beyond the triteness of the "madman's manuscript" ending, in that an explanation of vulgar illness is inherently far less melodramatic than actual supernatural events.

However, just as honesty is really only the second best policy, no matter what the proverb might allege, so the endorsement of the reality of supernatural trappings in fiction is only the second best literary option, beaten hands down by careful ambiguity, which ultimately refuses to reach an explicit conclusion as to whether apparent hauntings are real or delusory. For that reason, the disenchanting efforts of case-studies like William Gilbert and Walter Besant were never going to be able to hold up, in the literary arena, against the likes of J. Sheridan Le Fanu's "Green Tea" (1872) and *Strange Case of Dr. Jekyll and Mr. Hyde*, in which the boundary between the psychological and the parapsychological is deliberately obscured rather than clarified.

* * * *

Given the aesthetic effects to be gained from that kind of ambiguity, it is not entirely surprising that so few British writers were quick to follow William Gilbert's example, or that his two books of case studies were almost completely forgotten. For the same reason, it is not at all surprising that the author of the work on which Robert Hunt clearly modeled *Panthea*—Edward Bulwer-Lytton's *Godolphin* (1833)—should have subsequently recanted the choice seemingly made by that novel's narrative voice to plump for the rational rather than the mystical, and chosen instead to retain an interest in the occult that was, to say the least, teasing. The allure of the occult was such that Bulwer simply could not leave it alone, and he soon discovered that there were advantages in hesitation and obscurity.

The eponymous hero of Bulwer's *Ernest Maltravers* (1837) felt the same attraction as Percy Godolphin, further extrapolated in a sequel, *Alice; or, The Mysteries* (1838), and that narrative too eventually refused to endorse the truth of the mysteries in question, while also refusing to deny them, just as the narrative of *Godolphin* had. When Bulwer set out thereafter to write a more wholehearted occult novel in *Zicci*, he abandoned it part way through, but he eventually returned to it and completed a revised version, *Zanoni* (1842), which very carefully placed its mysteries in the deepest shadows of the grey area between science and mysticism, and was unprecedently lavish in dropping teasing hints regarding the possible reality of its sly assertions.

The eponymous hero of *Zanoni* is an immortal Brother of the Rose Cross, who is being guided in his education by a mentor, Mejnour. A young Englishman, Glyndon, is very ambitious to follow the same path, but comes into conflict with Zanoni when they both fall in love with the same woman. Zanoni wins that petty contest, although Mejnour has warned him that he will lose far more in consequence—as, indeed, he does, falling prey to the Terror in the aftermath of the French Revolution. Glyndon, however, falls victim to a terror of a different kind when, in the course of his initiation into the mysteries of the occult, he encounters the terrible Dweller of the Threshold, whose challenge he is unable to meet.

Zanoni was a huge best-seller, and its success acquired Bulwer the reputation of being not merely an ingenious writer of fiction but a secret occultist of great authority: a reputation that some might have considered tainted, but others would doubtless have deemed very precious—and that, too appeared to be a matter on which Bulwer was never quite able to make up his mind. The probability is that he found it politic, with respect to his readers if not his colleagues in Parliament, never to come clean about his confirmed skepticism.

Although it was clearly a work of fiction—Bulwer obligingly provided an "allegorical interpretation" for its supplementation in later editions—readers of *Zanoni* who were or wished to be believers in the occult could not bring themselves to accept that there was no truth "behind" it; the book became an enormously significant factor in the "occult revival" of the late nineteenth century, when occultism was reinvented in a wholesale manner, with all of its links with contemporary science carefully redesigned—and, naturally and inevitably, with far more prolific, wholehearted and ingenious literary assistance than genuine science had ever obtained. That literary assistance was exceedingly valuable, because the revival not only reinvented the present of occult science but its past as well, redesigning its history along with its supposed nature and declared ambitions. That was a project that involved a massive endeavor of scholarly fantasy, which was not merely akin to but intricately interwoven with endeavors in literary fantasy.

Critics and historians of science fiction have routinely attempted to free that retrospectively-constructed genre from associations with occult science, often attempting to draw sharp distinctions between science fiction and supernatural fiction, in imitation of the crusade undertaken by dedicated scientists, insisting in the same way that the claims made of behalf of occult science are not merely false but deliberately deceptive and dishonest. Even those critics and historians who recognize and admit that the claims of science fiction to be genuinely "scientific" are themselves, almost without exception, not merely false but deliberately deceptive and dishonest, still tend to draw the distinction and insist on its importance. Some will readily admit that "science fiction" is merely one category of a more generalized field of "fantastic fiction," but tend nevertheless to claim special and unique privileges for it by virtue of its supposed doctrinal allegiance to genuine science. Similar claims were advanced by the commentators who identified scientific romance as the field to which Jules Verne and H. G. Wells belonged.

In spite of that insistence, always crucial to the image of the genre, it would be a distortion of the historical picture to ignore all the co-options of scientific terminology and scientific theory attempted, with varying degrees of success, by participants in the occult revival, especially given their success in intruding a few elements of occult science into the standard lexicon of ideas accommodated by scientific romance, and subsequently by science fiction. Fitting that particular piece of the jigsaw to those more essential to the picture is bound to be a trifle awkward, and requires considerable caution, but it does need to be done.

* * * *

Such was the success of *Zanoni* that the consummately professional Bulwer, in spite of the increasing distractions of his political career, eventually followed it up with *A Strange Story*, serialized in Charles Dickens' *All the Year Round* in 1861-62. He peppered the story with footnotes referring to contemporary science and natural theology as well as various arcane sources, of which he had become a keen collector.

Bulwer always constrained such imaginative endeavors to his fiction, but that did not prevent the rumor spreading that he was the senior figure in the English branch of the Brotherhood of the Rose Cross: an opinion that has obtained some academic approval in such credulous accounts as Marie Roberts' *Gothic Immortals: The Fiction of the Brotherhood of the Rosy Cross* (1990). Some of Bulwer's contemporaries, however, cast away all hesitancy in becoming wholehearted lifestyle fantasists, embracing careers as occultists with all the verve expectable in an enthusiastic revival.

The most flamboyant of the pioneers of supernaturalized lifestyle fantasy was "Éliphas Lévi," the pseudonym adopted by the failed litterateur Alphonse Louis Constant, who created an important precedent by supposedly bringing the occult elements of his philosophy out into the light, not merely publishing them but doing so in the form of exoteric popularizations. His guide-book to *Dogme et rituel de la haut magie* (1854-56; tr. as *The Doctrine and Ritual of Transcendental Magic*) and the highly fanciful supportive *Histoire de la magie* (1859; tr. as *The History of Magic*) became the principal sources of all subsequent handbooks of "high magic" and reconstructed histories of the "Hermetic tradition."

The examples provided by *Zanoni* and Éliphas Lévi prompted the foundation of numerous "Rosicrucian lodges" modeled on, and in some instances evolving from, Masonic lodges. The most enthusiastic propagandists for the Parisian lodges included Joséphin Péladan and Édouard Schuré, both of whom made elaborate use of fiction in popularizing their ideas, and similarly intimate literary associations were formed when the fad spread to England. The most celebrated English organization of that stripe was the Order of the Golden Dawn, which attracted numerous literary men, some of considerable note—including W. B. Yeats and Arthur Machen—as well as Léviesque litterateurs-turned-lifestyle-fantasists, the most famous of whom was Aleister Crowley.

Most such organizations retained the pretence of being secret societies, into whose mysteries recruits had to be gradually initiated, but it was inevitable that the most successful of all would follow the Swedenborgian and Léviesque examples, by replacing, or at least combining, that stratagem with the production of new exoteric "scriptures" that could be used as incentives to credulity and affiliation. The most successful of all the new syntheses emergent from the nineteenth-century occult revival was Theosophy, founded by Helena Blavatsky, which combined Christian and Buddhist ideas and helped to promote a massive vogue for "the wisdom of the East," greatly assisted by information regarding Eastern beliefs and folkways transmitted back to Europe by conquerors and colonizers.

Blavatsky's first popularizing work was *Isis Unveiled: A Master-Key to the Mysteries of Ancient and Modern Science and Theology* (1877), which plundered ideas recklessly from a wide range of sources—including *Zanoni*—but only served to prepare the way for a much more extensive and robust account of *The Secret Doctrine: The Synthesis of Science, Religion, and Philosophy* (1888)—a work that had such an influence on early scientific romance and science fiction, directly or indirectly, that Everett Bleiler included an elaborate description of its contents in the "Background Books" section of *Science Fiction: The Early Years*. Not content to reinvent the history of magic, mysticism and religion, Blavatsky reinvented the evolutionary history of the planet and life on its surface, drawing extensively on the romantic aspects of contemporary biology and anthropology in compiling a highly imaginative account of the evolution of humankind, which featured seven "root races" (two of which had yet to materialize) associated with various fictitious primordial continents, including Hyperborea, Lemuria and Atlantis.

Theosophy's grandiose claim to be a synthesis of parallel religious traditions with scientific ideas gave it an advantage, in the eyes of many interested parties, over rival schools of "modernized" supernatural beliefs rooted more narrowly in Western religion, but the latter were not left behind in the quest for "scientifization." The most successful of them, in the late nineteenth century, was

"Spiritualism," which involved establishing communication between the living and the dead—the latter presumed to be enjoying a contented afterlife, although not necessarily in a Christian Heaven—by virtue of the intervention of specially gifted "mediums."

The Spiritualist fad originated within the rich tradition of American entrepreneurial quackery, with the exploits of the teenage Fox sisters of Connecticut in the late 1840s, whose production of mysterious "rappings," passed off as communications from the spirit world, spawned a host of confidence tricksters expert in "table-turning," the use of "Ouija boards" and the manifestation of ghostly forms by means of "ectoplasm." The idea of "mediums" had, however, been appropriated from the tradition of Mesmerism and "animal magnetism" that had spread to Britain and America from France.

Spiritualist mediums soon began not only to offer pseudoscientific explanations of what they were doing, but also to demand that their supposed gifts be subjected to scrupulous scientific investigation, like the French government's officially-commissioned investigations of the claims made by Mesmer. Such investigations usually produced negative results, but some of the investigators, perhaps inevitably, having failed to see through the conjuring tricks routinely employed by mediums, became convinced of the reality of the phenomena, thus giving birth to an entire new "science" that was eventually dubbed "parapsychology," although it was known in the nineteenth century simply as "psychic research."

The initial involvement of British scientists in psychic research owed a great deal to the efforts of the Scottish medium Daniel Dunglas Home, who had learned the tricks of the trade in America in the late 1840s, when he lived within a few miles of the Fox sisters' Connecticut home. While performing in America he attracted the attention of William Makepeace Thackeray, who became a fierce critic of his pretensions. Home moved to Britain in 1855, ostensibly for health reasons, and was swiftly introduced into London society, making a favorable impression on the Swedenborgian James Wilkinson and Edward Bulwer-Lytton, but annoying Charles Dickens and exciting a powerful antipathy in Robert Browning, who pilloried him as "Mr. Sludge, the Medium" (1864). Michael Faraday and Thomas Henry Huxley also criticized Home's claims. Spiritualism was satirized in Thomas Love Peacock's last novel,

Gryll Grange (1860), but was treated more reverently in some of the fiction that accompanied the occult revival, as in Frances Trollope's *Black Sprits and White* (1877).

Psychic research took off in Britain when the eminent physicist William Crookes undertook to investigate the abilities of mediums, including Home and Florence Cook, in 1869. He reported favorably on their claims in "Notes of an Enquiry into the Phenomena called Spiritual during the years 1870-1873," published in the *Quarterly Journal of Science*—after the *Proceedings of the Royal Society* had declined the paper—in 1874. Popular accounts of Crookes' findings, dramatically inflated in subsequent reportage by legend and rumor, played a considerable effect in confirming belief in mediumistic powers, especially in France.

The Society for Psychic Research was founded in 1882 by F. W. H. Myers and various associates, including the moral philosopher Henry Sidgwick and the physicist Sir William Barrett, but it followed in the tracks of an earlier investigative society that had chosen the less fortunate name of the Ghost Club, founded in Cambridge in 1855 and launched in London in 1862, with the enthusiastic support of Charles Dickens. Although the Ghost Club faded away in the 1870s it was revived alongside the S.P.R. in 1882 as a rival organization. Crookes appears to have been a member at that time, as was his fellow physicist Oliver Lodge, although it declined again and had to be revived for a second time in the 1920s, while the S.P.R. continued to thrive, soon inspiring an American counterpart, which eventually merged with it.

One of the S.P.R.'s six committees was set up to investigate telepathy—a term Myers had coined—while the others were devoted to the study of mediums, mesmerism, apparitions, Carl von Reichenbach's theory of the "odic force" and the collation of previously-published data; its first product was Myers and Edward Gurney's survey of *Phantasms of the Living* (1886). The activities and publications of the S.P.R. helped mediumistic powers to cross a significant boundary in public perception, which enabled literary accounts of mediumistic powers couched in the quasi-technical language to migrate from the perceived genres of supernatural fiction and religious fiction into the margins of scientific romance, where they took up a residence that they never surrendered. Most such works produced in the nineteenth century are perhaps more reasonably considered as items of supernatural fiction, but it would be a distortion to eliminate them from consideration in the present history.

The migration in question, accompanied by a marked hybridization, can easily be tracked through the second half of the nineteenth century from such philosophically-painstaking beginnings as George Eliot's "The Lifted Veil" (1859) to the fringes of the ghost story's standardization as a genre of popular fiction in the years preceding the emergence of generic scientific romance. Grant Allen's "Our Scientific Observations of a Ghost (1878) and "The Mysterious Occurrence in Piccadilly" (1884), both by-lined J. Arbuthnot Wilson, appeared in *The Belgravia*, which published several other tales of a similar hybrid kind, including two personality-exchange stories, Arthur Conan Doyle's "The Great Keinplatz Experiment" (1885) and B. F. Cresswell's "A Psychical Experiment" (1887), as well as W. H. Stacpoole's account of a delusory teleportation device, "The Teleporon" (1886) and Fergus Hume's "Professor Brankel's Secret" (1889), in which a chemist researching the activities of Medieval alchemist discovers a formula that will permit access to various past eras—and, it seems, future ones too, albeit at a cost. Stacpoole, the elder brother of H. de Vere Stacpoole, who went on to much greater success as a novelist, expanded the theme of his story considerably in the novel *Herr Richter's Strange Experiment* (1886), which also includes obvious echoes of "The Great Keinplatz Experiment."

The principal means by which Spiritualists attempted to concoct a new "scientific" warrant for mediumistic powers led to their extensive development of the mathematical notion of a "fourth dimension" of space. The notion was popularized by the astrophysicist Johann Zöllner, who visited William Crookes in London in 1875 and then conducted a series of investigations of his own with the medium Henry Slade, trying hard to explain Slade's "spirit manifestations" with the aid of the notion that the spirits in question were resident in a fourth spatial dimension. He published his thesis in a book translated into English as *Transcendental Physics* in 1880.

The adoption of the fourth and other dimensions into occult thought was only natural, given that hypothetical geometry was one of the most significant arcane realms within mathematics—a realm of thought whose initial arcana dated back to Pythagoras, and whose stock had been increased dramatically since Isaac Newton's development of "fluxions" in order to explain the geometry of the planetary orbits in the context of the theory of universal gravitation. The arcana of mathematics did not often prompt literary endeavors, but a classic of that esoteric kind appeared in 1884 with the publication of *Flatland: A Romance of Many Dimensions*, issued under the by-line "A Square."

Flatland was the work of Edwin Abbott, a clergyman, Shakespearean scholar and headmaster of the City of London School, who wrote several other books on literary and theological subjects. *Flatland* is partly a didactic thought-experiment and partly a social satire. Describing life in a two-dimensional world inhabited by triangles, squares, polygons and circles, whose social hierarchy, so far as males are concerned, is determined by the quantity of their angles—circles being conceived as having an infinite number, and therefore constituting an aristocracy. Females, on the other hand, are so slender as to be almost linear, and hence extremely sharp. Perception of shape by sight is, however, difficult by virtue of the dimensional limitation, and has generated a complex etiquette.

In the second part of the novel, an inhabitant of Flatland discovers a one-dimensional world, Lineland, and has difficulty trying to explain the second dimension to a Linelander—an experience that helps to prepare him for an encounter with a Spacelander who similar tries to explain the third dimension to him. With the aid of logic and imagination, the Flatlander does contrive to obtain some understanding, although his subsequent attempt to share that understanding with his fellow Flatlanders results in his being deemed insane and imprisoned. The invitation to other Spacelanders is obvious, complete with warning notice, but discreetly understated.

Although Abbott makes no reference to Zöllner's "transcendental physics" or to the use of dimensional jargon by occultists and psychic researchers, it is possible to read a certain theological allegorizing into *Flatland*, which was surely intentional. At any rate, the temptation to continue intertwining the two kinds of arcana was irresistible, and continued apace, most ingeniously in the work of Charles Howard Hinton, a mathematician who approached the issue from the same direction as Abbott, but attempted to take the theological allegorizing much further—as will be described when his contribution to generic scientific romance is described in detail in Chapter Three. The other significant writer to take inspiration from Abbott was Alfred Taylor Schofield, who was a physician, not a clergyman, but nevertheless wrote numerous essays in support of Biblical prophecies; his *Another World; or, The Fourth Dimension* (1888) also features a square flatlander who ventures into a lineland before being progressively raised into a three-dimensional world and a four-dimensional world, where the explanation of various Old Testament miracles becomes clear to him.

* * * *

Spiritualism was by no means the only significant stimulant to literary hybrids of scientific romance and supernatural fiction, nor was dimensional fantasy the only productive strategy attempting to reaccommodate the supernatural within the manifold of scientific theory. Substantial groundwork for some such accommodation had already been laid by such visionary fantasies as Christiaan Huygens's *Cosmotheoros*, Emmanuel Swedenborg's *Arcana of Heaven* and many nineteenth-century accounts of cosmic voyages, including those featured in *Queen Mab* and *Consolations in Travel*, which combined the imagery of scientific romance and religious mysticism, providing an obvious sector of hybridization.

The Anglican clergyman W. S. Lach-Szyrma provided a particularly significant example of this kind of fictional development in a series of works, beginning with *A Voice from Another World* (1874), in which an apparent hunchback turns out to be a winged Venusian. The character offers a much more elaborate account of himself in *Aleriel; or, A Voyage to Other Worlds* (1883), including a description of his exploration of Mars, Jupiter and Saturn, all of which are inhabited by humanoid beings, but with considerable physical modifications, in accordance with a divine plan. Between 1887 and 1893 Lach-Szyrma then contributed a series of less mystically-inclined "Letters from the Planets" to *Cassell's Magazine*, offering more detailed accounts of the relics of a long-dead lunar civilization, and various regions of Mars, Mercury and one of Jupiter's moons, although the explorers are warned off approaching the sun too closely by a strange cloud. The earlier stories in the sequence had the distinction of being translated for serialization in the French popular science magazine *La Science Illustrée*, in a regular section headed *roman scientifique*.

Having minimized the religious aspects of the interplanetary letters, however, Lach-Szyrma restored it to far greater prominence in *Under Other Conditions* (1892), in which another mysterious personage, who calls himself Ezariel, reveals his true identity as a superhuman being made of a variant form of matter, and argues strenuously that the plurality of worlds inhabited by beings adapted to various local environments is not in conflict with scripture, but reveals a cosmic dimension of the divine plan.

By far the most successful writer of occult fiction in Britain was "Marie Corelli," the adopted (and probably natural) daughter of the Scottish poet Charles Mackay, who became the best-selling writer in the English language during the *fin-de-siècle* period, promoting her own idiosyncratic synthesis of ideas drawn from contemporary science—including electricity and radioactivity—with Christian mysticism. Charles Mackay had earlier been a successful "debunker" of all manner of occult notions in his *Extraordinary Popular Delusions and the Madness of Crowds*, divided into sections on "National Delusions," "Peculiar Follies" and "Philosophical Delusions," including chapters on alchemy, prophecy, fortune-telling, animal magnetism, witch-hunting, haunted houses and holy relics. The book's essays on the phenomena of economic "bubbles" and crowd psychology became oft-quoted classics. His daughter, however, not only became a notorious supporter of several such delusions but fell prey to self-delusion to an extraordinary extent, with an enthusiasm that fueled her fiction and presumably helped it to attain an enormous success.

Marie Corelli's spectacular debut in this curious hybrid fiction was *A Romance of Two Worlds* (1886), in which a charismatic "Chaldean" named Casimir Heliobas reveals the secrets of the Electric Creed to the sickly heroine, laying the foundations for her physical and moral rearmament. As part of her re-education he sends her on a cosmic journey, in the company of an angel, which eventually ranges further afield than Aleriel's excursions, although it similarly takes in Venus, Saturn and Jupiter; its climax is a trip to the central sphere of the universe, the heart of Creation, where a great electric circle spins off the fabric of souls. The excursion also reveals that the Earth is the unhappiest world in the universe, because only there have people failed so completely to embrace the true faith. Corelli went on to develop variants of the thesis at intervals in the course of a sequence of novels in various genres, published during the next thirty years and more.

In *Ardath: The Story of a Dead Self* (1889), Heliobas mesmerizes a disenchanted poet and enables him encounter the beautiful Edris. When he subsequently undertakes a visionary journey through time to the city of Al-Kyris, seven thousand years in the past, and falls in love with a *femme fatale*, Edris comes to his rescue and revisits him in the present; although she is an angel, she consents to marry him. *The Soul of Lilith* (1892) describes experiments conducted by the superhuman magus El-Rami with the aid of a girl maintained in suspended animation for centuries, who undertakes cosmic journeys in spirit and reports back on life on other worlds. Eventually, however, he falls in love with her and decides to wake her up, with tragic results. The sequence reached an apogee of sorts in *The Sorrows of Satan* (1895), in which a young novelist makes a deal with the Devil, the progress of which is disrupted when the Devil, now repentant, falls in love with Mavis Clair a brilliant female novelist unjustly persecuted by contemporary critics. Corelli feigned surprise when reviewers suggested that the latter was a self-portrait, and modestly denied the resemblance. The novel vastly outsold *The Time Machine*, which was published in the same year, conclusively demonstrating the priorities of popular taste with regard to works of the literary imagination.

Not so very far behind Corelli as a *fin-de-siècle* best-seller was Henry Rider Haggard, whose *She: A History of Adventure*, also first appeared in 1886 in America, although its English book edition was held up until its serialization in *The Graphic* had finished in January 1887. Although it was read primarily as an adventure novel, following up the classic *King Solomon's Mines* (1885), *She* is also a hybrid of scientific romance and supernatural fiction, in that its anti-heroine, She-Who-Must-Be-Obeyed—who is even more charismatic, in her fashion, than Corelli's Heliobas—insists that her immortality and seemingly magical gifts, obtained from the Flame of Life, as well as the hero's alleged reincarnation, are entirely natural, No explanations of their functioning are, however, offered in support of this contention. Perhaps, wittingly or unwittingly, that was the point; *She* set a crucial example in the exoticization of adventure fiction, in which fantastic things could henceforth happen without any particular attention being paid to the how or why, such notions as immortality being simply taken for granted as potentially justifiable.

The immediate sequel to *King Solomon's Mines, Allan Quatermain* (1887), is considerably more exotic than its predecessor, featuring the discovery in the heart of Africa of the unknown civilization of Zu-Vendi, with a culture approximately parallel to Classical Greece. The novel thus established a key reference point for the rapidly-proliferating genre of modern traveler's tales that came to be known as "lost race stories," featuring exotic enclaves hidden in the last remaining geographical regions, where occult knowledge and "forgotten science" often survive. Haggard did not invent that subgenre—significant examples with a slight priority had been provided by William Westall in *A Phantom City: A Volcanic Romance* (1886) and *A Queer Race: The Story of a Strange People* (1887)—but he went on to make prolific and productive use of it, and proved it to be a device whose time had come.

Allan Quatermain was swiftly followed by the anonymous *Thoth: A romance* (1888; by Joseph Shield Nicholson), in which an enclave of the same sort is discovered in the time of Periclean Athens, the inhabitants of which are already equipped with flying machines, submarines, electrical technology and other trappings of nineteenth-century science, including advanced weaponry held in store for an anticipated conquest of the world—which is inevitably aborted—and by G. G. A. Murray's *Gobi or Shamo: A Story of Three Songs* (1889), in which a scientifically-advanced culture is discovered lurking in the Gobi desert. Marie Corelli was quick to introduce similar notions into *Ardath*, in which the priests of Al-Kyris have custody of a secret science and advanced electrical technology. Like Marie Corelli, Rider Haggard went on to produce novels in various genres, frequently embracing the same favorite themes, especially that of reincarnation, rationalized in terms of "ancestral memories," and helped pave the way for other writers of adventure stories and thrillers to spice up their plots with similar exotic cocktails of ideas plundered at will from the reconfigured stocks of theosophy and psychic research.

No matter how hard purist historians try to draw clear boundaries isolating such works of fiction from scientifically-based speculations, the decision as to exactly what can count as "scientific" in the context of such stories is difficult and sometimes impossible to make. Discrimination is especially awkward with respect to such commonplace notions as hypnotism and telepathy, which had long been granted an ambiguity in relation to science and occult science—an ambiguity that only became more confusing when "psychic research" made its bid to become a science in its own right.

Generic scientific romance was never free of such ambiguities, nor did most of its major exponents make very strenuous efforts to liberate it. To some extent, that was because the writers were genuinely uncertain as to where the boundaries of rational plausibility lay, and were all the more eager to explore them in consequence. Partly, too, it was because they were well aware of the roles that purely and admittedly fantastic devices could play in philosophical speculation, and whenever such speculation was a significant objective in their work—as it almost invariably was in the work of the more ambitious writers—they knew that it did not pay to be overly scrupulous in ruling out equivalents of the ring of Gyges on logical grounds.

* * * *

The complex penumbra of occult science was not the only shadow cast by science to which it is desirable to pay attention here, although there is a wry paradoxicality in the assertion that some of the most interesting literary reactions to the advancement of knowledge are to be found in what is arguably the blackest shadow of all: that of frank and flagrant nonsense. It is a mistake to think of nonsense merely as an absence of sense, and all nonsensical productions as essentially similar; the most interesting nonsense is the nonsense that is most determined and most vehement in its denial of sense, and most judicious in its choice of the sense that it is determined to deny, defy and undermine.

All satire is to some extent deliberate nonsense, but there is a species of satire that is ambitious to test what is taken for sense to destruction; if possible, it desires to prove that what is taken for sense is actually nonsense, and all the more pernicious for being unadmitted nonsense clad in a plausible mask. The Swiftian satirization of science has already been illustrated in previous sections of this history, but it is also appropriate to point out that a new kind of nonsense emerged in the second half of the nineteenth century that seemed somewhat distinct from satire, and unlike anything that had been done before. It had three outstanding practitioners, one of whom, coincidentally, was the son of William Gilbert, the pioneer of psychoanalytical case-study fiction: William Schwenck Gilbert, most of whose work was manifest in the form of librettos for comic operas. The second was the great proponent of nonsense verse, Edward Lear. The third and most significant of all was a mathematician and logician, a contemporary of George Boole and Edwin Abbott, and also a clergyman: the Reverend Charles Lutwidge Dodgson, better known as Lewis Carroll.

In *Alice's Adventures in Wonderland* (1865) and its sequel *Through the Looking Glass and What Alice Found There* (1871) Carroll played games with logic and paradox, the literalization of metaphors and literary parody, producing a series of comic archetypes that have become part of the symbolic landscape of English discourse. Although the stories feature some impish dissent from Victorian moralism, especially as applied to the education of children, their real assault is upon styles of reasoning, and their clever inversions and perversions helped lay groundwork for a new species of wit, soon taken to its elegant extreme by Oscar Wilde. Although perfectly capable of delighting children—their primary motive—the two stories embody layers of subtext equally capable of delighting mathematicians and magicians. The breadth of their appeal is easily signified by the observation that they are included as significant items in the bibliographies of Julian Huxley's speculative essay "Philosophic Ants" (1923) and Aleister Crowley's *Magick in Theory and Practice* (1929), the latter annotating them as "invaluable to those who understand the Kabbalah"—as, indeed, they must be.

The Alice books provided spectacular exemplars of what would come to be known colloquially as "thinking outside the box" or, more sententiously, as "lateral thinking," providing maps of escape-routes from conventional ways of thinking-routes that were as potentially valuable to scientists in search of hypotheses as to artists in search of the surreal. Both texts make abundant use of poetry, in order to use its formal devices to mock their own determinism, deftly substituting rhyme and unreason for rhyme and reason. Carroll's third great work, *The Hunting of the Snark* (1876) was a mock-epic poem, which similarly added new concepts to the language, although not quite as many as the brilliantly concise "Jabberwocky" in *Through the Looking Glass*.

Edward Lear's first collection, *A Book of Nonsense* (1846), which predated Alice, had popularized the limerick as a form of verse, but Lear's crucial contributions to the lexicon of symbolic nonsense began with "The Owl and the Pussycat" (1867) and continued in such classics as "The Jumblies," in *Nonsense Songs and Stories* (1870), and the "The Dong with a Luminous Nose" and "The Pobble Who Has No Toes" in *Laughable Lyrics* (1876). W. S. Gilbert's "Bab Ballads" were mostly published in the same interval, between 1866 and 1870, and provided much of the source material later adapted such musical plays as "Topsyturveydom" (1874) and the more famous librettos set to music during the late 1870s and 1880s by Arthur Sullivan.

There is not a trace of science in any of the latter material—Gilbert's belated *Utopia Limited* (1893) is a satire on party politics, not Utopias—and if there is romance, it is romance of a very special kind; but that is precisely why the subgenre, and the Alice books in particular, retained a perverse relationship with scientific romance when the genre eventually developed: a relationship foreshadowed, in an inverse fashion, in Isaac d'Israeli's *Flim-Flams!* and the *Anti-Jacobin* parody "The Love of the Triangles"—which would surely be entitled to be reckoned a much better poem if Erasmus Darwin had never written "The Loves of the Plants," the prior existence of which relegates it from nonsensical brilliance to mere caricature.

* * * *

The evolution of Carrollian nonsense in the late 1860s is merely the extreme of a much more general tendency in Victorian literature to oppose the perceived nexus of oppressions of thought that continued to be called "Victorianism" throughout the twentieth century. Although there was a manifest opposition between the advancing tide of skeptical materialistic science on the one hand, and stubborn religious faith on the other, both sides in that dispute were antipathetic to the literary uses and manifestations of motifs drawn from folklore. The free and eclectic use of such motifs by

Erasmus Darwin and Percy Shelley was soon subject to a dual censure, attacked by the champions of science on the grounds of imaginative obsolescence and by the champions of religion on the grounds of unorthodoxy.

The educative crusade launched by the members of the Lunar Society and their contemporaries, and continued by such writers as Robert Hunt, inevitably provoked an adversarial response from older educational institutions like the Society for Promoting Christian Knowledge, founded in 1698 by Thomas Bray. The Society's publications became more profuse and more assertive in the nineteenth century, in response to the perceived threat, and also more definite in their ideology. As well as disapproving of science, many enthusiasts for religious education also disapproved of the "pagan survivals" that were so prominent in "fairy tales" told to children, and began actively attacking such inclusions. That attack inevitably brought forth counter-attacks by expert foes, most prominently Charles Dickens, whose sterling defense of the right to innocent amusement prompted the production of his Christmas Books.

Dickens was not the only person troubled by the assaults on the imagination conducted by the stern exponents of Victorianism, and they brought a particularly robust response from a number of clergymen who felt that their faith was being traduced, and perhaps endangered. Lewis Carroll was one, and his friend Charles Kingsley was another, but the one whose literary response was most prolific was George MacDonald. Like Kingsley, he framed his response as allegory rather than deliberate nonsense, and he used allegory not merely to secure the educative functions of his endeavor but also to work through some of his own spiritual doubts.

Although it might seem to be a rather distant digression from the subject-matter of this history, there is some purpose in giving brief consideration to MacDonald's work in this vein, and to a distinctive tradition in British fantastic fiction that it launched, and which continued, not merely throughout the Victorian era but long into the twentieth century. Although this "pure" variety of British fantasy is more easily separated from British scientific romance than British occult fiction, its evolution proceeded in step with it, responsive to the same historical events and consequent cultural shifts, and ultimately achieved a crucial interaction with it that will justify further brief digressions in the course of this history.

MacDonald's first major allegorical work was *Phantastes: A Faerie Romance for Men and Women* (1858), which takes its primary inspiration from the German Romantic Movement and the *kunstmärchen* [art fairy tales] produced in connection with it, although MacDonald was undoubtedly familiar with such precursory products of the English Romantic Movement as the writings of Nathan Drake and John Sterling, and might also have read the moralistic fantasies of James Dalton. *Phantastes* is a portal fantasy in which the protagonist, Anodos, embarks upon a quest modeled on those featured in chivalric romances in pursuit of his ideal of female beauty, embodied in a statue by Pygmalion he calls the "Marble Lady"—a quest made problematic by the suspicion that, because lust is a sin, virtue might lie in failure rather than success.

Although the children's stories MacDonald then began to publish in *Adela Cathcart* (1864) and *Dealings with the Fairies* (1867) were written primarily to amuse, they are haunted by similar allegorical implications, which become darker by degrees in *At the Back of the North Wind* (1871), *The Princess and the Goblin* (1872), *The Lost Princess* (1875) and *The Princess and Curdie* (1883). The sequence ultimately produced another allegorical, and deeply enigmatic, portal fantasy for adult readers in *Lilith* (1895), which delves into the primordial materials of the Christian Mythos. Although it would be hard to stretch the Wellsian notion of "scientific romance" far enough to include *Lilith*, the novel is an exceedingly "scholarly" fantasy; it is not a "scientific romance" in James Ibbetson's understanding of the term either, but nor is it devoid of scientific method in the manner in which it attempts to analyze the metaphysical and psychological roots of Christian faith. Not all the contrived modern Romances that came after it involved the same intensity of philosophical speculation, but philosophical speculation remained sufficiently important within the subgenre to maintain an intellectual kinship with more serious endeavors in scientific romance—a kinship recognized by H. G. Wells in his insistence that his classic definitive scientific romances were not fundamentally distinct from the philosophical fantasies *The Wonderful Visit* and *The Sea Lady*.

Such sophisticated endeavors in philosophical fantasy were not confined to the work of clergymen. Victorianism had other ideological opponents, among the most significant of whom, from an artistic viewpoint, were the members of the Pre-Raphaelite Brotherhood founded in 1848 as a belated component of the Romantic revolution against Classicism. Although not formally a member, by virtue of being female, Christina Rossetti, the sister of one of the founders of the Brotherhood, Dante Gabriel Rossetti, produced what is perhaps the most strikingly defiant of all responses to imaginative oppression in the graphic "Goblin Market" (1862), whose subject-matter is the consumption of forbidden fruit and the possibility of redemption from its effects. Another of the founder-members of the P.R.B., William Morris, went on to become a fantasist almost as prolific and influential as MacDonald.

Morris does have some direct entitlement to be mentioned in a history of scientific romance because of his two utopian works, *A Dream of John Ball* (1888) and *New from Nowhere* (1890), the latter of which is an explicit reply to Edward Bellamy's description of Utopian socialism in *Looking Backward, 2000-1887*. Morris' idea of an ideal society, however, involves a retreat from mechanical technology toward earlier ideals of craftsmanship, and thus places his work in the same reactive category as Richard Jefferies and W. H. Hudson. His other fantasies are, in essence, reactions of a similar kind, which go to further extremes in their nostalgia for imaginary Medieval settings, carefully modifying those of Norman romance in several different ways. The modifications usually involve the injection of a strong dose of Scandinavian inspiration derived from Norse sagas, of which Morris became an enthusiastic translator.

Following the early allegorical novella "The Hollow Land" (1856) most of Morris' early works in this vein were given poetic form, including an elaborate account of Vikings searching for *The Earthly Paradise* (1868-70). After a couple of relatively straightforward pseudohistorical novels, however, he imported more fantastic and allegorical devices into a series of novels begun with *The Story of the Glittering Plain* (1891)—issued by his own Kelmscott Press—and continued with *The Wood Beyond the World* (1894), *The Well at the World's End* (1896) and *The Water of the Wondrous Isles* (1897). As with MacDonald's *Lilith*, the novels draw heavily on the legacy of Morris' scholarship, and represent a reaction, albeit in a markedly different fashion, to some of the same contemporary concerns that are reflected in the scientific romances that enjoyed a heyday of sorts in the same decade.

Although works of the kind produced by MacDonald and Morris have evident links with German *kunstmärchen* and French stories produced under similar theoretical and reactive influences, they remain distinct in their outlook and the manner of their allegorical concerns by virtue of their specifically Victorian origin, and the same is true of a number of other works, by such writers as Oscar Wilde, Richard Garnett, "Vernon Lee" (Violet Paget), William Butler Yeats, Laurence Housman and "Fiona MacLeod" (William Sharp), which became sufficiently prolific in the 1890s to constitute a retrospectively-discernible genre developing alongside the genre of scientific romance, although it went unnoticed by contemporary commentators.

There are several significant crossovers between the two genres, including works by M. P. Shiel and Arthur Conan Doyle as well as H. G. Wells, and there were more complex interactions in terms of the influence exerted upon them by, and the influence they exerted upon, contemporary scholarly fantasies. The continuing overlap was very different in kind, however, from the overlaps between either genre and occult fiction. The latter overlaps blurred boundaries, whereas there was a sense in which the juxtaposition of scientific romance and fantasies of the kind descended from MacDonald and Morris highlighted them as polar opposites.

That manifest opposition greatly encouraged subsequent literary historians interested in drawing sharp boundaries between "science fiction" and "fantasy fiction," but the assistance it lent in matters of discrimination should not be allowed to obscure the fact that the poles in question had a certain mutual attraction, and often functioned as termini in the same energizing circuits. To write a comprehensive history of British fantasy would require a book of the same dimensions as this one, and it is a project best left for another occasion, but there are good reasons for inserting occasional brief digressions within the present project, even where obvious overlaps of endeavor are not manifest within the work of individual writers.

www.ingramcontent.com/pod-product-compliance
Lightning Source LLC
Chambersburg PA
CBHW032101090426
42743CB00007B/193